Hugh Dunn Fisher

The Gun and the Gospel

Second Edition

Hugh Dunn Fisher

The Gun and the Gospel
Second Edition

ISBN/EAN: 9783337067465

Printed in Europe, USA, Canada, Australia, Japan

Cover: Foto ©Lupo / pixelio.de

More available books at **www.hansebooks.com**

THE GUN
AND THE GOSPEL

EARLY KANSAS
AND
CHAPLAIN FISHER.

...By...
Rev. H. D. FISHER, D. D.
Topeka.

Relation of Kansas to Freedom. John Brown. Jim Lane. Days that Tried Men's Souls. Circuit Riding in the Fifties. Quantrell's Raid. Army Life in the Southwest. Work Among the Contrabands. Church Life Among the Mormons. Congressional Chaplaincy Canvass.

SECOND EDITION
1897
MEDICAL CENTURY COMPANY
CHICAGO   NEW YORK

Copyrighted by
H. D. FISHER,
1896

To
the wife of my youth,
whose counsel
has made my success in life possible,
and
whose wonderful heroism and self-possession
saved me from death by
Quantrell's murderous band of guerrillas,
this volume is
affectionately dedicated.

PREFATORY.

MUCH of the history and many of the incidents herein narrated are so related to the conflict between Slavery and Freedom and the defeat and destruction of the former, "the sum of all villainies," as to justify me in interweaving a resumé of its introduction and growth into a national disgrace, its insolence and downfall, with the more personal features of my autobiography. The subject is necessarily treated imperfectly for the sake of brevity, yet, I believe, with accuracy. This volume is written in response to oft-repeated solicitations of friends of the author to put on record the more eventful incidents of a life devoted to God and Freedom in days that tried men's souls, but not without the hope that it may awaken additional interest in the important part played by Kansas in securing the freedom of a bonded race, and that it may also, by its record of national and individual accomplishments, encourage the further bridling and eventual abolition by the people of "God and Home and Native Land" of that greatest crime remaining in the wake of slavery—the rum traffic.

I have tried, moreover, to portray an occasional thrilling incident with the idea in view of entertaining and instructing the young people of Kansas and the Church into whose hands the volume may come, and into whose hearts I would instill the patriotism of the heroes whose achievements are herein depicted and a love for those principles which carry with them a confident hope of Eternal Life.

THE AUTHOR.

INTRODUCTORY.

If we were to seek by first analysis the cause of the great agitation that gave Kansas her prestige and made her name illustrious we would find that it rests in "the agitation that precedes the organization of society." In each physical sense of mankind a passion lies latent. Each sense, appetite, desire, obtains gratification by reprisal and appropriates what is obtained from others as a trophy of conquest. Hence the origin and perpetuation of slavery. Enlightened conscience recognizes the rights of the person and forms the basis of justice. Multiplied antagonisms result from the consciousness of right and wrong. The strong oppress the weak. Agitation appears in the defense of human rights. To oppose wrong-doing and oppression, self-protection develops as a law of nature. Here begins the tendency toward association—or society. As all society recognizes this necessity, favorable conditions are created for mutual as well as for self-protection.

The Anglo-Saxon had and still possesses a strong consciousness of the ego; the African slave in our America had it in a less pronounced type; the Indian tribes to a yet lesser degree; consequently their disappearance before a more pronounced type of personality and more closely banded association. The Caucasions find highest culture in refined society; the slaves in field and cabin association; the redmen only in clans and tribes.

The soldier, though a product of war, is a necessity of civilization. The time was when there were no soldiers, no severe antagonisms of interests, either individual or social. But under aggression the natural rights of others appeal for redress; hence, from time immemorial the soldier has been seemingly an indispensable factor in the crystallization of society and the formation of states and nations, as well as toward their perpetuity.

The gun as an emblem of soldierly prowess has often changed the maps of the world, has destroyed inquisitions and prisons in which tyranny has gloried and liberty has been incarcerated; it has furnished themes for poets, material for historians, and made a highway for civilization; it has tunneled the hills and scaled the mountains, crossed seas and continents, and planted symbols of christianity upon the islands of the seas; it has preserved and it has demolished nations; and with the sword, an emblem of power, has established the prerogatives of those mightier weapons of civilization and christianity,—the pen and the pulpit.

The gun has furnished painters and sculptors subjects for brush and chisel; pictures, pedestals, gardens, museums and triumphal arches proclaim and perpetuate the triumphs of the gun over barbarism and the gospel of peace over war!

The tall columns of Trojan, Marcus Aurelius and Washington, the column of Vendome, the triumphal arches of Titus, Constantine and Napoleon, and the magnificent mausoleum of Grant would not have stood save for the Gun and the Sword. But the Evangel of Peace on Earth, the Gospel, follows in the wake of conquering armies, healing the wounds that cruel war has caused, and establishing here and there and yonder, everywhere, eleemosynary institutions as trophies redeemed from the barbarism of war, and points to them with pride as evidences of peace established with God and man, peace on earth and good will to men.

All over the world float the emblems of war. Even from the cathedral of Milan the image of Napoleon looks down upon the church. But in the gateway to America, Liberty Enlightening the World stands with radiant brow and uplifted hand, flashing out the light of the gospel of peace and a welcome to all who seek a home in a christian land.

Society is the threshold of civilization. But in society agitation never ceases, though form and field of action may change. Divergent ideas give rise to strife, and strife continues to the conflict of arms, which is simply the antagonism of ideas materialized into brute force and signalized by the sabre and the gun.

The preaching of peace contemplates a changed condition of the senses. Life is to be no longer sensual, carnal, devlish, but spiritual and elevated. Barbarism gives place to civilization, slavery to freedom, cruelty to charity, hatred to love; and men are fitted for the highest development and happiness.

The history and condition of Mexico, as well as our southern states, within the period of Kansas' history, shows clearly the oppressive, repellant, destructive trend of power and the triumphant spirit of conservative peace.

Just after the rebellion it was found that in Mexico the Romish church was losing control of the people, and that the revenues of the church were failing. An appeal was made to the Pope of Rome for relief. He cast about among the Catholic nations for aid to more firmly establish the authority of the church. Money and soldiers were needed. France could furnish the men but not the money. Austria found in Arch Duke Maximillian an eligible and wealthy prince who could supply the latter. But the occupancy of

Mexico by a foreign potentate and troops was so contrary to the Monroe doctrine that Mr. Seward, then secretary of state, notified Napoleon III. to withdraw his troops within a given time or General Logan with two hundred thousand veteran troops fresh from the victorious fields of the south would be sent to help them vacate. The French troops were withdrawn. Maximillian sought refuge in Queretaro, where he was captured and tried by court martial by the Mexican authorities, and shot. Thus ended monarchy in America!

President Juarez confiscated the church property, sold it, and sequestrated the proceeds to the use of the states, and Mexico entered upon an era of unprecedented prosperity. The oppressive and repellant action of power ceased. The conservatism of peace was enthroned, and even leaders of banditti were controlled by its assertive influence for good.

So in Kansas. The right of way for peace was secured by the gun, and the right of moral and intellectual darkness gave way before the insistent flashes of gospel light. Even more so has it been in the fair southland, until now, in the history of a generation, the power of oppression has given way to intelligent conservatism, with education, science and religion dominating, and half a continent, once dark as midnight with human woe, then scarred and scorched and blighted by war, now blossoms like the rose and is filled by the gospel with joy and song and prosperity. Even the poor chattel sold from the auction block has become a scholar, a christian, and a leader in higher education.

Such is the transforming power of the Gun and the Gospel.

It is intensely interesting to trace the marked trial of the two types of civilization, or rather the barbarism of slavery and the refinement of christianity, that met on this chosen battle field of Kansas. There was Franklin, a pro-slavery town, now a cluster of farm houses and barns. West of this, four miles, is the free-state centre, the historic city, the Athens of the west,—Lawrence,—destroyed twice by rebel hatred, now the seat of the Kansas State University, whither annually go up ten hundred young men and women, students from Kansas' homes, to obtain thorough equipment for life's higher destinies. Twelve miles up the Kansas River is Lecompton, the old pro-slavery capital, where was expended a hundred thousand dollars by the general government to erect a slave state capital building. The ruins, and even the site itself, would have been obliterated ere this had not the loyal United Brethren located thereon a university, calling it after the grim Kansas chieftan, "Lane University." Tecumseh, another pro-slavery town site, would have gone into obnoxious desuetude had not the Methodist Episcopal church made it the head of a circuit and planted a church and parsonage here. Just west stands Topeka, the home of churches, schools, prohibition and refinement, saved by the gospel. Up the river farther you can see the old stone house, without window or door, roof or floor, none of which it ever had, where the first pro-slavery legislature met, armed cap-a-pie, organized—and adjourned to the border of Missouri because the gospel of peace had located a college on Blue Mont, and by Methodist money and devotion consecrated it to civilization, education and christianity.

All over the state, in close proximity, are seen the evidences of the relationship of "The Gun and the Gospel;" in incorporating that relationship in the title of this book, I am but conserving the unity of the already written record of history.

EARLY KANSAS AND CHAPLAIN FISHER.

CHAPTER I.

THE RELATION OF KANSAS TO FREEDOM.

The careful reader of history cannot have failed to discover that from the earliest dawn of human society there has been an almost unintermittent struggle between the weak and the strong, the rich and the poor, the good and the bad, for equality—social and religious—before the law. Oppression by the strong was the source of human slavery, which has darkened and blighted almost every continent and realm, as well as cursed almost every tribe and nation and people. It was the exhibition of this spirit of oppression and the opposing spirit of freedom and religion that led our pilgrim fathers and mothers, in the year of our Lord 1620, on August 5, to leave the comforts and blessings of the civilization of the old world and cross the untried ocean to plant a new civilization on a new continent, amid the savage and untutored tribes of the forests and plains of North America, and which prompted them, when they landed at Plymouth Rock on Monday, December 11, O. S., 1620, before they left the cabin of the Mayflower to consecrate the continent to God and Freedom, to enter into a perpetual covenant "to live in peace and harmony, with equal rights to all, obedient to just laws made for the common good." To this simple but sublime constitution of the oldest New England states all the heads of the families (forty-one in number) solemnly set their names.

The astonishing feature of our history is the fact that very early in colonial days human slavery was introduced. In 1617 and 1618 King James had conferred upon the council of Plymouth a charter to all that part of America lying between the fortieth and forty-eighth parallels of north latitude, extending from ocean to ocean. The oldest Virginia colonists were idle, improvident and dissolute. They came from Newport in 1607. Of these only twelve were laborers, four carpenters, six or eight masons and blacksmiths, and forty-eight "gentlemen." The first families of Virginia, chronologically speaking, were the result of the sending of women to supply the lack of wives, their transportation being paid by the men in tobacco, the first cargo costing one hundred and twenty pounds and the second one hundred pounds per capita, passage money, which the men cheerfully paid. In 1619 negroes were brought to the colony as slaves, as both the English and Germans had held them for a term of service of a few months or years. In the month of August, 1619, a Dutch man-of-war sailed up the James River and offered twenty Africans for sale by auction. They were purchased by the wealthier planters and made slaves for life. Nearly fifty years later Negro slavery became well established in the English colonies; so that at the time the Declaration of Independence was adopted declaring that "these truths are self-evident, that all men are created equal; that they are endowed by the Creator with certain inalienable rights that among these rights are life, liberty and the pursuit of happiness," almost all the signatory colonies were involved in the inconsistency of holding their fellow-men in slavery. The first bloodshed in freedom's holy cause was that of a black man, Crispus Atticus, who died in the streets of Boston, almost under the shadow of Faneuil Hall, the birthplace and cradle of American liberty.

During the revolutionary war the colonies were holding slaves, and when the war ended and a national constitution came to be framed the most stubborn difficulty that confronted the patriots who had gained American independence was the problem, What shall be done with American slavery? Six of the thirteen states became absolute slave-holding states.

It was hoped that slavery would die out of its own inertia, but it was fostered and grew and extended until Virginia, "the mother of presidents," became debased and ruined by becoming a slave-breeding and slave-trading commonwealth. The admission of Vermont as a free state and Kentucky and Tennessee as slave states made the number of slave and free states equal, and made the senate half for freedom and half for slavery. In 1818 Illinois was admitted to free statehood and Alabama as a slave state. But when, in 1820, it was proposed to admit Missouri the North became alarmed on account of the encroachment of slavery northward. Maine was proposed as a free state, and a compromise was agreed upon that all that part of the Louisiana purchase lying north of Mason's and Dixon's line, or 36 degrees 30 minutes North latitude, should be forever free. Finally, the abolition of slavery was demanded by the American Anti-Slavery Society. The agitation spread. Slavery became arrogant and dictatorial. It controlled the dominant party. It held executive, administrative, judicial and legislative control. The plow-share of discord furrowed deep in church and state. In 1844 the Methodist Episcopal Church was rent asunder, and other Christian bodies were later divided on this question. In 1845 Texas was annexed that she might counterbalance the possible growth of free states. Michigan balanced Arkansas, Iowa and Wisconsin balanced Florida and Texas. In 1850 California was admitted and the North thus gained an extra state. New Mexico and Utah could not become slave states. Where could the South look? All remaining territory was free under the Missouri Compromise. Part of this must be overwhelmed by slavery, or all would be lost to the slave power.

Herein lay the importance to civilization of the struggle for supremacy in Kansas.

In 1853 and 1854 Senator Stephen A. Douglas, of Illinois, wished to become president, and launched a new political dogma—that of "Squatter Sovereignty"—which meant that the people of a territory should settle at the ballot box the character of their domestic institutions, and he became the champion of the Kansas and Nebraska bill. This bill repealed, in its passage, the Missouri Compromise, and threw Kansas open to settlement by the slave-ocracy of the South. Mr. Douglas said he did not care whether slavery was voted "up or down, in or out." Kansas thus became the providential battle-ground upon which we believe God intended should be settled the struggle going on for six thousand years—the equality of man before law. Here the minions of the slave power met the representatives of the Christian civilization of the best and brightest pages in the world's history, worthy sons and daughters of the Puritan Pilgrim Fathers, ready to die in Freedom's holy cause. As Christ died to make men happy they were ready to die to make men free.

South of Mason's and Dixon's line were the rich planters and families, unsuited by all their training, conditons and inclinations to become pioneers to settle a new state. There was a large number of whites (poor people) called by the rich "white trash," upon whom and their families the burdens of slavery rested with more cruel and crushing weight than upon the blacks. These were helpless, ignorant, and so poor that to emigrate was impossible. Had they found their way to Kansas they would probably have voted to make Kansas free that they might get homes. The negroes were of no use, having no vote, and if they had been brought in numbers it would have required an army to keep them from fleeing to Canada. So the slave power was here represented by border ruffians and refugees from justice, who came in armed bands with whisky, bowie-knives and revolvers. Thus they came, a motley crew, fit representatives of the barbarism of slavery, to make Kansas a slave state and then retire and leave the occupancy of the land to the planter. No thrifty towns, beautiful school houses and stately churches would have bedecked and crowned this fairest gem of all God's beautiful world had their efforts prevailed.

North of Mason's and Dixon's line there was a surplusage of population, especially in the Northern and Middle States. Here were large families of educated people. These had married and were elbowing their neighbors for room. Many of them were small merchants, tradesmen, mechanics—adaptable men; they could make a living almost anywhere. Their wives were like them, and, used to work, able to help their husbands in a new state, and to the new state of Kansas they made their way.

Many instances are recorded exemplifying unusual courage upon the part of these brave people. One little woman near Portis, Kansas, whose husband was an invalid, with the aid of her little boys made a dugout and afterward dug a well thirty feet deep, securing an abundant supply of pure water. Another west of Atwood, in Rawlins county, while her husband was working out at an average of $62\frac{1}{2}$ cents per day, broke forty acres of prairie ground and raised a crop of sod corn. Next spring she broke twenty acres more, plowed the forty she had formerly broken, and raised a crop on the forty and sod corn on the twenty. I had the pleasure of dedicating a sod church near their home.

Such people as these came from the North and East in colonies and brought their children and their school books, and in some cases the school teacher and the preacher. They brought their Bibles and hymn-books along, and at even-tide had family prayer in camp or on boat; and on Sabbath they had class meeting or preaching. A Christian movement was this. and they came to make Kansas a free state. No marvel if when this stream of patriotic Christian civilization, involving love for "God and Home and Native Land," met the barbarism of slavery there should be a conflict, resulting in bloodshed and death. And so it was. More than two hundred patriot lives were sacrificed on freedom's holy altar to make Kansas free, and hundreds of other loyal, liberty loving men lost all they had in the strife. "Bleeding Kansas" was no unmeaning phrase, and but for this sacrifice Kansas, fairest of the fair, would have been blighted and seared and scorched by slavery.

THE RELATION OF KANSAS TO FREEDOM.

Kansas was admitted to statehood January 29, 1861. It is four hundred and six miles East and West and two hundred and four miles North and South—the central state of the sisterhood—well organized, a veritable sanitarium physically, morally, socially, religiously and educationally. It is composed of one hundred and five counties, with nine thousand, one hundred and seventy-four organized school districts, and eleven thousand, four hundred and ninety-six school rooms, almost all of which are furnished with modern conveniences for educational advantages for both teacher and pupil. It has the most salubrious climate, fertile and easily-cultivatable soil, the best and highest average (taking seven years as a period) of delightful weather, and more clear days and balmy nights than any other state in the Union.

Taking all constitutional and statuary enactments, the laws that govern this sublime commonwealth are the result of the best minds, based upon experiment and experience, and really need less amendment to constitute a perfect system of civil jurisprudence than the laws of perhaps any other state in the Union. There has been wonderful and satisfactory unanimity of action considering the heterogeneous character of our citizency, in all these enactments except in the prohibitory law; and want of harmony arises here from the very nature of that twin relic of barbarism—always an outlaw—the rum traffic, opposed to the peace and purity of the state. But even in this the great seal of the state is prophetic.

This seal, without which no public document is of force, was adopted by the first legislature, having been designed by a joint committee of the lower and upper houses, and is at once a history and a prophecy. The original was designed by John J. Ingalls, at that time secretary of the senate. The motto "ad astra per aspera" "to the stars through difficulties"—was illustrated in the original design by a lone bright star, representing Kansas rising above a field of cloud to join a constellation of stars numbering twenty-seven, as many as there were states composing the Union when Kansas was admitted to the sisterhood.

The clouds of strife were rifted, territorial wars were dissipated. Bleeding but bright with the effulgence of liberty Kansas attracted the gaze of nations. Another star had arisen to bedeck the brow of liberty. The motto was adopted, but the design was changed so that the sky is murky and bedizened. This, too, may be prophetic for a season. But the clouds will roll away and Kansas will yet appear as the bright and morning star of the American firmament.

CHAPTER II.

JOHN BROWN.

Every great epoch in history is preceded by widespread agitation, is ushered in by action, springing from thought and motive of extreme intensity on the part of the actor, and is always in advance of the mentality of the age and always stamped by the idiosyncrasies of the reformer whose soul is so wrapt in the oncoming, inevitable event as to be precipitated into action without counting the results to self or fortune. Thus it ever has been and doubtless ever will be in human life and history.

The first act of Moses, Deliverer and Law-Giver, in slaying the Egyptian oppressor, prefigured the deliverance of Israel, voiced the universal desire for freedom, lost him the throne of Egypt, drove him personally into banishment, inaugurated a new epoch in the destruction of Egypt, the then mightiest nation on earth, and quickened into birth a nation whose perpetuation without home or country or king, prince or ruler, is the standing miracle of the ages even until this day. So it was with John the Baptist. At the time of his appearance the world was full of desire and expectation for a new form of worship and spiritual service. Suddenly, without plan or forethought for personal safety or emolument, he burst upon the expectant world with the startling declaration "The Kingdom of Heaven is At Hand," and inaugurated a new era and a new salvation, even at the loss of his own head. The greatest character in human history, one whose every act was a sermon and whose every word was a revelation, perfected the era introduced by John the Baptist and crowned the ages with immortality by dying that most ignominious of all deaths, crucifixion, and so demonstrated his infinite love for suffering humanity, as well as the most exalted plan and purpose for establishing the universal brotherhood of mankind.

We need not multiply examples. Bridging from the fairest ensample of devotion to a cause the world has ever known, turning from the greater to the less, from the pattern to the follower, we have in the case of John Brown, of Osawatomie, the subject of these paragraphs, one in whom all that we have predicated of era-makers had full scope and concentration. He appeared in the arena of action when the public mind was surcharged with the electric impetus of coming events, when the dawn of a new age of broader freedom trembled upon the horizon, when the watchers looked intently for the full rising of that sun which should warm the half-born thought to sturdy life and set reform in motion.

John Brown was born at Torrington, Connecticut, May 9th, 1800, and died on the scaffold at Charleston, West Virginia, December 2nd, 1859. He was sixth in descent from that Peter Brown who came to New England in the Mayflower in 1620, and was a grandson of Captain John Brown, a revolutionary officer who died in the American revolution. He was honorably and well connected, numbering among his immediate kinsfolk conspicuous Puritans, revolutionists, soldiers, lawyers, professors, doctors of divinity, orators, physicians and farmers. His father and family moved to Hudson, Ohio, when John was five years old. Here in the Ohio wilderness he grew, a stalwart youth. At the age of sixteen he joined the Congregational church and began studying for the ministry. Ohio, especially Hudson, was at this time thoroughly imbued with anti-slavery doctrine, and young Brown imbibed the sentiment freely as he grew toward manhood. Tall, athletic, studious, having the bearing of a theologue, he had, like the immortal Simon and Grant, been a tanner, and when from excessive application to study his eyes failed him he returned to his early vocation in Hudson. Here he married and partially reared his family of six children. He was farmer, tanner and land-surveyor while living at Hudson. In 1826 he moved to Richmond, Pennsylvania, near Meadville, where he remained until 1835, when he located at Franklin Miles, Portage County, Ohio. His life being one of change, his business while in this locality was one of speculative adventure in land and sheep until he finally moved to Boston and became a wool merchant. Here he made the acquaintance of such men as Caleb Cushing, Rufus Choate, Gerrett Smith and that greatest of all ex-slaves, Frederick Douglass.

In 1848-49 he visited England to open a wool market and also to visit noted battle-fields. The world was one day to know why!

On his return he went at once to live among the colored farmers of North Elba, in the Adirondack woods, for the purpose of drilling a company of liberators from among them. The life of the people at North Elba was strictly pioneer, but though there were few roads, churches or school-houses the people were inclined to religion, education and thrift. Mrs. Brown's dwelling had but two rooms and in this house two families lived. In these humble surroundings, sowing what seeds they might toward a future reaping, they lived for several years.

In the winter of 1854-55, after Kansas had been opened for settlement, the Browns prepared to settle there. The brothers—John Brown, Jr., Jason, Owen, Frederick and a half-brother, Salmon—established themselves in Miami County, near Osawatomie. To supplement their anti-slavery struggles in the new land they wrote to their father for aid. Through his efforts a mass-meeting was held in Utica and an anti-slavery society was formed to help settle Kansas. At this meeting the father pleaded eloquently for the cause for which his sons were doing valiant battle on the Western fields. "Without shedding of blood," he cried, "there is no remission of sins!" He asked for arms, dwelt upon the violent spirit of the pro-slavery people and pledged himself to join his sons and make good report of their doings. Arms were provided and funds were furnished and the father was sent to his sons in Kansas. Such were the material results from Kansas meetings on both sides of Mason's and Dixon's line!

The Brown contingent already in Kansas had selected claims and were serving in the free-state conventions. John Jr., had been elected to the free-state legislature at Topeka. They were all radical free-state men. When John Brown, Sr., had joined his sons at Osawotamie he found his sphere, and from and after October of 1855 he became a colossal figure in the nation's history, a bold picture down time's perspective. His wife was ever his counsellor and ally, his sons, like the sons of the patriarchs of old, were his trusted lieutenants, and even his sons-in-law became part of his invincible cohort. So early as 1839 John

Brown had declared that by blood atonement alone could the chattel slavery of human beings be destroyed, and virtually from that date he had become bound with them in bonds to stay with them and be of them until the bitter end. His forecast was unerring—events proved it. He took his wife and three eldest sons and a colored preacher into his plans and purposes and bound them all to secrecy as to the place of the inauguration of the epoch of liberty. His eldest son records that the first time he saw his father kneel to pray—he was a Presbyterian—was when he first vowed himself then and there to attack slavery by force.

Hinton says John Brown equipped his brain as well as his conscience. He made himself familiar with military tactics and guerrilla methods, for he was a thinker as well as a believer in destiny. Kansas was to him a splendid opportunity for a demonstration of himself. It was here that he began to think and write, and none can measure the depths of his desire and doing. He resolved to make the Declaration of American Independence a verity and the constitution an instrument whereby to liberate and elevate a race. His matured plan was to form, by means of picked men, a line penetrating to the very heart of the Southland, to be held by adroit and persuasive men who should receive, protect and pass on to safety all slave-fugitives, and thus create a mobilized force. The specifications of the plan are too great to be given in detail here.

This plan, though miscarrying at Harper's Ferry, showed consummate skill and remarkable geographical knowledge of the Southern states and the fastnesses thereof, covering the whole land like a vast net-work. And if once those meshes had been drawn, the hundreds of thousands of lives lost and the hundreds of millions of dollars spent in civil war would have been saved and John Brown's soul in it's "marching on" would have lead the brothers in black from slavery to freedom through a bloodless victory. There would then have been no confederacy nor a semblance of war against the Union. His chain of mountain forts and defiles and draws, as a means of communication along the great divides and slopes of southern mountains, would have done honor to Napoleon's best civil engineer corps. He has been pronounced insane by men whose conception could never by any chance rise to the compass of such a scheme as was his. No general of the age showed such thoroughness of topographical knowledge of his territory as did John Brown, and few have showed engineering skill of such scope and ability. He sincerely believed that the slave power was designed to cripple and destroy the Republic, and he as sincerely hoped to abolish that power, root and branch, by aiding the slaves to secure their freedom. He lived under this profound conviction as under a guiding star and acted under the light of it. There was nothing in his Puritan nature that could by any possibility compromise with what he intelligently conceived to be an evil oppressive to humanity. To him that crime against liberty, as enacted in the over-riding of eight hundred legally cast votes by four thousand invading Missourians, whereby a citizen of Texas was elected as a delegate to Congress to represent Kansas, could not be condoned or palliated.

Robbery, murder and arson had marked the march of Buford, Titus and other commanders of the border ruffians who had invaded Kansas, while free-state men had come as came the Pilgrims from across the ocean, with wives and children, Bibles and hymn-books, school books and teachers—to establish a type of Christian civilization superior to any yet developed on the American continent. It was with this last named band that John Brown had become identified with all the zeal and enthusiasm of his rugged and devout nature. Struggling against mighty odds, this purposeful people had written on high their legend, "Resistance to Tyranny is Obedience to God." They resisted—and to what end the Pottawotamie Creek disaster to the pro-slavery men bore testimony of supremest force. This—always to be lamented—sanguinary encounter by no means lessened the asperities between the pro-slavery and anti-slavery forces. The results of it have been censured and they have been commended, but they fixed upon this hero the significant sobriquet, "Osawotamie" Brown—he whose soul in poetry, history and song goes forever "marching on." From that time he was an aggressive figure in free-state movements for the rescue of Kansas from the desires of the slave power.

John Brown was conspicuously connected with the obtaining and colporteurage of the noted "Sharp's Rifles," known as "Beecher's Bibles," and in his visits to Chicago, Buffalo and elsewhere he aided greatly in kindling a public sentiment in favor of free Kansas and the integrity of the Union. Anticipating the determined purpose of state's rights men to dissolve the Union to make way for the extension of African slavery he fought zealously in the van-guard.

Among his various supporters he counted upon the full confidence of that non-combative, peace-loving people, the Quakers, as the following incident will show: On one of his visits East he stopped in the

Springdale Settlement in Iowa. A friend named Townsend kept a house significantly called "Traveler's Rest." Riding up to the door of this unpretentious hostelry on a very gaunt mule the spare, dust-begrimed, sun-burned traveler dismounted. "Have you ever heard of John Brown, of Kansas?" was his question to the landlord. With no word of welcome, recognition or introduction, the landlord calmly took from his pocket a piece of chalk and lifting Brown's hat from a head covered with grizzled hair he drew a broad "X" on the hat and then turned him about to make two "X's" on his back. "Walk right in and make yourself at home," said the landlord then. And for the sake of the cause the faithful mule, as well as his owner, were gratuitously entertained. The Unitarians of New England, and the Congregationalists and Presbyterians, as well as all philanthropic people, were deeply interested in the mission in which John Brown was engaged and bade him a hearty "God Speed" from day to day.

Finally, concentrating his attention upon Virginia as a starting point, Brown began assembling his chosen lieutenants at Harper's Ferry. On the 16th of October, 1859, they took possession of the United States arsenal. They then set about destroying telegraph communications, captured a railroad train, and at last got into imperfect fortifications in the Erskine House. The grounds, the bridge and the entire town passed into their possession, their declaration being that they wanted only liberty. The stopping of the train was the one fatal blunder in the well-conceived plan, for its detention gave the passengers and trainmen an opportunity to learn the situation and to spread the news to telegraph stations. All hope of

secrecy was lost at once. On the morning of the 17th of October, 1859, the country from ocean to ocean was ablaze with flaming bulletins like these:
"Fearful and Exciting Intelligence!"
"Negro Insurrection at Harper's Ferry!"
"Hundreds of Insurrectionists in Arms!"
"Arsenal and Works Seized!'
"The Leader, 'Osawatomie Brown,' of Kansas!"
"Several Killed. Troops on the Way!"
Such were the startling echoes which filled the air, were to be heard on the streets, discussed on the cars, in the papers and whizzed from every telegraph wire.

The smouldering public sentiment, already kindled by dread and excitement, burst into flame at the name of "Osawatomie Brown" and Kansas. It was to the American people as the war cry of old, "The sword of the Lord and Gideon!" It was as the breaking of pitchers and the glowing of lamps and the clarion notes of bugles on the hill-tops in the midnight stillness. "Negro insurrection;" "Led by Osawatomie Brown of Kansas." The words became a slogan of horror. I was in Baltimore that day—and such a day! When many of the great cutlasses provided by Brown were captured and brought to Baltimore the people went wild. Men's hearts failed them for fear. It was the beginning of the end, and the air was thick with direful prophecy.

While the enormity of the crime of human slavery justified an expiation by blood it is but just to say of John Brown that his was not intended to be a bloody insurrection. He hoped for a vast uprising and a peaceable manumission. His methods proved unwise, inefficient and disastrous. He and his men were captured, though not without an effort at defence; some were killed in the struggle, among them

Oliver Brown, one of the sons of the leader. "Osawatomie Brown" had undeniably committed an offence against the United States government by having taken forcible possession of the arsenal, and against the dignity of Virginia by occupying her soil with an armed force. What was to be the penalty? On the night of the 16th some of Brown's men had captured Colonel Washington. The Virginian had surrendered the "sword of Frederick the Great" and "the pistol of Lafayette" and he and his sons had then been marched to the ferry. Here the slain of the party had already aggregated ten. Brown, wounded and bleeding, was taken shortly afterward by United States marines and turned over to the state authorities. Tried by a Virginia court, he was found guilty of treason against the state and condemned to death by hanging.

On the 2nd of December, 1859, the execution took place at Charleston in the presence of thousands of people who had gathered to witness this first and last execution for "treason" on such grounds. Just before his execution Brown wrote in a clear hand: "I, John Brown, am now quite certain that the crimes of this guilty land will never be purged away but with blood. I had, as I now think vainly, flattered myself that without much bloodshed it might be done."

* * * * * *

When the body was laid to rest at North Elba, Wendell Phillips said of him, "Marvellous old man! History will date Virginia's emancipation from Harper's Ferry. John Brown has loosened the roots of the slave system. He sleeps in the blessings of the crushed and the poor, and men believe more firmly in virtue now that such a man has lived."

His body rests at North Elba, New York, 'neath

the shadow of a great rock which is made his monument, but his record is on high. As Christ died to make men happy he died to make men free. His short-lived movement crystallized and projected into tangible form the spirit of the age. Even from the time the first innocent blood baptized the fair soil of freedom's chosen battle-field, Kansas, the die was cast, the time chosen and the methods fixed by which the crime of crimes must be undone. And from that time until now the name of John Brown, Christian, patriot, liberator, has stood out broadly in the chronicles of our country's struggle for freedom. Brown's name, like that of James H. Lane of Lawrence, is so interwoven with Kansas history and that history is so interwoven with the larger history of universal American freedom that no discussion of either would be complete or just without giving to him the large meed of credit which rightfully is his for the part he played in starting the nation upon a vaster conception of its obligations to liberty and the individual.*

―――――――――――――――――――――――――――――――

*The summer of 1896 has seen the realization of a hope dear to the heart of the late Kate Field, its instigator, and to all those who take pleasure in the rendering unto Caesar the things that are Caesar's. The John Brown Association, organized by Miss Field, and numbering among its members some prominent New Yorkers, has purchased the John Brown farm and homestead and formally presented this historic property to the state with the agreement that the Commonwealth of New York shall defray the expenses of taking proper care of it. Upon the occasion of the presentation an appropriate monument was unveiled, situated near the old headstone marking John Brown's grave.

CHAPTER III.

JIM LANE.

The fact of the existence of human slavery under the Aegis of American freedom is so monstrous an idea that if it were not history it would be unbelievable. But the fact admitted, with it was carried all the atrocities of this barbarism and from it developed all the theories of the Northern abolitionists, as well as the direct and stubborn antagonism of the earnest, unconquerable West.

Every great epoch develops men of action, following close upon the sentimental and educational stages of reform. Thus we find Mr. Wesley declaring human slavery "The sum of all villainies," and Garretson and Phillips thundering their anathemas and arousing the slumbering conscience of the American people, and the New England Emigrant Aid Society, with the Methodist itinerant force in the field, to help families obtain homes and keep the moral tone of society firm, and John Brown, of immortal fame, and Jim Lane, the brave Kansas defender and liberator, as leading actors in freedom's cause.

James H. Lane was born at Lawrenceburgh, Indiana, June 22d, 1814. His environments were those of patriotic enthusiasm. The war of 1812, Jackson's great exploits at New Orleans, and the exciting political campaigns which soon followed all afforded for the boy, the youth, the young man, intellectual and sentimental food which incorporated itself into the

GENERAL JAMES H. LANE.

warp and woof of his life. He was a child of the frontier.

He was of Scotch-Irish and Puritanic extraction, his father and mother, both of patriotic connection, numbering among their immediate relatives judges, lawyers, statesmen, patriots and honorable politicians. His father was the first speaker of the house in Indiana and afterwards a judge and member of congress. His mother was regarded one of the most devout and intelligent Christian women in Lawrenceburgh, an ornament to the ranks of Methodism in that great Methodist state.

The son imbibed from the mother's teachings and example the highest reverence for religion and true Christian character. We have no doubt that in the development of character the co-mingling of influences so sacred in home life with the attrition of political surroundings, had large influence in forming the idiosyncracies of the man, which made Jim Lane the enigma he was and the historic character he is. His like cannot be found until another necessity like Kansas' border-ruffian warfare shall call him forth to lead in the contest for the right. I knew him intimately and long and well, and never knew a man who, when with good men and in refined surroundings, was so wholly and powerfully under the influence of mother's teachings. Her memory was a veritable presence; her example a perpetual admonition. In the company of politicians his Scotch-Irish pater-master politician's example led him, and he often fell into censurable mirthfulness and conversation; but his mother's name and life was ever before him in thoughtful mood, like a benediction.

He was in partisan politics a democrat. When the war occurred between Mexico and the United States he enlisted as a private, but was early made colonel of the regiment. He gallantly led his men through all the engagements up to the battle of Buena Vista, and here rallied the scattered regiment of Col. Bowles, and honorably commanded until the close of the war. He became lieutenant-governor of Indiana and elector at large, voting for Franklin Pierce for president, and was also a member of congress and voted with Douglas for the Kansas-Nebraska bill.

With such experience and honors he came to Kansas, arriving one bright April morning in 1855, and with jug in hand (not for liquor, for he was an abstainer, but to get water), he walked into the free-state hamlet, now the historic city of Lawrence. Here he took up his abode, and wrought and fought, and was buried. He came a born, developed, firm son of democracy, but his high chivalric nature could not and would not approve the methods introduced by the vice-president of the United States, David Atchison, and his border-ruffians, to foist slavery upon the soil of Kansas, and also to fetter free-thought, suppress free-speech, and drive out of the territory the free-state men of the United States, who came from almost every state and territory in the Union, bonafide settlers, to secure homes for themselves and families.

The first trial of the forces by count at the ballot-box occurred on November 29, 1854, and resulted as follows: Democrats 305, Anti-slavery 248, and Pro-slavery 2,258, for delegate to congress. On this day occurred the first homicide, when Davis, a pro-slavery man, assaulted unprovoked, Kibby, a free-state man. Davis was killed by Kibby in self defense. On March 30, 1855, a regular invasion of ballot-box stuffers and repeaters from Missouri and other Southern states took place, when at Lawrence, Leavenworth, Kickapoo, Atchison and elsewhere a pro-slavery legislature was chosen by the boldest and most wicked assault ever made on the ballot-box in the name of popular suffrage. Loyal men were disfranchised, border-ruffians were triumphant. They passed a code blacker than barbarity itself.

In such an emergency free-state men needed a leader, and in Jim Lane they found one whose name was worth a thousand men, and whose bugle-blast became a terrifying tocsin to the enemies of freedom. Up to this date he had simply tried to organize the democracy, but now his lion-heart revolted from the unprecedented crimes of the slave oligarchy. With such aggravations it were marvelous if the free-state citizens had felt no resentment. They were not freebooters, nor were they nor their neighbors thieves or adventurers, but a body of honorable men and women and children, home-seekers, who came to make the prairies bloom as the rose. To such the field of battle was the field of honor. They came to build churches, school-houses, mills, manufactories and cities. It is safe to say that there never was a better, more industrious, more law-abiding people in all respects than were the emigrants who came to Kansas from the non-slaveholding states. Their purpose, as the sequel shows, as the present demonstrates, was to establish a commonwealth in which education, religion, patriotism and righteousness could have their best opportunity and their highest development.

The "Grim Chieftain" combined in himself all the elements of fiery oratory and magnetism, being possessed of a ready flow of forceful language, a vocabulary redundant in expressive adjectives. He charmed his admirers, terrified his opponents, comforted the discouraged, fired with zeal those whose impulsive natures flamed with freedom's fires, so that every assembly he addressed was thrilled and swayed by a master hand, and even his avowed foes became his admiring friends. In his first alignment with the free-state men, which was looked upon by some New Englanders as rather dubious, he gave utterance to words that would honor the head and heart of a solon. In the "Herald of Freedom," for August 18th, 1855, he is quoted as follows: "If I believed a prayer from me for you would do any good it would be that you might be endowed with the wisdom of Solomon, the caution of Washington and the justice of Franklin. It requires wisdom, it requires manhood, to restrain passion. I say, as a citizen of Kansas, I wish we had wisdom to-day. There is the existence of a nation hanging upon the action of the citizens of Kansas. Moderation, Moderation, Moderation, Gentlemen!! I am here, as anxious as any of you, to secure a free constitution to Kansas."

There was no small contention on the question of excluding all black people from the state, both slaves and free. Some declared that if blacks settled in Kansas they would prefer that they should be slaves. Some Western states had these exclusive laws. Lane was at first a black-law man. This gave him prestige with Western free-state men.

But he discovered very early that such a clause in the proposed constitution would lose all the sympathy and influence of such men as Giddings, Sumner, Wade, Wilson, Stevens, Seward, Grow, and Chase. He gave up his exclusive views, and became a giant, armed cap-a-pie in freedom's camp for all men, without reference to color, race, or previous condition. He became a member of the constitutional convention, and was sent to Washington with the constitution.

Senator Douglas accused him of forgery, in having struck out the black-law clause. Lane promptly challenged him to deadly combat, but Douglas declined the challenge because Lane was not his peer, not being a senator.

He used to say, "Douglas has carefully put away a challenge which he declined because I was not a senator. You owe it alike to yourselves and me to put me where I can make him fish up that paper." Later Lane was elected senator and he and Douglas became fast friends, and perhaps no senator felt more keenly the loss of a great actor in the national crisis which resulted in making Kansas free, precipitating an already determined rebellion and determining the emancipation of the slave, than Lane felt at the death of Douglas. The war had made them friends to be separated only by death.

The murder of Charles W. Dow by F. M. Coleman was followed by the pro-slavery invaders' arresting Dow's neighbor, one Branson, to prevent him from being a witness against Coleman, who thus went free. This deplorable event was quickly followed by the Wakarusa war. Invasion, murder, arson, and outrages called for resistance and defense. Here was a new chance for the appearance of conflicting jealousies, even among free-state men. The New England men had their preferences, and the Western men were suspected of lack of radicalism. Especially were Southern anti-slavery men distrusted as not sufficiently Puritanical.

Dr. Charles Robinson, afterward Governor, was commander-in-chief of the anti-slavery men during this war and Jim Lane, who was the best equipped by experience, drill, courage and skill in military affairs was second in command. Like a true soldier he did his duty well and faithfully. He accepted his subordinate rank as other great souls have done and at once began drilling and organizing the troops.

His energy was unflagging, his presence an inspiration everywhere. The free-state forces were less than half the number of the invading enemy. Breastworks and rifle-pits were speedily constructed in regular military style under Lane's supervision, so that the fortifications and earthworks could have resisted an invading force four times the strength mustered by the invading border-ruffians. Every man did his part well, and the name of Jim Lane was now, as ever afterward, a terror to his enemies. As he reviewed the troops and works nearly completed he commended them, at the same time cautioning against rashness, alarm or surprise. His were magical words; they nerved every arm, and fired every breast with courage. He was not alone in words of encouragement during the siege. Jimmie McGee, an old Irishman, came and said, "Work away, boys, be-dad; there's 2,000 bushels of corn in McGee's crib, and you shan't starve as long as there is a kernel left!" To indicate the spirit of the times, two brave boys brought a howitzer to Lane's camp and two loyal women brought kegs of powder under a buggy seat to aid in defense of their homes.

On the 29th of December, 1855, Gov. Shannon proclaimed internecine war. Lane hastened to Lawrence and wrote to friends to hurry up the "baggage," meaning munitions of war, and the conflict thus and then commenced did not cease until the slaves were emancipated and Lee had surrendered to the "Silent Man of Destiny."

Lane's management of local affairs won the approval of all the free-state men, and the invading ruffians were compelled to leave the territory, while the Wakarusa war was the initiation of a victory for freedom. Even Shannon, though backed by United States authority, was compelled to admit that the men whom he had called into action were an invading force. All this while Lane scrupulously avoided conflict with United States laws, and the governor issued an order that Lane's men should defend the town, the people and their lives and property. Very soon after receiving such order Lane called his force into line and addressing the motley company as "United States dragoons," ordered them to hold themselves in readiness for action. The invaders made a mad rush for the Missouri line, and thus the Wakarusa war was ended, with Lane as the idol of the free-state dragoons.

Lane's utterances on disbanding the brave defenders of home and freedom were words of wisdom and patriotism which still ring down the aisles of freedom's history. His greatest speech was afterwards delivered in Chicago, and struck a popular chord which produced a national crisis. It was only realized when in the national republican convention in which Mr. Lincoln was renominated; it was then seen that a master-hand had planned that result. There was great dissatisfaction and unrest throughout the country, and a contest which boded no good for the Union cause was imminent. But in the grand council of the Union League the evening before the convention, after many able speeches favoring other candidates had been made,

Mr. Lane arose and made the political speech of his life, carrying the League with him almost to a man. In the closing of his speech he said: "We shall together be watched in breathless listening by all this country—by all the civilized world—and if we seem to waver as to our set purpose we destroy hope, and if we permit private feeling to break forth into discussion we discuss defeat, and if we nominate any other man than Abraham Lincoln we nominate ruin. Gentlemen of the Union League, I have done." The next day Mr. Lincoln was nominated on the first ballot. The grim chieftain had won his cause and ruin was averted.

Hon. John Speer has truly said of Lane: "To the experience, skill and perseverance of the gallant Gen. James H. Lane all credit is due for the thorough discipline of our forces, and the complete and extensive preparations for defense. His services cannot be overestimated. Kansas can never forget them."

In 1861 I was stationed in Lawrence. Gen. Lane had recently professed conversion at a camp-meeting near Palmyra. He and Col. H. P. Johnson, a local preacher, and Capt. McLean attended church one evening in Lawrence. Lane related his recent experience, and Johnson spoke after Lane. All three had served in the Mexican war, and both referred to their army life. McLean, who was evidently under the influence of liquor, arose and said: "Yes—hic!—Lane and Johnson—hic!—were good—hic!—soldiers, and fought—hic!—and bled and died—hic!—and I was there too—hic!—and I fought—hic!—and bled—and died, nary a time—hic!—and this—hic!—is the first—hic!—time I've—hic!—said anything about it—hic!" With this Johnston helped him to a seat, and we sang a verse or two of "Come, ye sinners," to avoid a scene.

Soon after this the rebels fired on Fort Sumter and invested Washington. Lane and the Kansas men who were in Washington offered their services to Mr. Lincoln, and were bivouacked one hundred and eighty strong in the East Room, by concurrence of Gen. Hunter and the Secretary of War. At midnight Mr. Stanton and President Lincoln, arm in arm, walked into the camp in the White House, guarded by Lane and his Kansas heroes, who thus thwarted a well devised plan to kidnap the president and secretary.

President Buchanan, in 1857, had in his message to congress said, "The people of Kansas are in rebellion against the government with a military leader of most turbulent and dangerous character at their head." In reply Gen. Lane said: "I venture the assertion that the message stands without a parallel in its falsificaiton of history. Never have the people of Kansas been in arms, except to resist invasion from other states. When the territory was occupied by four distinct armies from foreign states, laying waste the country and avowing to exterminate the people of Kansas, before resisting them we called upon the territorial authorities and the commandant of the United States troops for protection. Let Buchanan howl and congress enact! Kansas is free, and all the powers of the earth cannot enslave her! To-day the people of Kansas are a unit, and so long as that unity is preserved, nothing can prevail against her." War existed. Civil rights were secured at the cost of precious lives, and equality before the law was made a verity for the first time in history of Kansas, long before the first gun was fired on Fort Sumter. And the "Grim Chieftain" had much to do in thus immortalizing Kansas. The war thus inaugurated closed only with Sherman's march to the sea and Grant's acceptance of Lee's surrender at Appomattox.

Lane was authorized in 1861, by the President and Secretary Stanton, though then a United States senator, to raise troops on the frontier to protect Kansas from invasion. The company remained on duty until the danger of kidnaping the President was over. Senator Lane sent a squad to capture Robert E. Lee, but he had left for Richmond before Hon. Charles H. Holmes and his squad reached Arlington. What untold slaughter of human life would have been averted had his plan not miscarried no human pen can describe or tongue proclaim.

In accordance with instructions referred to Senator Lane came home through Missouri incognito, and immediately organized the Third, Fourth and Fifth Kansas Volunteers, appointing Col. Montgomery to the command of the Third, Col. Wear to the Fourth, and Col. H. P. Johnson to command the Fifth, a cavalry regiment. I was made chaplain of the Fifth regiment, and we were immediately ordered on forced march to Fort Scott to protect valuable quartermaster stores and ammunition, stored for the army of the frontier. The militia were called to concentrate at Ft. Scott. When we arrived there were about 4,000 men, all told, poorly armed, and very poorly mounted; with no cannon, only one howitzer, and a small Rodman gun. Lane sent two women over the line to report to the rebel army approaching, 18,000 strong, under command of Gens. Price, Raines and Slack, that there were 40,000 Iowa, Nebraska and Kansas troops, armed and equipped, in and around Fort Scott, under command of Gen. Jim Lane, awaiting their arrival and ready to receive them. The rebel army came to the line at Dry Wood and formed in battle array. Lane sent Montgomery, Wear and Johnson, with 380 men, and Capt. Moonlight with the howitzer, to meet the enemy's main force of 13,000 men, flushed with the victory they had won at Wilson Creek over Gens. Lyon and Sigel. They were to be reinforced by Gen. Slack. Moonlight planted his howitzer on a commanding Kansas knob. The Kansas boys dismounted and with Sharp's rifles in hand crept up through the tall prairie-grass and hazel-brush within convenient reach of the rebel force. Moonlight opened fire, and his first shell burst in the midst of Capt. Bledsoe's splendid battery of field guns, wounding the captain, killing three gunners, upsetting two of his guns, and wounding several others of his men. Lane's men turned loose their Sharp's rifles, and in a few minutes seventy-two rebels lay dead and many others wounded. The rebels overshot Lane's troops and they had but one wounded. The presence of less than 400 men in action soon became to the enemy the mysterious 40,000—and Jim Lane in command! Gen. Slack was hastily brought up with his splendid force to sustain Price and Raines, but found them in full retreat. In his official report to Calib Jackson, governor of Missouri, he says that when he came upon the field to reinforce Price and Raines he found them and their very efficient army under rapid retreat on the verge of a general stampede, in the presence of a greatly superior force under command of Gen. Jas. H. Lane.

Lane's name was worth a thousand men, his multiplication table answered instead of numbers; and 380 Kansans, inspired by patriotism and their intrepid leader's presence, put 18,000 men to flight, saved Kansas from invasion, and hundreds of thousands of dollars worth worth of army stores.

Gen. Lane moved his command to Kansas City to prevent Gens. Price, Raines and Slack from advancing on Fort Leavenworth. They attacked Lexington, Mo., captured Col. Mulligan and his command, and then started to retreat and attack Gen. Fremont at Springfield. Lane ordered an advance to support Freemont. When we reached Osceola the enemy had burned the town and destroyed the ferry boat on the Osage River. The water was up, and nothing was left but an old abandoned scow, within 40 miles, on which to cross. Not an officer in the command would undertake to cross the command on that old boat. Lane called upon me to help him out of his dilemna. By my request he detailed six men from each company, and with these we beached the old boat, calked her seams with old clothes, nailed fence boards on the cracks to keep the calking in place, and put six men to work with battery buckets, to bail the water out. With hearty good will the men obeyed my directions and followed my example while the other chaplains and officers sat on the bank and watched us ferry the command safely over the river.

In due time we reached Springfield, and went into camp to await orders to march and meet the rebel forces under McCullough. Gen. Fremont was in command when we arrived, but was soon superseded by Gen. Hunter. Here transpired under my own observation two of the most trying ordeals of nerve I ever witnessed. Several trained and experienced French soldiers, fine looking fellows, came to America with Fremont. Some of them were attached to Lane's staff. It was Sabbath morning. Gen. Lane had sent for me. I reported at headquarters, and the general said he wished me to preach to the brigade and visitors, as many would be over to camp by 11 o'clock. While we were talking, in came the French officers, in a high state of excitement. Gen. Fremont had been removed and their anger was unbounded. They laid down their arms on the table and said they were going to leave the camp and return to Paris at once. They stood pale with rage. Lane sprang to his feet like a lion. He seemed taller than ever before. Seizing a revolver in each hand, he said: "You shan't resign. It is the order of the Secretary of War. We must obey. You will disgrace yourselves, dishonor France, and disgust the army." And fairly foaming with rage he stalked up to the men, and with uplifted revolvers, said, hissing it out: "By the eternal, I'll kill you both before you shall disgrace yourselves. Go back to your tents and remain until Gen. Fremont goes east, and like true soldiers remain with your superior."

In the afternoon review took place, and Gen. Fremont's staff came over. Gen. Lane reviewed the troops and put them through the manual of arms. One regiment was cavalry, another was mounted infantry, the rest infantry, so that the troops were not supposed to be well-drilled. But when Lane's command rang along the line every man seemed to be electrified. When they heard his voice, "Ground arms!" every gun dropped as if by magic, and they awaited in breathless expectancy his next word of command. He glanced up and down the long line, and then called, "Shoulder arms!" Every gun leaped to its place so simultaneously that the visitors were filled with surprise, and though out of place, suppressed applause passed from lip to lip. I never saw automatic movement more perfect than that "Shoulder arms" under Jim Lane's inspiring command.

Gen. Hunter assumed command, and immediately ordered the main army to St. Louis, while Lane's command, which never retreated, countermarched by way of Lamar to Kansas. The whole negro population of Missouri which had followed Fremont's march and Lane's brigade were shaken off by Gen. Hunter's army and took up their march with the Kansas troops, bound for Kansas and freedom. We, in turn, were followed by McCullough's army, beset on either hand by Coffee's and other noted guerrilla bands, and liable to be attacked at any hour. The second day out Lane sent for me on the march, and explaining our imminent danger of attack and the helpless condition of the great multitude of blacks, said: "What shall I do with them?" I replied that all the men were in the army, and the women and children in Kansas needed help to save the crop and provide fuel for winter, and I advised to send the negroes to Kansas to help the women and children. His laconic reply was, "I'll do it." When we went into camp he issued an order that all the refugees and blacks should meet on the parade ground next morning at 8 o'clock, ready to go to Kansas; and his first order was, "Chaplains Fisher, Moore and Fish will take charge of these people, escort them to Kansas, divide their property among them as best they can, find homes for them, and report to headquarters."

Jim Lane was a striking character. Without him Kansas would not likely have become what she is. He was a leader of men. His long strain of excitement, with perhaps inherited suicidal tendency, and his extreme sensitiveness to criticism on defeat, at last broke his indomitable energy and will, and in an unfortunate desire to control presidential patronage he found himself as United States Senator supporting the president, Andrew Johnson, in his opposition to Mr. Sumner's civil rights bill, thus antagonising the very sentiment which in Kansas gave him such victories and honors.

When he awoke to see the fatal blunder he had committed he became despondent, a spell of illness ensued, his mind gave way, and while out driving at Fort Leavenworth, where he had sought rest and treatment, he stepped behind the ambulance and placing a pistol in his mouth sent a bullet crashing through his brain. Though fatally wounded he regained consciousness and at times was able to recognize his particular friends and members of his family. I was called by telegram to his dying bed and as he took my hand in his and placed it upon the site of his wound he said plaintively, "Bad, Bad," and soon afterward died. The spirit of a leader, a man who had never known defeat at the hands of others, had been ushered before his maker by his own hand while smarting under the sting of political defeat wrought by an error in judgment. In times of war and strife a giant, in times of peace and politics he was but mortal.

The most trying ordeal of my ministerial life was thrown upon me by his death. I was called upon to preach the funeral sermon in Lawrence on the Sunday following his demise. There were present men who had carried a rope to hang him on account of the early tragedy which had resulted in the death of Jenkins, and there were present men who had stood watch the livelong night to prevent his mobbing; there were men who were with him during the border-ruffian war and during the war of the rebellion and who had become a part of him, and there were men who were against him in spirit during those trying times and who had often secretly wished for his removal. There were present neighbors, friends, family, foes political and foes personal—all testifying to the greatness of the man and to the wonderful works he had done for Kansas and the Union. Many of those present knew his virtues, which were many, and others knew his faults, which were pronounced though few.

How to preach the truth and yet vindicate the gospel was a question. The text chosen was "God is love." I believed then and believe now that in his partially conscious moments, after he had accomplished what all the demons of hell composing the guerrilla army of the border had failed to accomplish though often tried, before he breathed his last expiring breath the teachings of his sainted mother and her prayers, which had exampled him unto her Savior and the Savior of sinners, took hold upon him and, repenting of his sins, he died believing in the Savior of all mankind. I have always had hope that through the saving grace of the Master Jim Lane is saved, saved for the good he has done for the cause of freedom and humanity.

His life was a life of ambitions, successes, triumphs —and one grave failure.

CHAPTER IV.

EARLY EDUCATIONAL HISTORY.

The colonial families and their immediate descendants felt the need of and believed in common school education, and early provided for the schooling of all children. They not only planted Yale, Cambridge, Williams, Brown, Johns Hopkins and other great universities, but planned a common school system which to-day meets the exigencies of the present advanced state of education and civilization.

Within the last fifty years there has been a revival of popular education, beginning with the labors of Horace Mann, in every Northern state. Improved methods and an enormous growth of moral, intellectual and industrial agencies have marked a new era in both hemispheres. The Year of Our Lord 1897 has beholden in Kansas half a million children and youths daily responding to the chime of the school-house bell, with joyous step, bright and cheerful countenance and an ever increasing thirst for instruction from her thousands of well qualified teachers. For the accomplishment of this great work willing taxpayers (except an occasional, grumbling old bachelor "without pride of ancestry or hope of posterity") and whole-souled philanthropists have invested three hundred and fifty millions of dollars in school property, and pay annually one hundred and fifty millions of dollars for the maintenance of these schools. The southern states, since Kansas repelled invasion and set the mark of equality before the law and made common education the inheritance of all, have kindly and enthusiastically taken to the common school system, and in this good year of their opening prosperity have expended two millions of dollars for the children and youths of all races in her borders, that they, too, may enjoy the advantages of the common school. Her eight millions of colored population, who by law were debarred from education when Kansas cast her determining influence for freedom, now enjoy with their white brothers the opportunities of an education.

The matters of deepest concern to the free-state families coming to Kansas in her early history were school and church facilities. These were of paramount importance, and from the beginning the greatest interest was taken in schools, academies and universities. Many of these ventures had precarious lives; others struggled through weary years of poverty and discouragement, and while many noble young men and women were consumed by the desire for an education, yet because of reverses incident to settling a new state under such disadvantages and the poverty entailed by a long and expensive removal from older communities, they were unable to attend unendowed schools, many of which were literally starving their agents and professors because of inadequate salaries.

It is a serious question whether later-comers can have adequate conception of the struggle through which we passed to plant the standard of free and higher education. Mercenary men have censured the early efforts to build and maintain our schools because it cost something, and others have censured the noble men who early planned so wisely because they did not wait until the state became rich. But even in territorial times, while the sky was lurid with war and famine was staring them in the face the people provided for the intellectual and moral culture of their children, willing, if need be, to stint their bodies rather than dwarf the minds and souls of the coming generation. School houses were erected to accommodate the church of the neighborhood as well as the school. The chapels of some of the best colleges in the state were made to answer a double purpose, and became citadels of scientific, moral and religious truth, while every pulpit was a rock of defense for the liberties and education of the people. When the constitution was adopted Kansas incorporated the best educational system known to Europe and America, and from small beginnings her school interests have grown until they now stand at the head of the column.

Among the earliest educational institutions of the territory was Blue Mont College, located at Manhattan and built by Methodist money and enterprise. This became a successful school under the presidency of Joseph Denison, D. D., and the agency of Professor Isaac T. Goodnow. Finally Congress gave to Kansas a large grant of the public domain for agricultural educational purposes, conditionally; the state being unable to comply with the conditions, and rather than that the grant should revert from the state, the Methodists magnanimously donated their college buildings, apparatus, furniture, students, president, etc., to the state, thus securing the land grant, with the result that our agricultural college stands second to none in the nation.

From those grass roots of Kansas, now thirty-five years old, there has grown and developed a state school system which numbers nine thousand three hundred and thirty-four school-houses with eleven thousand four hundred and ninety-six school-rooms, employing eleven thousand nine hundred and three well qualified teachers, with an enrollment of three hundred and ninety-three thousand eight hundred and forty pupils between five and twenty-one years of age. The average salary of teachers per month is $43.91, with an average term of twenty-five weeks. The estimated value of school property, buildings and grounds is $11,193,396. There are one state superintendent and one hundred and five county superintendents who make nine thousand five hundred and fifteen visits to the schools during the year. There are eight thousand seven hundred and ninety-nine districts that sustain school at least three months in the year, and but three hundred and seventy-five that do not sustain them that long. The school system is a very satisfactory one, and the results are in almost every district exceedingly gratifying.

The qualification of our young people for public service is seen in the fact that every department of business activity is being well supplied therefrom. In December of last year while I was in the capital of the nation I was requested by Rev. A. B. Leonard, Secretary of the Missionary Society of the Methodist Episcopal Church, to make a missionary address to a large audience in Waugh Methodist Church, on Home Mission Work. I complied, and in the course of my remarks referred to the fact that the greatest solicitude I had felt in moving to Kansas was the apparent privation my boys would experience in getting an education. After describing what the Church had accomplished in extending the Kingdom of Christ by the aid of the Home Missionary Society I referred to the planting of schools, their growth and development, especially as exhibited in the educational department of the Columbian Exposition at Chicago, where, on a great map, with lines like those on a field chart, were shown the rise and progress of common education. Beginning in Massachusetts, crossing westward with varied depressions and upward inflections of the lines, the rise was so perceptible that when the stream of educational influence touched Kansas it almost reached the highest line on the map, showing that Kansas stood at the head of the procession. When I saw this I called my wife, who is sharer of all my toils, privations and joys and said to her, "Kansas leads the Nation! If I were not afraid of being arrested I would shout." At the close of the meeting a large number of persons came forward and congratulated me on the growth of Kansas, among them the chairman of the sub-committee on civil service examination, who, in the presence of a number of gentlemen, thanked me, saying my remarks about educational matters had given him the key to an explanation which had long been lacking in his committee room; for it had been observable for four or five years past that the best prepared papers presented for examination by applicants for positions in the various departments were almost invariably from Kansas. So marked was this that whenever a paper showing thoroughness of preparation came before them they were disposed to say, "Here is another application from a Kansan." "Now," said he, "I understand the matter perfectly, and your people are to be congratulated upon their successful educational advantages."

Seventeen church denominations have organized seminaries, colleges or universities, some of these more than one of such school of higher grade, and there is one, "Campbell University," undenominational. The Methodist Episcopal Church, always and everywhere the friend of education, founded the first schools for the higher instruction in the territory. Baker University was chartered in 1858 and opened her halls for the reception of students the same year; since which time through border strife, drought, grasshopper raids, poverty and civil war, class recitations in regular terms have never been suspended for a single school day. From the first president, Rev. Dr. W. R. Davis, and his devoted faculty to the present Baker University has been blessed with as competent and self-sacrificing a class of professors and instructors as ever attempted the deveioping and upbuilding of an educational institution in America, and since she graduated her first class in the state has maintained a front rank among the institutions of Kansas. She has had a hard struggle, but has passed the crucial period and won the right to live—as well as having demonstrated her providential mission. Her work has been well and successfully begun and must not fail for want of funds or students. The church and state can well afford to cherish and maintain this first and high-grade university. From the beginning the scholarship and curriculum of this school were on a par with the older schools of the East; so that students who went East to complete their courses of studies matriculated ahead of their home classes. The moral and religious influences of Baker have always been of the highest order and are among her greatest agencies and causes of commendation.

Blue Mont College (referred to as the State Agricultural College) was the next in order of the Methodist Colleges, and as such did noble work until transferred, when it took a wider sweep in scientific studies of climate, soil, seeds, trees, animals and all husbandry and agriculture, with but a limited range in the classics.

A school under the quasi-patronage of the Methodist Church was started at Circleville, Jackson County, but had a precarious life and finally succumbed to the pressure of poverty and died an honorable death, her memory still living because of the good she did.

Southwest Kansas College was founded at Winfield in 1885, opened for the reception of students in 1886, and has associated with its curriculum a Young Men's Christian Association and other Christian agencies, which make it not only a center of classical attainments but also of broad, philanthropic culture and equipment. The Kansas Wesleyan University, located at Salina, was founded in 1886, and is in all respects a counterpart of the Southwest College, with very nearly identical purposes, courses of study and addenda. The work these are doing is being well and faithfully done. These two properties are valued at $172,000, thus making an aggregate value of the three college properties under Methodist control of $270,000, besides their endowments. These are large and encouraging, but not enough. A Central enterprise at Topeka suddenly suspended (with a foundation worth $30,000) when the cyclone of contraction took place because of the "bursting of the boom."

Critics have severely deprecated the multiplying of schools; I never have. I believe there should be ten thousand young Methodist people crowding the halls of learning, preparing for more active and useful lives in the cause of humanity. I never did and do not now believe in an aristocracy, either in the commercial or monetary world, much less in the educational field. It should be the ambition of every parent to help his posterity to the best equipment for a life of usefulness, and the church does well to provide liberally for the education of her children under her own thoroughly equipped faculties and Christian agencies.

CHAPTER V.

THE PLANTING OF THE CHURCH.

The Methodist Episcopal Church, always a pioneer of evangelism, was first to enter the door of occupancy of the sacred territory of Kansas. Among the advance guards were such men as Abraham Still, W. H. Goode, J. S. Griffing, L. B. Dennis and B. F. Bowman. The Kansas and Nebraska Conference was organized in a large tent in Lawrence, the historic city, by Bishop Osman C. Baker, on Thursday, October 23, A. D., 1856, the session closing on Saturday, the 25th, showing a ministerial force of twenty members and two probationers. These, with five supplies, were expected to occupy Kansas, Nebraska, Colorado and New Mexico, with the Indian Territory. Within these vast bounds there were nine hundred and ninety-six (996) members and one hundred and eight (108) probationers, with twenty (20) Sunday Schools, having one thousand five hundred and eighty-two (1,582) teachers, officers and scholars, with but five (5) meeting houses in all that empire, and these but shanties. These ministers and their wives were the advance guard of God's chosen servants, who endured hardships as good soldiers of the cross, as seeing Him who is invisible and His victories. The history of the struggle of church building and organizing would make a volume, and in all this work the preachers and their families bore the heaviest part of the burden.

The growth in church membership and Sunday

School, church property and accommodations, following within forty years on such territory and under such conditions, including two great upheavals, resulting in bloody strife lasting nearly as long as the revolutionary war, coupled with wild speculation and gold panics, is truly phenomenal. The results are lesson-fraught with lasting interest, showing a self-denying spirit, a heroism unexcelled by any aggressive army of itinerants—like the angel of the Apocalypse flying through the air, having the everlasting gospel to preach to the inhabitants of the earth—and a wonderful responsiveness of the people in answering to the call to organize and establish the opportunities of church association for themselves, their families, and their neighbors. For the churches of the state are the bulwarks of the civil, religious, moral and educational liberties of the people, and wonderfully promotive of civil peace, financial success, intellectual culture and the highest and best of religious life and joy.

The number of those early churchmen who have come and gone is by far the larger list. Only two of the charter members of the conference remain in the Kansas conference, Rev. Joseph Denison, D. D., and B. F. Bowman. Now Kansas alone has four (4) annual conferences, which have just stationed nearly four hundred and seventy (470) preachers and thirty (30) probationers, with over one thousand (1,000) stations and circuits to be supplied by them. She has ninety-five thousand, eight hundred (95,800) full members and one thousand, five hundred (1,500) probationers. Her Sunday School army under the loyal banner of the Methodist Episcopal Church alone numbers eighteen thousand (18,000) officers and teachers with over one hundred thousand (100,000) pupils. In

Nebraska there are four (4) annual conferences and forty-five thousand (45,000) communicants; in Colorado one conference and twelve thousand (12,000) members; in Oklahoma one conference and fifteen thousand (15,000) members, and in New Mexico a mission with two hundred and fifty (250) members. In these, at a reasonable estimate, are eight hundred and fifty (850) preachers with one hundred thousand and forty-five (100,045) members loyal to the flag that made us free, to the American Sabbath, the Bible and common school education for all the people. The valuation of church property within our organic lines amounts to the enormous sum of $5,170,000, and our churches have a seating capacity for one hundred thousand people.

It is a question of gravest importance whether the multiplication of distinct denominations has not seriously and censurably hindered the spread and influence of Christianity in Kansas; and it appears reasonable that all those denominations of like religious faith and church discipline and piety should at the earliest possible date so unite as to make all the available influences and conveniences for church work and evangelical success more potent for good, as well as less burdensome. There are seventy-nine of these varying denominations, and yet these may be traced in first analysis to four or five great cardinal doctrines. These denominations are reported as numbering three hundred and fifty thousand communicants, and a great army of pastors.

If all these were united in a spirit of broad, universal evangelism what a mighty host it would be!

CHAPTER VI.

"I AM BORN."

I, Hugh Dunn Fisher, was born in Steubenville, Jefferson county, Ohio, March 14, 1824. My father was William Fisher, the son of John Christopher and Elizabeth Bratton Fisher. These grandparents were German, by a long line of Teutonic extraction. Both were born in the land of Huss, were Lutheran protestants "from principle," and members of the Protestant Episcopal Church "of choice." Their children were all baptized according to the beautiful ritual of that Church. The family was a large one, most of the children living to a good old age. William, my father, was the third son and favorite brother, always regarded with that peculiar respect and courtesy that is the pride of a well-ordered German family in recognizing a beloved parent or brother. He was born in Staunton, a beautiful little town on the South branch of the famous "Potomac" River in "East Virginia," on the 26th of March, 1793.

In 1805 the family emigrated to what was then regarded as the "Great Wilderness," as all that region west of the Alleghenies, and especially the Ohio Valley, was called. So rude and barbarous were the methods of emigration at that early day that they crossed the mountains on pack-saddles in company with a "salt train," no wagon roads being yet opened. The trail was so steep and rough and narrow in places that many times were they compelled to unburden their laboring horses and assist them in the ascent of the mountains with ropes, carrying the goods and children to a place of rest where they could remount in safety to pursue their difficult and dangerous journey. They were compelled to kindle fires at night to protect themselves from the wild beasts inhabiting the mountains. Not infrequently did they startle the bear, deer and wolf from the dense thickets of flowering laurel and underbrush which skirted their crooked and rugged trail to the gateway of the West. When the family at last descended from the mountain the first settlement they came upon was a point near the present site of West Newton, Pennsylvania, where there was a village called Plump Sauk, then a miserable apology for a town, but a real frontier village, full of drunken and debauched men. After reaching the banks of the Youghiogheny River the family stopped and established the first pottery West of the Allegheny mountains.

The following spring they descended the Yougheogheny River in a small family boat to its confluence with the Monongahela at the point now occupied by McKeesport, a few miles above the noted place of Braddock's defeat, still called "Braddock's Field." The history of Braddock's fall and Washington's bravery was fresh in the minds of the emigrant family and they felt no little anxiety in passing down the river in so unprotected a manner. They were compelled to row the boat with oarsmen hidden from view to keep the men from being picked off by the Indians, who appeared on the banks at several points and by signs and various devices sought to induce the emigrants to come near enough to be captured. But the men kept her well out into the stream and by careful watching and earnest rowing landed the family in safety after several days and nights at the site of Steubenville.

* * * * * * *

There were but eight or ten houses in the village in that day, and these were principally built of logs. Among the rest there was a "block house," or kind of ancient citadel of defense, into which the settlers might gather in times of alarm and danger from the Indians. These alarms were frequent and the danger so great that much of the daily labor was performed with gun in hand, ready for an emergency. Several years later the Indians came into this settlement and carried away captive Daniel Pursley, a lad in his teens, and his playmate, Seth Bickerstaff, about his own age. The latter escaped through the superstition of the savages, by the interposition of the Great Spirit, as they supposed. Young Pursley was retained in the tribe until he became a young man. The writer has often heard "Father Pursley," as he was later called, narrate the most thrilling incidents of his Indian slavery, his escape and conversion to God. As he would stand in the class room to relate his strange, wild experience, with uplifted hand and pointed finger he would shout in Indian style, "The Victory! The Victory!!" crying "Who-o-o, Who-o-o, Who-o-o, Who-o-o-pe!" until the class room would ring. He was indeed a shouting Methodist."

Grandfather Fisher established a pottery in Steubenville, but there being little demand for his wares it did not prove a success. Here he died, but the rest of the family remained together until death called a dear son named Joseph. The other sons and daughters became so permanently located as ever to remain within easy reach of each other, the last one dying in 1890.

My father went to live with Barnard Lucas, a typical

Baltimorean Methodist. There were at this time eight or nine persons in Steubenville who had brought certificates of membership in the Methodist church to their Western home. These organized a class of which Mr. Lucas became leader. The Sabbath after the organization my father, then a mere boy, gave his name as a probationer in the Methodist Episcopal Church, thus identifying himself for life with this then hated people. This step greatly exposed him to the persecution and hatred of wicked boys and men. He was often followed and stoned as he returned from evening prayer and other Christian meetings, but this in no wise daunted or discouraged him in his life of devotion to his Master's service. He became a class leader in the church, which relation he held for more than thirty-five consecutive years. He was a remarkably useful leader, sometimes having charge of three classes at once, always leading with skill and acceptability and being almost a second Corvoso. At times as many as thirty persons who belonged to his class would pray in public, and many useful leaders were trained under his care.

Father was happy in his choice of a helpmeet, in the person of Isabella Dunn, daughter of Hugh and Rebecca Dunn, of Scotch descent. From early girlhood she had been a devoted Christian and became a great help to my father in his Christian life, her patient, quiet spirit toning down his impulsive and somewhat hasty temperament. My parents were poor, like most of the citizens in that early day, but by diligence and frugality were enabled to rear their family in reasonable comfort.

* * * * * * *

My mother was an invalid for years, so greatly afflicted that for long periods she was deprived of the privilege of attending public religious services with those she loved. My recollections of her are associated with my earliest religious impressions, made by her example and teachings. The Bible was her daily companion and she early inclined me to read and reverence the Word of God. I remember a most impressive lesson given me under these circumstances. A little girl by the name of Carroll, whose sister was a very dear friend of my sister, died. My sister took me to Mr. Carroll's the morning of the funeral to see the corpse. This was the first time I had ever stood beside a coffin looking upon the lifeless form of a human being. My heart was deeply touched. In the afternoon when the bell was tolling slowly and solemnly my mother drew me near her side as she sat in her chair and talked to me of God and heaven, and told me with much tenderness that if I would be pious and serve God in life when I should die my spirit would go to heaven. I remember I believed that the soul of that little girl was with the angels, singing the praises of God. That lesson has not lost its effect upon my mind to this hour. Soon after this occurrence mother took me to her bedroom and caused me to kneel by her side and there prayed for her little son while the warm tears ran down her cheeks and fell on my upturned face. I wondered why my mother wept.

I know now why she wept and prayed!

It was the established custom of my father to have family prayers. Often did father and mother become so wonderfully blessed on such occasions that they shouted the praises of God, rejoicing with exceeding joy. Very frequently class leaders and others would come and spend the evening at our home, when a season of song and prayer would end in a grand shout of praise to Christ the Redeemer.

In 1829 my father rented and took charge of a ferry at the foot of Market street in Steubenville. We lived near the river where we had a neighbor, Mr. Robert Hering, who was a warm friend of Sabbath schools, and a kind man to little boys. On the day that I was eight years old he presented me with a little book called "The Pilgrims." I prized that book very highly and read it with great delight and profit. I had a playhouse in the yard into which I used to go to read and pray. On that day I took my new book and went there to read. While there I know my heart was renewed. I was exceedingly happy, and I felt as distinctly as I ever have since that I was inwardly moved by the Holy Ghost to be a preacher of the gospel. From that day all my reading was with a view to a preparation for that great work, and I did not pass a week without the conviction that I was to be a minister of the gospel of Christ.

During our residence here my father engaged in keeping a store. This, with the ferry, was helping him to recover losses sustained by going security for a brother who had failed in business. But a band of desperadoes, some of whom were afterward hanged in Wheeling for murder, broke into his store and robbed it of a large quantity of valuable goods, money and papers, which so embarrassed him that he never fully recovered from the loss sustained. Thus embarrassed in business and having sickness to contend with he had ever after a hard struggle to support his family, and could give his children only a limited education. We were all of a studious turn, however, and made reasonable progress for our opportunities. By my sister's side I took my first lesson in a little Sunday school primer. Both my sisters were early in life converted and became active in the service of God. Two other sisters had died in infancy. My older brother, who was named for Grandfather Fisher—John Christopher—was happily converted while our mother still lived. He became a useful class leader, an efficient steward and trustee in the church, and lived and died an exemplary member of the church of our father.

After the death of mother, on September 7, 1837, we were left in the care of our second sister, who took charge of the home and family, the older sister having married just one week before mother died. Father, sister and three brothers were now left without a mother's counsel to guide them in domestic cares or the affairs of life. Our home was gloomy; but the triumph of mother was so complete that heaven seemed nearer and the Savior dearer than ever before. Her last words were, "Jesus is mine, and I am His."

Father's second wife was Miss Elizabeth Permar, a maiden lady of considerable experience in domestic affairs, having in girlhood been charged with the care of her father's family upon the death of her own mother. She was also a devout Christian woman and proved to be a good mother and a great blessing to our home. I was asked when father brought her to us: "What are you going to call her?" I answered: "I am going to call her mother, and if I do my duty she will do hers," and so it proved. She was always as a mother to me.

CHAPTER VII.

MY CONVERSION AND CALL.

In 1838 Rev. George S. Holmes was the pastor of the church of which my father and family were members. During the winter there was a remarkable revival, taking in its range the old and young of both sexes. Among the converts was the pastor's son, Charles Avery. He and I were nearly of an age and very intimate friends. On the evening of Monday, February 15, 1838, Charles was converted. Next morning our Sunday school superintendent, Mr. Francis Bates, came to the shop where I was working and said to me, "Hugh, you should have been at the meeting last night to have seen how happy Charles Holmes was. He was converted." I could not reply. I went out of the shop and passed around the large chimney used by the shop (we were coopers) and wept like a child. My young friend had obtained salvation and I was without a satisfying assurance of mine, for though my childhood's conversion had never lost its influence upon me, the years had brought increasing need of a larger grace. That evening I went to church and during the sermon my heart was broken. When the invitation for mourners was given I went and knelt as a seeker of conscious salvation. That night I found no clear evidence of peace. On the next afternoon I attended a private prayer meeting led by my father and again presented myself at the altar of prayer. I felt some relief of mind from the fact that I knew I was in the line of duty. At night I again presented myself as a seeker, resolved that I would not leave the place until consciously saved. My case grew desperate. I felt that it was all dark, that I was sinking into despair. The floor on which I was kneeling seemed to be sinking beneath me and I appeared hopelessly lost. Suddenly and to my great astonishment my tears ceased to flow. Just then my kind Sabbath school teacher, Mr. John Taylor, came to my side and laying his arm tenderly around my neck with deep sympathy, said to me earnestly, "Believe on the Lord Jesus Christ and thou shalt be saved."

That was exactly what I was trying to do, but just what I did not know how to do. His words sank deep into my ear and seemed to possess a wonderful charm, especially when he spoke the name of "Jesus." This strengthened my heart. I raised erect upon my knees and stretching my hands to heaven cried out in anguish, "Lord, save or I perish." I lost sight of myself and my surroundings. The ceiling seemed to vanish as I gazed upward, the roof to part asunder, and by faith I beheld Christ standing at the right hand of the Father looking tenderly down upon me. I ventured out of myself and sins, being helped by the Holy Ghost, into the arms of Jesus, and as quick as a spark from smitten steel light fell upon me and filled the house with glory. My sins were pardoned! My soul was free! I rejoiced in the clearest possible evidence that I was born again and adopted into the family of God. I bounded over the mourners' bench and across the altar into the arms of my young friend and we shouted together the praises of God in the presence of the vast congregation, most of whom had known me from childhood and many of whom deeply sympathized with me in my new found joy, and praised God in my behalf. When my joy had subsided a little

I wondered why I had not believed earlier—it now appeared so pleasant and easy. The evidence of my acceptance was so clear that I have never for a single moment since that night been tempted to doubt it.

Immediately my impressions of duty grew clearer and I felt with new force that I was called to preach Jesus and the resurrection. As I walked home with my brother and sister it appeared to me that the moon and stars shone with greater brilliancy than ever before. All nature seemed changed into one vast scene of delight and praise. My soul was exceedingly peaceful and happy.

With renewed assiduity I began to study everything that I thought would fit me for a useful ministerial life. I found great difficulties to be overcome. My education was of necessity very limited. Schools were not accessible. My father was getting old and had to struggle to provide for his family. His previous losses had so reduced him financially that all his children found it necessary to do what they could to help him. Therefore we were raised to very active habits, which, however, are perhaps as great a fortune as land or money. My opportunities for obtaining an education were greater than any of the family, as I was acquiring a trade which enabled me to study. But another difficulty confronted me. Our church was always clamoring for "educated preachers," and at this time there was much talk about higher education for ministers of the gospel, though not so much as to how those called to this work were to obtain education. I knew little, indeed almost nothing, about circuit work, except as my ideas had been formed from what I knew of full grown and able preachers, such as Waterman, Bascom, Holmes, Babcock, Swazey, Kinney, Cook,

Battell and their class of expounders of the truth. I could not expect to preach as they did, but how my heart panted for the knowledge that would fit me for the ministry! My soul thirsted for the learning that lay beyond my reach.

A third difficulty stood in the way to hinder me. Several young men had felt "called" and were persuaded that they should preach. The church encouraged them and for a season they did well, but before getting into conference they broke down and utterly failed. The fear of a like failure became the greatest barrier in my way. Looking back upon those early needs and fears I am led to think that it is much easier for a young man to start in the ministry from a rural district or country charge than from a city station. With these difficulties in my way on one hand and my convictions of duty on the other I had a terrible warfare running through all the years of my young life and manhood. Sometimes I was almost driven to despair, when I would conclude to give up the idea of becoming a preacher. But in this conclusion I found no rest. Then I would resolve to go forward. If God had called me he was responsible and would clear the path before me as I advanced. I had adopted as my motto that quaint saying of Davy Crockett's, "Be sure you are right and then go ahead;" and again and again under its quickening influence my courage would arouse and I would press on through the darkness until light would come upon my soul.

All this time I was reading, studying and praying while I continued to help my father maintain his family and pay my way through school. For months I worked from early in the morning until nine o'clock, then met my classes in the academy and recited with them, returning immediately to my work, where I

MY CONVERSION AND CALL. 67

would continue until 4 p. m., again returning to recite, then working until dark and studying until midnight. My lessons in the languages, higher mathematics and astronomy were studied with my books lying or standing open on my bench held in position by a block of wood. I would catch a sentence and while champering a head or setting a hoop would repeat it over and over until I could catch another and settle it in my mind. Very many nights when the town bell in the old tower would toll out the noon of night I was on my knees with the open Bible spread on the shop chair praying to the Giver of Wisdom, who upbraideth not, that he would guide my path aright.

I continued thus to study and work until our family physician enjoined my father to no longer allow me to do so lest I should ruin my health, which, greatly to my sorrow, was already impaired. So I was compelled to change my habits of study and devote less time to my books. Still my soul thirsted for knowledge that I might be qualified for usefulness as a preacher of salvation. Often I went under the river bank into coves washed by the eddying waters of the beautiful Ohio, and imagining the stream a congregation of sinners I would preach repentance, faith and salvation, weeping at the story of the cross while my soul was moved with a desire to do good. There were times when the sense of responsibility upon me was so great that I prayed in agony of soul to be released and have another called in my stead.

Just opposite where we lived there was a deep defile between the towering Virginia hills which skirt the Ohio opposite Steubenville. This formed a dark, romantic canon, bowered with stately pines and graceful birch. Vast cliffs of rocks stood bare on either side, and away up the winding canon was an old moss-covered rock sheltered by a beautiful birch, so dense in its foliage and so interlacing its comrades that the sunlight scarce ever fell upon the secluded spot. I sometimes went there to pray, and more than once did I think I would go, like Elijah in the wilderness, and hide behind that rock and fast and pray until God would either relieve me from the call to the ministry or by audible voice tell me in unmistakable words what he would have me do and how he would have me do it. Then the Holy Spirit would ask "What more or greater evidence would a voice give than that thou hast in the inward call of the Holy Ghost?" The conflict was continuous and consuming, notwithstanding I doubted neither my conversion nor call. Not a day or hour has passed without that deep, constant urgent voice as clear as the hour I first heard it.

Some years later I formed the acquaintance of John R. Shearer, a young man who afterward became a member of the Pittsburg conference. One beautiful Sabbath afternoon as we walked together I revealed to him what I had kept locked up in my heart so long—my convictions of duty and the severity of my struggle. He entered into full sympathy with me, gave me excellent advice, and soon after wrote me a letter containing good and profitable direction. Following upon this, I conferred with the presiding elder concerning the subject of my desire and hope, but was sadly disappointed in receiving from him whose duty it was to help me little of encouragement and no valuable advice.

I was at this time a member of the Young Men's prayer meeting, and, as the discipline recommended and required, several young men about my age had organized a "Band Meeting." We met in band in an upper room, with closed doors, for the purpose of scrutinizing our hearts and conduct. This was the best means of grace I ever attended. Here we laid our souls open before God and each other and prayed with and for each other. The Lord heard and answered us. I was also greatly aided in preparation by a "Youth's Lyceum" in which we debated questions of a strictly moral character. On a memorable occasion we had the question "Has Man the Power of Volition?" For once and only once I turned Calvanist, and taking the "Westminster Confession of Faith" and "Buck's Theological Dictionary" for text books, made a pretty fair defense of the negative. Indeed, it was placed to my credit that I won a decided victory—it was unfortunate, however, that it should have been on the wrong side!

These opportunities with regular attendance upon Sabbath schools, Bible classes, and teachers' meetings, became as schooling to me. In fact I graduated from the Sabbath school into the ministry. It was my theological Alma Mater. My Sunday school commencement was the beginning of my itinerancy. Few in the church or Sabbath school knew that I was preparing for the ministry, only as they surmised it from my close application to study, though the church seemed to have a conviction that I would preach. Meantime the lessons I had taken in vocal music were proving of great use in my work, and I was early elected chorister to the Sabbath school and subsequently to the church.

CHAPTER VIII.

BETROTHAL AND FIRST WORK.

Our Sabbath school was a model school. We had forty-four regular teachers besides a full corps of officers. Most of these were deeply devoted to the school and church. It was here that I became acquainted with Miss Elizabeth M. Acheson, who subsequently became my wife. She was the oldest daughter of John and Ann Jane Acheson, who were Scotch Presbyterians and of Scotch-Irish extraction. Elizabeth being warmly enwrapped in the Sabbath school, a congeniality of interests ensued. Acquaintance became intimacy. This became a matter of prayer; for I was not free to marry, as that would effectually prevent my becoming an itinerant. Yet, believing as I did, that this young woman, who is by my side at the age of seventy years as I write these lines, would make me a helpmeet indeed, I proposed to her and in due time was accepted, and the time agreed upon for marrying was put five years in the future—unless the Lord should open my way earlier into the itinerancy.

This was a fortunate contract for me, for not infrequently when, discouraged on account of the difficulties in my way, I would say, "I have a notion to give up the idea of being a preacher, get married and settle down in life; the church needs devoted laymen, as well as preachers," my betrothed would reply: "You believe you are called of God to be a preacher; if you disobey Him you cannot prosper; I don't want to marry a failure; do you remember Jonah? I don't want a whale to swallow my husband. He might not escape as well as Jonah did; we will wait God's own time." Thus, at the time I most needed help God gave me a counsellor whose advice has always been in the line of duty. My brother-in-law, Joseph Laning, though not a professed Christian, also gave me advice which wonderfully strengthened me in the overcoming of obstacles which appeared to me almost insurmountable.

Thus helped I pressed onward. My early efforts at public leadership and speaking were trying ordeals, almost crucifixions, but usually resulted in victory, increase of strength and high resolve. My sermons to imaginary congregations were prophecies, many of them already fulfilled. The scenes of my youthful vision became realities in fact and form. My first attempt at leading was in a young men's prayer meeting. Clark Huff and William Richards were the responsible leaders. It was their duty to see that the meeting was properly conducted. I had been appointed to open the devotions with reading, singing and prayer. I had learned my scripture lesson almost by heart. My hymn was number seven hundred and one. When the hour came for commencing the service I was so seized with fear that I could not stand up to read. Brother Huff seeing my embarrassment sang a verse or two and then said: "Take up the cross, Brother Hugh, there is a blessing under it." With great trembling and fear I arose, read my scripture lesson and knelt and prayed. This meeting proved a great benefit to my soul, lessening my timidity and increasing my spiritual strength.

My first public speech was a missionary address

before the Sabbath school of nearly eight hundred. I was then but a lad. God gave me help and the result of that effort lives yet, though the majority who heard it have fallen asleep in Jesus.

Soon after this, upon my motion in teachers' meeting, we planned a Sabbath school in the district in the north part of the city. I was its first secretary and commissioned to secure the use of the house. The school developed very rapidly and grew into a good appointment, finally becoming a self-sustaining station. It was in this house that several years later I preached my first and trial sermon, and it was in this house that I was afterwards regularly licensed to preach on Christmas Day, 1847, and it was in this house that I was, in December, 1895, introduced by the pastor of the now prosperous church as the founder and planter of it.

About the time we organized this Sabbath school I was appointed class leader. With much fear and trembling I attempted to lead. Good results followed from my efforts, and the class, though almost broken up at the time I took charge, soon recovered a good attendance.

My leadership here ended only to give place to more active duties as an exhorter. The first meeting I held in this latter relation was in Sycamore school-house on Florence Circuit, of which Rev. Israel Dallas was pastor. He was called home on account of the sickness of his father in the fall of 1844, just after the presidential election in which Polk and Dallas were made president and vice-president. I had been absent from home when Brother Dallas called to secure my services to fill appointments during his absence. When I returned my father told me Mr. Dallas had

BETROTHAL AND FIRST WORK.

called to see me. I wondered why the vice-president of the United States should call up on me, especially as all my political feelings were on the other side. Seeing my quandary and misconception, father humored the joke a little until I became thoroughly interested to know what the vice-president wished with me, when I was gravely informed that it was the Rev. Mr. Dallas who had called and who wanted me to preach or hold a meeting at Sycamore school-house, in Virginia.

At the appointed time I went to the place of meeting and found it full of people anxious to hear the gospel. I spoke to them from the language of John the Baptist. "He must increase but I decrease," and we had what was to me a glorious meeting. This, almost the beginning of my ministerial work, was indicative of the larger duties soon to overtake me, in whose struggles and conflicts encouragement and victories were often to mingle.

Hill's school-house in Ohio, and Beatie's school-house in Virginia were points where occasional visits afforded me the opportunity of holding religious services for exhortation and prayer. Sometimes, also, I accompanied Mr. Frederic Risher, a local preacher of some repute, to appointments in Annapolis, called Old Blue Salem. These journeys afforded me opportunity to converse with one who had larger experience than I and proved very profitable, yielding to me the treasures of a knowledge I could not hope for by reading alone, though I was all the while applying myself to study with the greatest possible diligence. I read, visited, exhorted, and attended all the meetings I could reach with a single view of qualifying myself for the work to which I felt called.

Finally I commenced the study of "Systematic Divinity" under the direction of Rev. Geo. S. Holmes, of the Pittsburg conference, a clear thinker and a sound gospel preacher, who said to me encouragingly, "My boy, if you master Watson's Theological Institutes you will be able to preach anywhere."

About this time I made the acquaintance of Rev. Mr. Hoagland, pastor of the Methodist Protestant Church in Steubenville. Together we studied that most beautiful science, astronomy. I found him to be a clever and spiritual gentleman. My advantages soon almost equalled those able to attend theological schools; for I had the acquaintance of Rev. C. C. Beatty, D. D., president and proprietor of Steubenville's celebrated female seminary, over which Dr. Read, a friend of later years, now presides, and also of Rev. Intripit Moss, D. D., of the Protestant Episcopal Church. Both were able ministers of the Lord Jesus Christ, whose lives and advices to me were rich in blessing.

My first knowledge of Sabbath school celebrations dates back to the very initiation of them—a union celebration on the Fourth of July, 1832, consisting in singing and appropriate addresses delivered in the First Presbyterian Church, after which we formed a procession and marched to Dr. Beatty's seminary where we were refreshed in body as well as in soul. The singing was very unlike our present Sabbath school songs, but it was the beginning of that wonderful change which has come over society by which the Sabbath school has sanctified our national holidays to the remembrance of patriotism and the promotion of religion, thus doing away with the general or militia musters which used to be attended with drunkenness and rioting. 'Tis a happy and blessed change!

In after years it was my privilege to visit all the Protestant Sabbath schools in Steubenville by invitation of a union teachers' meeting to teach new tunes and songs to be used on similar but grander scale. Such was the progress of Sabbath school influence that the Episcopalians, and even the Seceders, not only allowed me to teach their schools the songs, but were zealous to have me do so. This beautiful exhibition of Christian union influenced my after life; early I learned "How good and pleasant it is for brethren to dwell together in unity!"

The years rolled by while my soul was being thus enriched and my mind stored with valuable material for use in the saving work of the Christian ministry, and almost imperceptibly I was learning the great benefit of pastoral visitation and pleasant intercourse with Christian workers.

In addition to the above cited means of Christian culture and experience I occasionally attended a field or out-door meeting for religious service on the hillside under the shade of the stately oak and poplar. These meetings were usually led by a band of zealous English people called "Primitive Methodists." Chief among them were Mr. and Mrs. Riley. She, especially, was mighty in word and prayer and her labors were acknowledged by the spirit in the salvation of precious souls. These out-door meetings were schools whose lessons have been of great service to me in many similar public services, religious, patriotic and reformatory. While I felt intensely diffident, by such example and in varied ways it was being impressed upon me that duty and success demand promptness of action, and my aim was growing more directly toward results. Having frequent opporunity of hearing class leaders converse in my father's family, especially on the subject of pastoral visitation and its absolute necessity to a successful ministry, I early resolved I would try to become a faithful pastor. In subsequent years I have found great pleasure and profit in pastoral work, and deeply regret that this important department of church work should be so largely neglected at the present day.

To-day I look back upon those years of varied and trying experiences to see that they were only preparatory—that I had yet to realize that there are more and greater trials to follow. I was truly in the furnace which was to be heated seven times hotter than it was used to be heated. But the fire has not consumed, only refined, and given me such an estimate of the world, its poverty-stricken riches and its unmitigated and miserably pleasurable munificence, that the hardships of an itinerant life have become luxurious and its privations have no discouragements, the severest conflicts no terror.

CHAPTER IX.

"DOUBT NO MORE."

But while these young years were wearing away I often almost gave up the thought of pressing on to the ministry. Waves of darkness, mountain high, would roll over my despairing soul and out of the darkness I would cry unto the Lord as out of the depths of hell and He would hear my cry and deliver me. Then up I would rise again to the determination of duty or death!

The time came at last when the path opened before me bright and clear. I had most solemnly promised God on my knees that if he would open the way I would go even to the ends of the earth, claiming the promise, "Lo, I am with thee to the ends of the world." In the fall of 1847 my father and I were engaged at coopering. We had laid in a stock for the winter and had made all calculations for success in the business, when early in November Rev. David S. Welling of the Pittsburg conference, an able and eloquent preacher stationed on the Jefferson circuit, came to Steubenville to get help in holding a series of meetings on his circuit. He was directed to call on me with the information that I was studying for the ministry and would be of service if he could persuade me to go. My way was open. After consulting with father I consented to help him. We traveled in a "hack" to a little town where we took supper, thence proceeded to Annapolis on horseback, and from this point to Hopewell

Church. Here we had a glorious meeting, resulting in the conversion of about forty precious souls, among the number a Quakeress and her husband by the name of Scott. I never before witnessed such a wonderful change in the expression of a human countenance as was shown in the face of this woman. The divine power of saving faith had a truly wonderful illustration in her conversion.

One Sabbath night there occurred in this church a scene which deserves description. The house was a good-sized, old-fashioned log church, rudely seated and generally well filled with attentive hearers. It was warmed by the use of a large wood-burning stove, the chimney passing out through the center of the loft and roof. On the occasion referred to there was an unusually large congregation in attendance. I had preached in the church in Annapolis in the morning, and at night was preaching at a full church from the words, "Behold He cometh and every eye shall see Him, and they also that pierced Him and all flesh shall wail because of Him. Even so. Amen!" Just as I reached the climax on the last part of the text and the people were listening with rapt attention there came the sound of a mighty crash, an apparent trembling of the whole house, a flickering of the lights, followed by a slow and confused rumbling lasting for a few seconds—then silence as of death. Men and women turned pale, glanced at each other terror-stricken, looked at the preacher as he stood with uplifted hands and streaming eyes, and as if by one common impulse of terror uttered a wail of anguish as if the judgment was set and the judge descending had heralded his coming. For a moment all was mystery. Then it flashed upon me that the chimney had fallen, which proved correct. While taking advantage of the solemnity of the ocasion I applied the truth to the awakened and interested congregation. Several were converted that evening. I remained at a neighbor's over night and the next day joined his sons in rebuilding the chimney, whose fall had aided me in the application of the doctrine of the judgment to come.

A little later we held another meeting at a point where there was a large log church, floored, and seated with puncheons—benches of split logs hewn smoothly on the upper side with legs made of short, stiff sticks stuck in augur holes in the under side of the slabs. The people came from a considerable distance in wagons, in the winter in sledges, bringing all the members of the family. The high old pulpit was of ample dimensions, utterly destitute of pretension to architectural design or finish. It was a compact box entered by several steps through a door which when closed and buttoned so completely sheltered the preacher that the congregation could not see him nor he them until he arose to preach, and even then only part of his body was visible above the "book board." It was a "bust view" only. This proved to be an admirable device for preachers who stood in all manner of wriggling attitudes or whose brogans were strangers to brush and blacking. Imagine a spare, pale-faced, uninitiated youth from the midst of a fastidious city congregation taking his place in such a pulpit and facing such a congregation alone! The opening services were gone through with without perceptible embarrassment. I had just read my text and begun to speak when my attention was attracted by an unusual noise. It was as regular and deliberate as the ticking of the old wall-sweeping clock that hung in my grandfather's house, sounding out a solemn "thump," "thump,"

"thump," "thump." Wondering, as wonder I would, and preaching on as best I could, I at last caught the direction of the sound and determined to discover the cause. I moved in the large pulpit in the direction from whence it came until I could look over and down into the "amen corner." Out of compassion for their wives and children and with an evident view to rock the children in the cradle of Methodism, the men had extemporized what would now be called a crib, an old-fashioned cradle of mammoth proportions, and had placed it in the right hand amen corner of the church near the pulpit. Into this omnibus crib went the babies when their mothers had wearied of holding them. Greatly to my discomfiture my eyes now rested on the rude cradle which was gently but regularly moved by the foot of a devoted grandmother and which contained four or five sleeping babies. When one little fellow would begin to squirm its mother would pick him out and thus make room soon to be filled by another mother's darling. The grandmothers —God bless our grandmothers—were devout in worshipping God and building up Methodism by training the children to love the Church and attend His worship. For a time that day both my sermon and gravity were upset by the picture, but I got away from that side of the pulpit, shut my eyes and drove right on.

While we were holding these meetings I occasionally visited a sick man in Salem whose name was Carter. He was a profane and violent infidel and would take his little son on his knee and teach him to swear, giving him money to induce him to excel in profanity. During this man's illness and on his death-bed neighbors who watched with him would sometimes become so terrified that they would flee the room. One morning I called to see the dying man. I was requested to read and pray, but my prayer was unavailing—the pitying heavens seemed to be closed. There was a fearful gloom over all; the room was filled with neighbors, many of them strong men, who had come to witness his death. The dying man struggled agonizingly, determined not to die, but at last gasped convulsively and was dead: His heart-broken wife stood beside the bedside transfixed with horror. Presently she threw her arms about the lifeless form of her husband and shrieked, "Oh, Carter! Carter! I could give you up, but where is your immortal soul?" A wail of woe went up from that company as from a lost vessel in the storm, heart-rending but ineffectual. May God in His mercy forbid that I should witness another such a death-bed scene!

In contrast with the death of Carter there occurred another a few miles distant from this place, the case of a young woman named Harriett Watson. Her mother was a widow, the family was in very moderate circumstances and Harriett was dying of consumption. I occasionally visited her and read, sang and prayed with the family at her bedside. She was confident in the prospect of immortality and joyous in the hope of heaven. When taking my last leave of her I asked, "Harriett, how is it with your soul?"

She replied, "All is well. I'll soon be at home. Hallelujah! Jesus saves me!"

"Have you any message to those to whom I preach?" I asked.

"Yes," said she, "tell every one, especially the young women and young men, to seek salvation and prepare for heaven."

Soon after this the angels carried her redeemed spirit to the Paradise of God. The chamber in which this good young woman died was privileged above the common walks of virtuous life, quite on the verge of heaven. Harriett rests from her labors but her works do follow her. I have delivered her message to thousands upon thousands and will repeat it and carry it onward through my remaining years until thousands more shall hear and obey.

Will you not hear her message too?

There were several converted in Anapolis who were in advanced life and could not pray in public for want of ready utterance. I advised that they should learn a prayer or repeat the Lord's prayer. A Brother Hutton got hold of a Sunday school book that had a very good prayer in it. This he learned by heart. At the next meeting he commenced his prayer, repeated a part of it, but, forgetting the rest, broke off into an extempore prayer which pleased and profited those who heard it. From that evening he had no need of books or formulas but became mighty in prayer, giving glory to God in his own good way.

After spending six weeks on this circuit, assisting in meetings, I returned to Steubenville to ask a license to preach. The official board on the circuit said if the quarterly conference at Steubenville did not grant the license they would. But I preferred a license from a board who had always known me. I returned, therefore, and made my request known. After due course of recommendation and thorough examination, on Christmas Day, 1847, I was licensed in regular form. The examination was very critical, led by Revs. Hiram Gilmore and George S. Holmes. I had tried in the few days after my return to review and be prepared, but the very anxiety of mind I was under rendered review next to impossible. But the Lord helped me and I was licensed and fully committed to the life of a preacher.

In ten days I was on my way as an itinerant. A good old brother gave me a pair of saddlebags, into which I put my scanty wardrobe and library and started on my life work on foot and alone. My father followed me to the gate and with tearful eyes, after giving me good advice, said to me: "My son, whatever you do, be yourself. Copy no man. Put your trust in God and always do well whatever you undertake. Never forsake Him, and He will not forsake you. God bless you! Goodbye!"

I walked part of the way and was conveyed part of the way by a countryman in a sled, through slush and mud and snow. On my return to the circuit I met a warm reception and entered at once on the work. Here I spent six months of unremitting toil, witnessing marvelous displays of saving grace and counting it all joy to preach Jesus Christ my Lord.

CHAPTER X.

"TO THE WORK!"

During the latter part of the year I became intensely interested in the cause of temperance. One place in the circuit, Annapolis, had become notorious as a resort of wicked men and drunkards. Dram-drinking and drunkenness were on the increase. One Sabbath afternoon at church I was wonderfully led by the spirit of God to pray for the destruction of this great and growing evil. I prayed that the Lord would convert or remove the occupants or destroy the place where this traffic was carried on. There was at the time of prayer a black cloud overspreading the heavens, and before the prayer was ended there came a flash of lightning from the inky bosom of the cloud, followed by a clanking crash, as if a hissing bolt from the hand of Jehovah would rend the very earth. Evidently the lightning had spent the force of its quick stroke not far from the place where we were assembled to worship. My hearers were startled and deep seriousness fell upon us all. When we were dismissed the report came that the house where the liquor was sold had been struck with lightning, the inmates severely shocked, and that it was with difficulty they had saved the house from burning. The proprietor was greatly alarmed, and after hearing of the prayer and reflecting upon the coincidence resolved to give up the business and remove to another place, fearing another stroke from heaven, and thus we were freed from the evil.

The people and preacher desired that I should remain on the circuit, but the people were poor and the preacher's family dependent, so that for six months' work I had received but fifty cents in money and about thirteen dollars worth of clothing and presents. Though I'd been happy as a king, I gave up the circuit and by the advice of the presiding elder was recommended for admission into the Pittsburg annual conference at its session in Wheeling, Virginia, on the 5th of July, 1848. At this session the West Virginia conference was set off from the Pittsburg conference. I was appointed to Paris circuit in Stark county, Ohio, with Dyas Neal as preacher in charge and Zarah Coston presiding elder.

Immediately on receiving my appointment I started on horseback to my new work. I had been ill during the session of conference and when I arrived at Waynesburgh, a town in the bounds of my circuit, I was very weary and weak. After resting a little I left an appointment for preaching in town at 3 p. m. on Sunday, and having met some of the brethren from Wesley Chapel sent an appointment there for 11 a. m. next day. Rest, medicine and kindly treatment soon set me right, so that on Sabbath I was able to preach three times. My friends were surprised by my early arrival from conference and pleased with my promptness.

Sabbath morning came. It was a charming day. The news of my arrival spread with rapidity and there was a large crowd to welcome the new preacher. When I reached the church the house was well filled with a number in the churchyard eager to see the young pastor. I reached the pulpit with no little trepidation and knelt, devoutly asking for the helpful influence of the Holy Spirit in preaching the gospel of salvation. When I took my seat in the pulpit an eager, anxious look met my eyes from every part of the large congregation. The concentrated gaze of the people was upon the trembling, inexperienced youth who fortunately, however, detected in the look of many of those before him more of real sympathy and anxiety than of censurably cold curiosity. Almost involuntarily, at least without intention or calculation of possible failure or reaction, I struck up in easy ringing cadences:

"Come thou fount of every blessing,
"Tune my heart to sing thy praise."

As I sang I surveyed my audience to see the effect; here and there I detected a pleased glance, suffused with tears; then an earnest and devout upturning of the eyes, a swelling bosom, breathing through parted lips the sentiment of the poet and singer. Here and yonder were seen to start the full, round tear drops, rolling down the furrowed cheeks of the fathers and mothers in Israel. On many a youthful face there was an expression of delight at hearing the shrill, clear notes of an old tune and hymn sung by the strange preacher. One verse sung and the whole audience was irresistibly swept into the channel of devotion, and with the stranger struck the first note of the second verse:

"Here I'll raise my Ebenezer,
Hither by Thy help I'm come."

By the time the last verse was sung the whole congregation belonged to God by solemn vow and was mine in every good sense to help in the work of saving souls from sin and death. A subdued wave of joy rolled over the audience, and when the prayer was offered many a hearty "Amen" lent its impulse like wings of light to carry the petition incited by the Holy Spirit through the gates of the heavenly temple to the throne where the Lamb performs the desires of His followers through the merits of His own death, and from whence came that day sweet answers of peace to the hungry hearts of God's children.

"The memory of that blessed day:
O, may it ever stay!"

This was my introduction, my installment. It has been interrupted by change, but never broken up. There was none to herald or introduce me, none to give seal or signet to my appearance. But I was here as the sent of the church, by her Bishop, and the Holy Ghost honored my coming. No pre-thought, or pre-arrangement, but only that song—that grand old battle song, of our church—springing as by magic to consecrated lips—had touched as by divine power and melted as by divine love all hearts into a happy union of song and praise. This was a glorious beginning of a pleasant pastorate of two years on my first circuit in the regular work.

My text on the occasion was "Only fear the Lord and serve Him in truth with all thy heart, for consider what great things He hath done for thee."

Having preached at 11 a. m. I returned home with a brother's family after having formed the acquaintance of a number of the prominent members of the church. After dinner I was accompanied by several of the brethren to Waynesburg, where at 3 p. m. I preached to a good congregation, many of whom welcomed me most cordially to my new field of labor. I was dissuaded by friends from going to the "Woods" appointment, some five miles distant, as there was no announcement out, and I therefore preached in Waynesburg at 7:30 p. m. to a larger congregation, the other churches having no evening service.

I immediately proceeded to adjust myself to the work before me. Arrangements were made that I should have a home at one of the stewards. I then started to bring my trunk containing my wardrobe and library, such as I had. On my way I was hailed by a man whose name was George Wood, who with his father and brothers were members of a small class at what was known as "Wood's Meeting House" on Paris circuit. These were large, strong men, very hard to govern or to keep near the mark of Christian duty. They kept whiskey in their houses and drank it. Election days were times with them of settling neighborhood troubles. They held the neighborhood and class in a state of terror, which made the exercise of discipline very difficult, indeed next to impossible. I was innocent of hint or knowledge of these facts.

Wood accosted me on the highway with "You are the young preacher sent to our circuit, are you?"

"I am the junior preacher sent by the Bishop to Paris circuit."

"We learn that you are a Son of Temperance," said he, "and we are determined that no member of a temperance society shall preach in our church."

I replied that I hoped there would be no difficulty on that subject, but that I would be on hand at the regular time and preach in the church—or on a stump.

I rode away wondering what manner of man this fellow could be. In accordance with the announcement (contrary to the advice of my colleague) I was on time to meet a good congregation. Many had heard of the interview between Wood and me and came expecting excitement. I preached, announced the next appointment and dismissed the people.

Immediately Wood rose and requested the members to remain, saying, "We want to know what the young preacher intends to do about leaving the Sons of Temperance." Then he sat down.

The unconverted, expecting fun or trouble, stood anxiously looking on, for I had fairly won them by my sermon. I afterward learned that they had resolved that I should not be harmed. As the first excitement lulled Wood rose again and said: "We want to know if you (addressing me) will leave the Sons of Temperance, for we are resolved that no member of that order shall preach here."

I was a stranger, but after surveying the situation leisurely, I arose and replied that I was born in Ohio, born free, that my father was a gentleman and a Christian, and had always taught me to mind my own business, and I had an opinion that the fathers of others should have done the same. As to leaving the "Sons of Temperance" I had simply to say if my colleague or my presiding elder, either or both, should so advise me I would do so; or, if the quarterly conference should so advise I would comply; but if they said I must leave the Sons of Temperance then I would exercise my rights as a man and do as I pleased—that I could be led but never driven.

All outside who could hear applauded. Wood and his party almost gnashed their teeth upon me. I took my hat and walked out amid subdued applause by the outsiders. So the matter rested until the quarterly conference. The preacher in charge, the elder, and the quarterly conference refused to interfere with my private rights, and I continued to preach regularly there for two years, with but little irritation and some success.

The most remarkable display of saving power was at Wesley Chapel and at Malvern. Hundreds were converted and added to the church. My colleague had a long spell of sickness which utterly disqualified him for his work for six months. At the meeting many very interesting cases of conversion occurred, one or two of which may be cited as illustrative of the power of grace.

Miss Brunson, a mute, with whose father I stopped when I first came to this circuit, had been married several years before to a Mr. George Miller. She was the mother of three children but had never been known to speak a word. She became deeply convicted of sin and sought salvation by faith in Christ. After long and prayerful seeking she accepted Christ and was gloriously saved. Rising from the altar, with a countenance all radiant with joy and hands raised toward heaven, she exclaimed audibly and distinctly, "Jesus, Jesus, Jesus saves me! Glory!" Such a thrill as went through the congregation I never witnessed before nor have I since. Strong men wept like children. Some wept aloud, others joined the shout, and it appeared that the Master was filling the house with divine light and life and power. The case was reported in the "Pittsburg Christian Advocate." This woman still lives a Godly life. Partially restored speech continues. I visited her and her family in Ohio in 1875.

The above occurrence brought men and women from near and far to attend our meetings, many of them unbelievers. Of the number there was a tall, fine looking young man, Barton Blygh, who was well posted in the objections of infidels, himself an unbeliever. On one occasion he came up near the altar to gaze and scoff at the scene. Some of the brethren thought he ought to be invited to a back seat, especially as he stood defiantly leaning against a column near the altar during prayer. I noticed his derisive sneer, and asked the brethren to pray that the Holy Spirit might touch his stony heart and awaken him. When we kneeled to pray I approached him, laid my hand on his shoulder and asked him if he did not feel the need of salvation. He replied that he neither knew nor cared for our religion and wanted nothing to do with it. I soon discovered that he was trembling violently, and leaning heavily against the column for support. The spirit of prayer continued to rise in fervor about him. As I stood with my hand on him I prayed God to have mercy and enlighten him and save him. Presently he cried aloud as though pierced with a dart, and fell in the aisle as one slain in a battle. There he lay until midnight, stiff and stark, as though indeed dead. Dr. Wilson and other physicians examined him and wanted to remove him to his home as dead, and were ready to say that life was gone; for he was as rigid as iron. I told them God could kill and make alive, and he would in this case. About midnight the sweet, low, subdued singing began to penetrate to his soul and he showed signs of returning animation. A heavenly smile came over his face, his lips moved, some of the brethren near by stooped to listen to his whispers; his words became more distinct as he repeated with indescribable sweetness, "Glory, Glory, Jesus saves me! Glory, Glory, to His Name!" This was a glorious conversion and its subject remained firm in the faith as long as I knew him.

CHAPTER XI.

THE WAIL OF A LOST SOUL.

At our meeting at Malvern we had a large ingathering of young men, while whole families were saved, to remain steadfast members of the church.

There came to our meeting here, on one occasion, a canal-boat captain named John Crandall. He was perhaps fifty years old, and had been on the canal for several years. Rev. J. H. Rogers preached from Luke xv-10. Captain Crandall listened to the sermon with attention and at the close while the exhortation was being pressed upon the people, arose and requested the privilege of speaking. I told him to speak on.

He said: "He that hath an ear to hear let him hear! I was the only son of religious parents. I was raised in the fear of the Lord. I grew up to young manhood, and my father died. I promised him on his death-bed that I would meet him in heaven. Months and years passed and often I thought of my promise but made no preparation for dying. Finally my mother was taken sick and called me to her side and said: 'My son, you promised your father you would be religious and meet him in heaven, but you have made no start yet. My dear boy, I cannot die satisfied unless you promise me you will prepare to meet me in heaven.' I then and there promised my dying mother I would lead a Christian life and meet her and father in heaven. The spirit of God strove with me, but I put off my return to Him from time to time I still kept on my wicked ways and sought the society of old companions. In a bar-room I cursed God and bade the spirit leave me. Soon after I attended a meeting in Pennsylvania. I was deeply convicted of sin. So powerfully did the spirit of God strive with me that I trembled like a leaf in the wind. I left my seat to go to the altar for prayer but my proud spirit rebelled and I stopped in the aisle and leaned against a column that supported the gallery. Here for some moments I parleyed with the spirit and finally, summoning my rebellious will with an oath, I determined I would run the risk of being lost rather than yield in that way. At that moment the spirit of God left me. I could almost see it departing. A deep, dark night settled down on my soul. I went out of the house and cursed God and heaven and dared Jehovah to do his worst. From that hour until this I have never had a conviction nor a desire for heaven. I know my doom is sealed."

Standing out in the aisle and raising himself to his full height he went on, "Look upon me and behold a man in his right mind and yet consciously and justly damned above ground! Language fails to describe the horror I feel and the anguish that is consuming my soul. Oh, the worm that dieth not is now preying on my lost soul!"

The poor man looked the personification of anguish.

Said he, "I would willingly give the world, did I own it, if I could but feel a desire to be saved. The only desire I have is for my broken-hearted wife and daughter, that they may not come into this torment. Some of you may say, 'Why, Crandall, if you have such a desire for others the Lord will save you! He will have mercy on you.' No! No! No! Mercy for me is gone forever. The rich man in hell desired that his brothers might not come into that place of torment, and he wanted God to send Lazarus to warn them. I warn my wife and daughter and all of you who know me to turn to God now, for now is your day of salvation. Mine is gone. My doom is sealed. I am lost, lost, lost!"

His exhortation to others to make peace with God and not hazard their salvation by delay or by resisting God's spirit was a horrifying appeal that thrilled all who heard it. I seem yet, after years have passed, to hear and see that man and feel the terror of that hour. The congregation was terror-stricken. A score or more pressed their way to the altar for prayers and before the meeting closed were converted. The revival continued several weeks and a great number professed religion.

After this Captain Crandall continued to run his canal-boat until taken sick at Bolivar, Ohio, where he died on his boat. His death was reported to me by Mr. Rogers: "John Crandall died in the winter of 1848-9 at Bolivar. I went down from Waynesburg for the purpose of learning how he died. I found his boat and his wife and nephew living in it. She was a Christian woman. I told her I had heard of the Captain's death and asked her how he had died. She said she could not endure telling me, but that his nephew would tell me. He told me his uncle died a most horrible death, cursing God and Jesus Christ. He would turn on his stomach and bite his own arms and gnaw his own flesh. "I would leave the boat, so terrible was it. It seemed to be full of devils, and he would tell us the devils were torturing him to death."

Thus he had lived and thus horribly did he die—a rejecter crying, "Remorse! Remorse!! Remorse!!!"

CHAPTER XII.

I AM MARRIED.

At Paris and other points on the circuit we held successful meetings, especially at Minerva. Here several very interesting conversions took place, which attracted much attention and became of lasting good to the church. There were three very amiable and intelligent sisters, by the name of Hostetter, who occasionally attended our meetings. The first one converted fell under the displeasure of the mother, who was strongly opposed to the Methodist Church. This so interested the other sisters that they took sides with the converted one and it was not many days until all three were happy in the Savior's love, sharers together of precious faith. In my subsequent visits to the family, by invitation of the father, I found the mother quite subdued by the beautiful lives of the three Christian sisters and almost persuaded to join with them in leading a Christian life. Their influence on society led many to accept Christ as their Savior. The conversion of these young women produced a remarkable change in their family, and the revivals of that year have also in other ways their fruitage even yet.

The sickness of my colleague, depriving the circuit of his services for half a year, my responsibility and work were greatly increased; for, in addition to the claims of the circuit I had my conference course of study on hand. My method was to study the textbooks closely and work up the material of the course into sermons. Thus as I went through the year I was utilizing my labor and preparing for conference, and while the lack of a colleague made it hard for me in my inexperience and youth yet the Lord was my strength and helper. We reported a large increase and finances in a reasonably good conditon. I received seventy-six dollars on salary with a good many presents as tokens of kindness from the people; among them was "a suit from top to toe." There were a great many farmers whom I visited and from these families I received numerous gifts, in some of which—not "the mitten"—the deft fingers of appreciative young ladies had inwrought the initials of my name; pleasant little marks of respect, by the way, one of which was to be a sign-manual for alarmed recollection far ahead in the future.

Near the close of this my first year of conference work, after due deliberation, prayer and counsel with my brethren who were acquainted with my betrothed, and by the advice of my presiding elder, I concluded that it would be of advantage to my work to marry before conference, and on the morning of May 1, 1849, at 6 o'clock, I was married to the wife whose counsel has never misled me, nor retarded me in my ministry, and whose helpful courage, piety and presence have always been a tower of strength in my various relations of life and my duties to the church.

We made an early start, both as to the hour of the day and the day of the month, as well as the month in spring. Our wedding tour was to Steubenville, where after two days' visiting we bade our friends farewell for an itinerant life, so full of incident, interest, fact and history that volumes might be written before the whole could be exhausted and recorded.

Returning to the circuit on May 5, we found a cor-

ELIZABETH MARGARET FISHER.

dial welcome at Mr. Simeon Westfall's, to whose family my wife became as a sister. Dinner over, we drove to Minerva and took supper with the family of David Kurtz, whose wife was as a mother to myself and bride. After supper we drove to Paris and lodged with Brother and Sister Gideon Smith, who had endeared themselves to me by kindnesses I can never forget. In their house I had found a home during the severest sickness of my life, which had occurred the fall previous. These good people always treated me as their son and my wife as a daughter. On Sabbath day I preached at 11 a. m. in Paris, at 3 p. m. at Franklin and again at night in Paris.

This was my introduction to a married life in the itinerancy, the beginning of unceasing activity. During six succeeding weeks we traveled over the circuit, visiting many families who had never had a visit from a preacher's wife before, and who took our attention to them as a remarkable treat. We thus visited over sixty families and so ingratiated ourselves into their affections that years of change have not obliterated the pleasant memories of the past nor broken up the endearing attachments.

Conference met this year at Brownsville, Pennsylvania, Bishop Waugh presiding. He said in his sermon on Sabbath day that "Christian perfection consisted in being emptied of sin and filled with the love of God." For this I hungered and thirsted. At the close of conference my name was announced, with Thomas Rucle, to Paris circuit. This surprised me, as well as others, for it was unusual to return a probationer the second year. I think the secret of my return was my method of visiting all the people, which had made me very generally acceptable.

Almost immediately we commenced house-keeping in Waynesburgh in a cosy little home of two rooms. But as my wife, who had been a school-teacher had been somewhat used to boarding around among the scholars, it was easy for her to make herself at home traveling the circuit, and we often traveled together to my appointments in a buggy. An occurrence took place in the fall of this year which deeply impressed us with the value of prayer and the providence of God. I had a regular Friday evening appointment about six miles from Waynesburgh on the Canton road. My wife was accompanying me as usual when, at the top of a long and very steep hill, whose road was washed out on the upper side and was very crooked and in places dangerous, my horse stumbled and fell, breaking both thills short off, but leaving the traces attached to the single-tree. The buggy ran upon the horse, which had fallen down. I sprang out and called to my wife to jump, but before she could do so the horse in its fright regained his feet and rushed wildly down the hillside. My wife rose deliberately and threw her cloak back off her shoulders and sat down in the buggy. Horse, buggy and wife went flying down the road. I thought she would be killed. I stood a moment as if paralyzed, and prayed, "Lord, save her, save her!" I ran after them, expecting to find my wife dead by the wayside. After running a third of a mile and turning a sharp curve in the road I beheld the buggy, a total wreck; the horse was not in sight but my wife, who had been thrown down the hillside by the upsetting of the buggy, was gathering herself together and clambering up the side of the bank shaking the dust from her clothing. When I reached the spot where she stood we knelt down in the road, wept for joy and thanked

God for His interposition in saving her life in answer to prayer. Some farmers at the foot of the hill caught our runaway horse and one came riding back expecting to find some one killed by the accident; but he found us alive and praising God. We stripped the remains of the harness from the horse, and gathering the broken buggy together put it into a brother's wagon and sent it back to be rebuilt. We then walked to the foot of the hill, borrowed a side-saddle, my wife took the reins of the prancing steed and rode on to the appointment while I walked by her side to meet a good congregation to which I attempted to preach. The event made a deep impression on all who heard of it, and was regarded as a special interposition of Providence in answer to prayer.

My colleague made one full round on the circuit when he was taken sick and after a short illness died, leaving clear testimony of the ability of Christ to save. His death was a sad loss to me, but it became an opportunity of development for future work; for larger responsibilities were thrown upon me which gave fuller scope to my former observation and experience.

CHAPTER XIII.

THE DOVE'S DESCENT.

At the close of the year conference was held in Canton, Ohio, Bishop Edmund Janes presiding. I was by special request quartered with Uncle Jimmie Armstrong, an old colored man strong in the faith, who entertained us in a princely manner. At the conference I was admitted into full connection, my probation having expired, and ordained as deacon in a class with Sheridan Baker, N. C. Worthington, J. J. McIlyar, James Beacon, G. B. Hudson, Robt. Cunningham, Joseph Woodrough, A. D. McCormac, D. B. Coleman, John Barker, D. D., Henry Snyder, Richard Clegg and J. T. W. Auld. Most of these have finished their work in holy triumph. Only two are still on the walls of Zion proclaiming the acceptable year of the Lord.

At this session of conference I was appointed colleague with Josiah Dillon to the New Brighton circuit, Pennsylvania, and crossed the country by private conveyance, stopping one night with the presiding elder, Father Monroe, in Beaver. On arriving at Freedom, a principal appointment in the circuit, we met with a cordial welcome notwithstanding some dissatisfaction because both the appointees were married men. Two preachers with two wives were more than they had bargained for. Money was scarce and the outlook rather forbidding. A good Brother McConnell consoled my wife with the thought that probably she could afford to wear "six cent calico" before the year ended. But nothing daunted, we went to work, visiting indiscriminately, and were soon installed in the affections of the people. We had a favorable initiation through a Sunday school celebration on the Fourth of July, where I made the eagle soar in a speech full of patriotism and temperance. Entertaining strong views on the temperance question, we entered the campaign to win and soon had the satisfaction of seeing the traffic of rum closed out. The circuit was large and required a great amount of labor to meet the expectation of the people. Some of our meetings impressed me so profoundly that I can never forget them. Many of them were very pleasant and are garnished with reminiscences which make them a delight to contemplate.

During the early part of our first year on this circuit there was a call made by Bishop Janes and Dr. Durbin for men to go to California to occupy that open field. Father Monroe, my presiding elder, wrote a letter commending me for the field. He deposited it in the post office, but as the mail only left twice a week, his letter remained in the office a day or two, during which time he relented, and being unwilling to have me leave his district lifted the letter of recommendation. It was never remailed, and thus I was retained on the circuit.

Among others, we held a very successful camp-meeting near Freedom. A great many were converted and scores of believers sanctified. Several incidents will bear recital. The meeting was attended with a display of divine power in a manner not before witnessed by the oldest Christians in attendance. Sister Dillon, wife of my colleague, a very sweet-spirited Christian, and Sister John Ansley, another preacher's wife, with my wife, were all young in Christian experience, as well as in the itinerancy, and were bound by these common ties in very dear relation to each other, and were wonderfully blessed, as the sequel will show. I know the reader will not only pardon the writer but thank him for the facts (though personal) that are here more minutely narrated, as incidentally connected with the meeting. My wife, who was reared a Presbyterian, had never been at a camp-meeting. Several weeks before the meeting she had a remarkable dream. I will allow her to relate it.

"I dreamed that there was a great concourse of people assembled on a beautiful plateau of ground; along one side a shining river ran eastwardly, while to the westward seemed to rise a beautiful sloping hill covered with stately oaks. The earth was carpeted with green. The company was shaded by the overhanging branches through which gleamed the subdued but clear sunlight of a mid-autumn day. All appeared to be filled with delight, while with upturned face and expectant eyes they were waiting and watching for some strange heavenly visitant. I drew near and asked what they were looking for so intently. Some one answered that they were looking for a dove that was promised to come that day, and that on whomsoever it should alight there should rest great peace and joy. Each one was filled with anxiety to be the first to see it and to have it alight on him. Presently a sensation of delight thrilled the throng as it was announced by some one of the company, 'The dove! The dove is coming!' I looked intently upward and away in the distance beheld a glittering speck as of burnished silver flashing in the sunlight. It came circling down in most graceful motion, seeming to survey every anxious spectator, while the vast, excited, breathless throng swayed to and fro with outstretched hands inviting the beautiful stranger to alight. It reviewed the large crowd with apparent satisfaction and then, to my surprise and extreme delight, perched upon my shoulder and nestled close to my face. Several persons pressed forward and put forth their hands to secure the dove but it shrank from their touch and settled closely down on my shoulder. The whole company joined in a shout, 'It has come! It has come!' I was so filled with joy that I shouted with inexpressible delight and awoke to find it but a dream, but so impressive a dream that even yet it seems a reality. My effort to shout awoke my husband, to whom I related my dream. Whereupon he replied that he hoped it was significant and that I might receive a visit from the heavenly dove at the approaching camp-meeting."

In due time the meeting began. It was largely attended. We held noon-day prayer meetings in a large tent, usually very much crowded. On one occasion Sisters Ansley, Dillon and my wife, neither of whom had ever prayed in public, were together in the meeting. I called on Sister Ansley to pray. She hesitated. I urged her to take up the cross. Finally she said in the most plaintive voice, "Oh, Lord, help me; I don't know how to pray."

I said, "Sister, you have made a good beginning; go right on and pray." She continued to plead with God in such supplicating terms as I had seldom heard. All were looking by faith for the fulfillment of the promise: "Whatsoever things ye ask, believe that ye have them, and ye shall receive them." And the Holy Ghost came upon all the company. None shared more largely in this baptism of power and glory than these three preachers' wives. My wife said to me, "My dream is fulfilled"; and for hours she rejoiced and told with wonderful clearness and simplicity the amazing power and sweetness of saving grace. Many Presbyterian ladies, hearing of her remarkable ecstacy and joy came to the tent purposely to hear from her own lips the glad story of salvation by simple faith. They were astonished and delighted to find one brought up as they had been testifying in such a manner.

Soon after this we visited my wife's father and mother. She resolved she would tell her mother all about her great blessing. When we reached the top of the hill overlooking the old homestead her heart failed her a little and she said to me, "I don't know how to begin to tell mother." I remarked she must not flinch now; that the way to commence would be open. On reaching home I said to mother I was sorry she had not been at the camp-meeting to have witnessed the wonderful blessing her daughter received. Then I retired, leaving the mother and daughter alone. My wife related her vision and the incidents of the meeting, and especially her own rich share of the Divine gift. They wept like children together and we have every reason to believe that from that day mother had a clearer knowledge of the way of salvation than ever before. She often said she had never heard such an experience, not even from her own favorite pastor, Dr. Duncan, of Baltimore. It was, indeed, as my wife told it, "The coming of the Holy Ghost and of power."

It was in this circuit that I was called upon to officiate in ministerial capacity under a reversion of circumstances unusually sad, and aptly illustrative of the fact that in the midst of life we are in death. In the neighborhood a young lady of twenty years of age was engaged to be married on a certain day and at a special hour. The wedding attire was complete, the guests invited, the minister engaged, the bridegroom came—to find his betrothed sick unto death. The very hour and day that should have sealed their nuptials became the burial hour of the intended bride. It was my solemn duty instead of performing the marriage ceremony to preach a funeral sermon over that beautiful young woman dressed in the chaste white silk meant for her bridal robe but now become the fit burial dress of one whose hopes had faded before and into the brighter bliss of a more intimate union with Christ. The sad termination of such an engagement almost crazed the affianced groom, who was only consoled by the doctrine of the resurrection of the dead and immortality at God's right hand.

CHAPTER XIV.

MY FATHER'S DEATH.

At the close of the first calendar year, as was my custom, we held a "watch-night meeting." It was held in the Methodist Church in Freedom, Pennsylvania, 1850-51. We had a very solemn time. The Lord was manifestly present. When we went home, very early in the morning, we received a telegram (the first in my life) from Steubenville, Ohio, saying, "Your father is dying and wishes to see you. Come home." He had long been a sufferer, but longer a Christian and active worker in the church. In addition to my natural affection for my father and my desire to be with him in the closing scene of life I had long cherished a desire to know how his faith would endure that severest of all tests, for I knew he would not deceive his children, and that he could not be deluded into a false trust or confidence, much less a false profession. We hastened to his bedside by the first steamer, as we did not have railroad communication.

On arriving we found father still alive. As I opened the door of his room he stretched forth his pale, thin hands, exclaiming: "My son, come while I tell you what great victory I have through our Lord Jesus Christ! Glory, glory to His precious name! The fear of dying is all taken away and I have perfect peace with God, and peace with all mankind. Preach a complete salvation, a full and perfect and finished salvation, in Jesus Christ our Lord."

Subsequently he said, "Satan has tempted me more severely than ever before in my life. He has tried to persuade me to trust in my good works and devotion to the church, and it has been a struggle to give up all these, but Jesus Christ is my only hope, Christ in me the hope of glory. Tho' Satan tempted me that the Savior would forsake me, I have had victory over that fear. He will never forsake me. Perfect love casteth out all fear, which hath torment."

He repeated and with effort sang parts of sacred hymns which he always admired, one of which I remember hearing him sing when a child:

"My span of life will soon be done,
 The passing moments say;
As lengthening shadows o'er the mead
 Proclaim the close of day.

Courage, my soul; thy bitter cross
 In every trial here
Shall bear thee to thy heaven above,
 But shall not enter there.

Courage, my soul; on God rely;
 Deliverance soon will come;
A thousand ways has Providence
 To bring believers home."

He also repeated the words of that glorious sonnet beginning:

"How firm a foundation, ye saints of the Lord,
Is laid for your faith on His excellent word."

And dwelt with manifest satisfaction upon the soul-stirring words:

"Amazing grace, how sweet the sound,
　That saved a wretch like me,
I once was lost, but now I'm found,
　Was blind but now I see.

'Twas grace that taught my heart to fear,
　And grace my fears relieved,
How precious did that grace appear,
　The hour I first believed!"

The scene was so overwhelming and inspiring that I have never doubted the power of Jesus to save to the uttermost, and to the close of life.

Father lingered until the 4th of January, 1851, during which time he was in constant ecstacy, frequently shouting the praises of God until his strength would be exhausted. His triumph and his experience were truly glorious. In the afternoon of the fourth day after my arrival, at about 4 o'clock, we were all gathered in the room where our mother had fallen asleep in Jesus on the 7th day of September, 1837, saying, "Jesus is mine and I am His," to witness the closing event of a life which was to us more a comment on Christianity than anything else. For this had always been our father's theme, and had led to an exemplification of it in his every day life in the most familiar and endearing relations of the family. He was now evidently and rapidly approaching the "Valley of the shadow of death." We gathered close to his bedside to catch the last utterances from his faltering tongue. None but those who have been blessed with such a father and who have been called to mourn his decease can appreciate our anxiety at that moment. His sight had evidently failed for he asked, "Who is in the room? Are you all here?" My oldest brother answered, "We are all here, father. Do you want anything?" He answered, "No." Then raising his hand and passing it over his sightless eyes he said:

"It is dark here, but glory is bright."

And the weary wheels of life stood still.

Angels caught the redeemed soul of our father in their loving arms and bore him to his home on high. To us all, but to me especially, it was a deeply solemn, gloriously triumphant hour. I have never since that hour felt like shouting the praises of God as then. It was victory, triumph over the last enemy by faith in our Lord Jesus Christ. The grave has lost its gloom and terror, and death his venomous sting. Since then Christ is dearer and heaven has been nearer. We made his grave beside our mother's, under the spreading branches of the old chestnut tree in the graveyard whose dust is sacred to the sainted dead, who sleep in hope of immortality.

I returned to my work a more sanctified and better man.

CHAPTER XIV.

AGENTS OF THE DEVIL—SERVANTS OF THE LORD.

I was called upon shortly to preach in a Calvinistic neighborhood near the seat of Rapp's colony of Economists in Butler County, Pennsylvania. When I arrived at the neighborhood school-house I met a goodly company assembled to hear what had never been heard there, a Methodist sermon. I chose for my text the eleventh verse of the 119th Psalm, read the verse, closed the Bible, and preached a plain but practical sermon. The Presbyterians were delighted, some regarding it as wonderful that a man could preach such a discourse without notes, and especially with the Bible closed. The truth sanctified and applied by the Holy Ghost led several persons into a clear Christian experience, and many became my regular hearers and fast friends.

* * * * * * *

While we were stationed at the beautiful little town of Freedom, in Beaver County, Pennsylvania, about three miles above the confluence of Big Beaver with the Ohio river, our home was blessed by the arrival of a little boy, our first born, whom we named for his grandfathers, John William. His birth occurred on the second day of June, 1851. His arrival was a matter of unusual moment to the young circuit rider and his wife, as may be expected, and was also hailed with satisfaction and delight by our members, all of whom took a greater interest in us on this account, if this were possible, and were exceedingly kind to us in our initial parentage.

Freedom was chiefly given over to the business of

JOHN WILLIAM FISHER.

steamboat building. While here I launched on one of the finest of the numerous craft built there for the river trade, the "John J. Simons," a boat upon whose decks I subsequently, eleven years later, took a company of contrabands from the Southern armies of the Union to homes of liberty in Kansas and Nebraska.

Our first son, whose portrait is given, is engaged in mercantile pursuits—a dealer in coal. For many years he engaged in farming on the "home farm" in Atchison County, but subsequently engaged in other pursuits in the city of Atchison, of whose council he was one term a member, and where he was for several years secretary and treasurer of the Pomeroy Coal Company, with yards and offices at Atchison, Topeka and Lincoln, Nebraska. For many years he has been a devoted Christian and an active and efficient worker in the church and Sabbath school. In recent years he has been deprived of the pleasure of regular church work because away from home most of the time, but he still delights in the service and church of his God.

Having spent two years on this circuit I was returned to Ohio and put in charge of Lima circuit with "one to be supplied." The circuit had thirteen appointments, with a membership of nearly five hundred, scattered over a territory twenty miles wide by thirty miles long. This territory included the hotbed of infidelity in Ohio. The noted "Come-out-ers," Abby Kelly, Foster, and H. C. Wright, had traveled the whole field, disseminating infidel doctrine, denouncing the church and the Bible, ministers, and the marriage contract as intolerable and to be repudiated. Abby Kelly, who had been a member of the Quaker church, was a woman of considerable intelligence and will, with fair address and force of character. She formed the center of attraction for a crowd of rude and irreligious people who composed her following. She and Foster traveled together, being entertained by those who, like themselves, held to very radical views relating to liberty from customs growing out of the marriage relation. But in some places public sentiment was so severely against the example of this free and easy way of evading the law of God and man that they finally formed a kind of "Hicksite-Quaker" copartnership, in the town of New Brighton, Pennsylvania, at the house of one Townsend, after which I believe they were recognized as man and wife, he being a kind of appendage or convenience, as is sometimes the case with strong-minded women and weak-minded men. Their teaching and example were subversive of morality and good order, because well suited to the baser passions of the human heart. Wright had been a local preacher in the Methodist Church, but left it and joined the ranks of the "Come-out-ers." The whole territory of the circuit of which I was placed in charge was poisoned with the false and vicious teaching of these people.

About the time I was sent to this circuit the Misses Fox, of Rochester, New York, began their spirit rappings—the origin of spiritualism in America—which was also a part of this infidelity. Abby Kelly and company had well prepared the way for this new theory and irreligion. Some incidents connected therewith will furnish a faint idea of the state of society under such influences.

Not far from Freedom, one of my appointments in Stark County, Ohio, there was an old log church, called Rucker's Church. It was arranged to hold in this house a convention of the infidels and sympathizers to consider what should be done relative to this new development called "Spirit Rappings" or Spiritualism. The appointment was made, the evening came, and with it a crowd of curiosity seekers. The old house was lighted in the rudest manner by the use of the light of past ages, tallow "dips" or candles. These were fastened here and there against the jambs of the windows by pocket-knives, while for front lights a board resting on the stand and window-sill supported several candles. Behind this were seated the leaders in the movement with a tall son of Anak, called Johnson, "the first letter of whose name" was "Jep." Acting as chairman, this young man was chief operator and held himself with much dignity. The company was a motley one, composed of railroad graders, "Come-out-ers," strong-minded old and young women, some of whom were dressed in bloomers, and young men with very long hair parted in the middle, easily and almost entirely covering the limited brains in their peanut-shaped craniums. Besides these there were numerous old moral cripples who had "come out" to the great relief of several churches. These, with a sprinkling of unbelievers, came to hear and see what the "Spirit had to knock." And they did.

The president began to state the object of the meeting to be the consideration of these new developments at Rochester, when a faint "Rap, Rap, Rap," was heard, as if immediately behind the president. At first all present were startled. Then came silence. By and by the president opened his astonished mouth to say that it was indeed mysterious; that they had met to consider this strange subject, and it appeared that the spirits were verily present; whereupon with greater vigor and emphasis than before the obtruding spirit gave its mystic "Rap, Rap, Rap," and all was again as silent as death. Cheeks were blanched, eyes flashed astonishment and surprise, knees quaked and smote together, all were amazed. Presently some one ventured to ask, "What do you want to communicate?" When, with greater vigor than before and much more deliberately and determinedly was heard the mystic "Rap, Rap, Rap," followed now by a most unearthly "Yeaow, Yeaow, Yeaow, Rap!" This brought the house to their feet and the president in gathering himself up overturned the board, upsetting every candle and extinguished most of the light. This served as a signal for a grand stampede, and out the door and through the windows went the astonished crowd, flying in every direction, some praying, others crying, while the Irish Catholics called on the "Howly Virgin" to pity Pat, and to forgive him for being at "sich a divil of a matin." One poor fellow who had recently been married, forgot his wife in his fright and ran as for his life. When he came back he found she had fainted for very fright, and was lying by the deserted house just recovering consciousness. When the truth was known the obtrusive spirit which had caused this confusion was none other than the materialized animus of an overgrown feline with a split stick on his tail which he used as a wrapper, and with which he had given a first-class "Spirit-rapping" seance, supplementing his efforts with the unearthly "Yeaow" which a Tom cat alone can give. Thus equipped and prepared for action some mischievous boys had dropped him through a broken window just behind the president's chair, to become the innocent cause of the sudden dissolution of the first and last spiritualistic gathering in all these parts.

The insolence of this class of people so outraged society that occasionally it had to be checked by law. There lived near Goshen Church two families named, respectively, Jenkins and Gibson, who, following the false teaching of the "Come-out-ers" and spiritualists, disregarded the sanctity of the marriage relation with such contempt that the civil authorities were compelled to interpose. They were brought in bloomers before Esquire Simeon Card, one of my class leaders, and were the first real spiritualists I had ever seen. I would they had been the last! The end was in disgrace and death—like Herod, they were eaten of worms.

We were compelled to meet these evils squarely and deal with them plainly from the pulpit. This sometimes led to public encounters. But truth, always mighty, prevailed, and the people were saved from the example of this heresy and ruin.

A very delightful occurrence took place while I was holding a protracted meeting at Marleborough. I was assisted by my old friend, Uncle Jimmie Armstrong. We held a meeting which was growing in interest, but which was much hindered by the clamor of want of union. There came to the neighborhood an itinerant Quaker preacher and his traveling companion, visiting the Quaker churches. It was announced that he would preach in the Friends' church at 11 o'clock a. m., and we were invited to attend the meeting. Uncle Jimmie, Brother John Swarts, and myself attended the services to hear a Quaker preacher for the first time. He preached a very orthodox sermon on the Resurrection of the Dead. I felt impressed with a desire to have him preach for my congregation. I told Uncle Jimmie I was going to ask him to preach for us. He replied, "O, it's no use. He won't do it." But I said, "I'll see."

So I went up to the preacher and assuming as much of the plain language as I could command, I said, "I am a Methodist preacher. We are holding a protracted meeting in Marleborough and I would like to have thee preach for me tonight. We will give thee the hour, and thee can do as the spirit leads thee."

He replied very kindly, "I will be very glad to preach for thee."

Notice was given and an invitation extended to the congregation to attend. When the hour for services came the house could not contain those who were anxious to enjoy such a union service. The Quakers came in great numbers and sat with hats on, presenting a strange appearance in a Methodist church. I told the preacher we would dispense with singing until the sermon was over, the hour was his. He prayed and sat down. All was as quiet as the grave. Then he arose and quoted a text or two of Scripture as a starting point and proceeded to preach a very evangelical sermon. In the midst of one of the most eloquent passages, in which he referred in beautiful language to the peaceable nature of the coming Kingdom of the Blessed Messiah and its near approach, and expressed a desire that it might speedily come, I was carried away with his eloquence and fervor, and endorsing his expressed desire I said "Amen."

Unused to such responses he was surprised, and turning around to me, asked, "What did thee say, Brother?"

I was confused, but had presence of mind enough to say, "Go on, Brother, go on."

Said he, "What did thee say?" I replied, "I said Amen."

He righted up and went on. The congregation was greatly amused and I felt woefully embarrassed. The Preacher finished well without any more of my "Amens."

While he was closing his sermon my mind was at work on how best to utilize the occasion. I knew all the Quakers were abolitionists and I had a good subject. So I determined I would take them with guile.

I arose and said: "A strange thing has occurred in Marleborough tonight. The quiet Quakers and noisy Methodists have held a meeting together and all ye are witnesses it has been a glorious meeting. And now I am going to ask Uncle Jimmie to sing the first hymn."

I gave him a sign and he promptly arose, attracting every eye and stood while I remarked that any who did not wish to hear him could retire. Every one remained. Uncle Jimmie struck the tune known as "Exhortation," singing,

> "O, for a thousand tongues to sing,
>   My great Redeemer's praise,
> The glories of my God and King,
>   The triumphs of his grace."

He sang as only he could sing. Under an inspiration every heart was moved. The whole company was swayed by this grand old hymn and tune sung by this dusky son of Methodism, as by the magic of a master.

When he had sung the last line I invited all to join in prayer and called on Uncle Jimmie to lead. Such a prayer had never been heard by that company, a prayer most eloquent and effective.

When it was over I stepped to the front of the altar to announce the appointments for the following evening, when the Quaker preacher came out of the pulpit and threw his arms around me and said audibly, "O, my brother, it is good to be here."

That meeting still lives and it will never be forgotten. Its far-reaching influence cannot be estimated.

This occurred in 1852 and in 1864, as I returned to Kansas from general conference at Philadelphia (of which body I was a member as a delegate from the Kansas conference) I met in the cars at Yellow Creek Station, Ohio, an itinerant Quaker preacher and his traveling companion. In the course of our journey I fell into conversation with them and learned that they were on a trip of visitation to the churches and were then going to Marleborough. I related to them the above incident, when they both rose to their feet and, grasping me warmly by the hand, exclaimed with unusual emotion for Quakers:

"Is it possible thee is the man that treated our Brother so kindly? We have heard him describe the singing and the singer, and the wonderful prayer, and the meeting, but we never expected to see the man that took such part in that interesting meeting."

They said that the relation of the incident pleased their friends very greatly. We had a joyful time talking over an incident of more than twelve years' standing. So far as I have been able to learn it was the first of the kind that occurred wherein Methodists and Quakers united in such a way to worship our common Savior and God.

At Mount Union, Stark County, one of my then appointments, there had been commenced a college three or four years previously, which is one of the many important institutions of Ohio. The president, Dr. O. N. Hartshorn, is a remarkable man, self-made in a striking sense, his whole life one of self-reliance. Coming up from obscurity and through poverty he has achieved wonders and assisted thousands of poor young men and women to the acquirement of an education and peculiarly fitted them for usefulness in life.

During my pastorate on the circuit I held four protracted meetings at this place, resulting in the conversion of more than one hundred of the students of the college. This was the beginning of active, open, effective Christian work in this locality, which was surrounded by infidel influences. In all these meetings I was heartily seconded and largely helped by all the professors, who continued to be a willing working band of Christian laborers. Every year since revivals have been enjoyed at this seat of Christian learning, resulting in the conversion of thousands of precious souls. The college is still sending men and women into every open field of usefulness. It was the first to adopt the co-education of the sexes, and from beginnings so small has gained upon popular sentiment until it has won its way to the front rank and today stands among the leading colleges of the West, owing much of its success to its decided religious caste and the faith and faithfulness of its faculty.

After more than twenty years absence from that field, ten of which were spent in Kansas, I returned to the Pittsburg conference and was made corresponding secretary of Mount Union College, in which relation I remained until called of the church and by the

Bishop to a field of vast moral importance. My early associations with this college as a religious instructor and helper so cemented my affections to the professors and institution that I still love to think, speak, pray, and write about them and its success.

When my time was up at Freedom we were assigned to a charge including North Benton, Mahoning County, Ohio. This was a pretty hamlet surrounded by well cultivated fields and beech and hickory forests. These abounded in game of various kinds, including flocks of wild turkeys. The circuit was thirty miles long and twenty miles wide, the parsonage being located at North Benton. Our removal was accomplished in part by rail and in part by wagon, and when we paid our teamsters our sole remaining funds in cash were three old fashioned copper cents. It was three months till quarterly meeting and we were among strangers. Furthermore, our larder was illy supplied with the necessaries of life. Such an experience would be accounted an unusual hardship even by a Methodist itinerant in these days, but it was not uncommon then.

When the situation became known to one of the stewards, Brother John Carter, he called to his aid Brother Henry Lewis and we were soon supplied, through their efforts and the kindly responses of the members of the local charge, with all that was necessary for our comfort.

There were thirteen appointments on this circuit, embracing, all told, about three hundred members. The people were unusually considerate of the needs of their pastor and his little family, and took excellent care of us all over the circuit. My work was success-

CHARLES EDMUND FISHER, M. D.

ful, it including thirteen protracted meetings during the first year and eleven the next.

Our second son, Charles Edmund, his second name being given him because of my love and admiration for Bishop Janes, was born during our residence in North Benton, on the seventh of March, 1853. I had been attending a special meeting sixteen miles from home and upon my return found the parsonage enlivened by the presence of this little black-eyed stranger. His coming greatly endeared us to the people, as he was the first new-comer ever arriving at the North Benton parsonage.

This son studied medicine, graduating at Detroit in 1872 and again in Cincinnati in 1875. He has also attended post-graduate study in New York and abroad, and has taken high rank in his profession. He early removed to Texas for his health, remaining there until 1893, when he removed to Chicago, where he now resides. He has been president of the Texas Homeopathic Medical Society, as also of the Southern Homeopathic Medical Association and, in 1895, of the American Institute of Homeopathy. It was my pleasure to attend the annual meeting of the latter body at Newport, Rhode Island, in June of last year, over which he presided. This doctor-son is editor of a prominent medical journal, the Medical Century, author of a standard work on Diseases of Children, and joint-author and editor of a large composite text-book of surgery. He has also served with distinction as a professor of surgery in one of Chicago's medical colleges.

At the close of my pastorate on the Limaville and Alliance circuit I was appointed to the Sewickly charge, in Pennsylvania. Here we spent a very pleasant year with a good degree of success. We finished a neat church, which had been commenced by my predecessor, Rev. Albert G. Williams, and Bishop Simpson dedicated it in his inimitable style. A pompous brother was to preach at 3 p. m. He announced that he would "endeavor to follow the Bishop at a deferential distance," and he did follow at a very deferential distance, and without special endeavor, too, greatly to the innocent amusement of the people.

On this charge we held successful meetings at Hopkins Chapel, where several persons were converted. Here we beheld the unusual sight of a beautiful rainbow by moonlight.

At Blackburn Chapel we held a meeting of great good to the many who attended. One evening there were eight or nine adults kneeling as seekers of salvation at the altar. A spirit of solemn supplication prevailed. The pastor's wife passed along from one end of the altar to the other, encouraging the seekers, with appropriate quotations and promises, and in less than ten minutes the whole number by faith entered into a joyful Christian experience and testified to the power of Christ to save those who believe. I seldom if ever witnessed such remarkable unanimity in belief and such simultaneous believing and rejoicing.

Sewicklyville had for a long time prior to our coming, presented a striking example of "how great a fire a little matter kindleth." Two otherwise good men had had a financial transaction about which they had disagreed, and for years they had kept the church in perpetual turmoil, until I finally succeeded in getting them to arbitrate their difficulties—to find that it was all about sixty-two and a half cents.

At the close of one year in the Sewicklyville charge

I was removed to what proved to be the most pleasant station I ever filled, viz., McKeesport, Pa. This was a beautiful town at the junction of the Monongahela and Yougheogheny rivers. Dr. Isaac N. Baird was my presiding elder. During the first year I united with the resident ministers of other denominations in a course of fifteen lectures on the Evidences of Christianity. There was much intemperance prevalent and a strong band of infidels, thoroughly organized in a club. This club held regular meetings for the purpose of reading what they termed "The Infidels' Bible," viz., Payne's Age of Reason, and other similar books. The club was popular, and was exerting a widespread influence among the young men of the town and neighborhood. Our course of lectures was designed to offset this plausible plan of the enemy and save the young men from infidelity. There were in the Baptist pulpit Dr. Penny and Dr. Remington; in the Presbyterian pulpit Dr. Nathaniel West, a man of learning, who was the author of "The Analysis of the Bible," and in the reformed Presbyterian church a Mr. Wallace. These brethren gave their best time and thought to the preparation of their lectures. From the beginning the course was so popular that the largest church in the town was crowded, and at the close of the third lecture, which I had the responsibility of preparing and delivering, Mr. Isaac Wampler, the president of the infidel club, arose in the midst of the vast audience and moved the lecture just delivered (which was on the Insufficiency of the Light of Nature as a Rule of Moral Conduct, and the Necessity of a Divinely Authorized Revelation of God's Will) be requested for publication in pamphlet form, and that he and his friends would pledge the payment of the cost of publication. His motion was seconded by another noted unbeliever, and put by Dr. West, in whose church the lecture was delivered, and unanimously adopted. The lecture was published accordingly, and was the means of doing much good. The infidel club never held another meeting, and at the close of these lectures many who were recorded unbelievers at the beginning became Christians, living and dying in the gospel of peace.

The churches had not only rest, but prosperity. Mr. Wampler became a member of the Presbyterian church, and Captain James Henderixson, Daniel Pollard, and other members of the club became members of the Methodist Episcopal church.

At Pine Run, some three miles above McKeesport, on the Monongahela river, we had a class of twelve members. With the efficient help and liberality of the class leader, Brother John O'Neal, I built a beautiful church, which was dedicated by Bishop Simpson. Our members here increased until the Society at the close of my pastorate, numbered eighty, with a flourishing Sabbath school.

During my pastorate here, on the 25th of May, 1856, our third son, Joseph Clarence, was born. He early became a devout and consistent Christian, and lived long enough to give great promise of usefulness, but was cut off in the midst of his preparation for life work by a very short illness, at Olathe, Kansas, before he attained his eighteenth birthday.

Our home in McKeesport was a delightful one, and the people were exceedingly kind and considerate. The town was picturesque and lovely, its situation being at the confluence of two of Pennsylvania's beautiful rivers. We spent two of our most delightful years in gospel work in this charge.

JOSEPH CLARENCE FISHER.

CHAPTER XV.

SAD INCIDENTS—WORK AT BIRMINGHAM.

In McKeesport there was a family by the name of Ludwick, most of them being very devoted members of the Methodist Church, though formerly Lutherans. They had built a large and beautiful flour mill, one of them being an experienced millwright and practical miller. He was a Lutheran. The day before the mill was to be tested was "Communion Sabbath." I had preached in the evening and administered the Holy Sacrament, of which a large company partook. It was a very solemn occasion. When we were about to formally finish the services I was profoundly impressed that there were others who should, on that occasion, commune. I urged upon the people their privilege and duty, with an inexpressible feeling that to some it would be the last time for such opportunity. While I was yet speaking this man arose, and coming to the altar knelt alone, and received with great solemnity the emblems of his Savior's passion and death. There was a holy reverence resting upon the entire audience, and he retired, his face bathed in tears. The following morning, very early, he went to the mill, only a few rods from his house, started the machinery to test it, and soon after was found in the lower story, where he had gone to adjust a wedge in the driving wheel, dead. Evidently his adz, which he had used in setting the wedge, had been caught by one of the swiftly revolving wheels and dashed with deadly effect against the side of his head, producing instantaneous death. I hurried to his house while yet the warmth of life was left, and when I entered the room where his body lay his aged father and mother and wife and little children were in tears of anguish. My coming in awakened the memories of the evening past, and one of them exclaimed, "Oh, what a comfort it is to think that the last public act of his life was to acknowledge his Savior! Now the Savior has acknowledged him before His father and the holy angels!"

"Oh," said his wife, "I can bear the parting, in the hope of blissful and eternal reunion."

Just at the close of the second year a most horrible double murder occurred above McKeesport, and nearly opposite my appointment at Pine Run. The parties murdered were an old couple who were living alone on a little farm, and had accumulated a few hundred dollars, which they had laid by in their house. This became known to a girl who was a niece of the old couple and whose name was Charlotte Jones. She became acquainted with a young Canadian, Henry Fife, and his accomplice in the crime, one Stewart. They planned the murder, and this trio of desperate characters, on their way to its execution, passed under my window, looking in where I was counting my missionary collection and other conference moneys, preparatory to starting to conference next morning. They did not molest us, however, but before daylight had killed and robbed the two old and helpless people. The man, Fife, and Charlotte Jones expiated their crime on the gallows in Pittsburg, while Stewart was reported as having died of smallpox. I have always believed that some other person died of the disease and he escaped, by means of unlawful influences.

Conference met the next day after this horrible murder, in Monongahela City, Bishop Simpson presiding. I had finished a successful two years' pastorate and the second day of conference the Bishop informed me that I might write to my wife that we were going to South Common Church in Allegheny City. On Monday following a committee from Birmingham called on the Bishop and requested that I should be sent to their station, to "take them out of the drag," as they said. They had a dilapidated church, in an out-of-the-way place, their congregation was run down, and though they had been trying for six years to change their condition it grew worse from year to year. The Bishop offered other names, but the committee hung for their first request. Having told me early that I was to go to South Common the Bishop, in the kindness of his great heart sent for me and very tenderly informed me of the Birmingham request and stated that he did not want to make the change without my concurrence, but he thought I could save our church interests in Birmingham, and as he was living in Pittsburg he desired the churches in and around the city to be put on a firm and healthy basis.

"I have always had a very profound respect for Episcopal authority," I said, "Bishop Simpson, you have the authority and the responsibility. I will obey orders."

As a result I was sent to Birmingham. My wife, though a heroine, felt afflicted at the change, but we went promptly and cheerfully, sending word in advance that I was coming to build a new church. This was taken by some as a jest. When we went to church on Sunday morning our little four-year-old boy, Charles Edmund, coming in sight of the old, dilapidated church, stopped short, and said, with characteristic vim: "Pa, if I were you I would not preach in such a dirty old church as that. I'd go back to McKeesport."

The congregation was very small, and sadly discouraged, but we had a melting service at the very beginning. Good Brother Fawcett came up immediately after service, and with tears on his cheeks, said to me:

"Brother Fisher, thank God! I love to see the people wiping off" while the tears ran down his own face. Many who were present wept with joy. The Sabbath school was very badly disorganized, but we began hopefully to plan and work. I arranged a series of cottage prayer meetings in the homes of the people, and appointed various leaders, giving each one something to do and directing that family worship be established everywhere. It was not many weeks until our little meetings had to be transferred to the lecture room of the old church and these, in turn, grew to be crowded. The Lord gave us favor in the eyes of the people, and I was enabled to buy a corner lot, right next to one our people had bartered away many years before, on which we soon began the erection of what is now Birmingham Street Methodist Church, which has been a center of power for years. It is in the very heart of the town, where the great manufacturing interests are.

But our chief energy and attention was directed to the conversion of souls. A deep religious feeling prevailed at every meeting, and in the families at pastoral visitation members of the family would often leave the room at close of prayer, their faces bathed in tears. The congregation grew until every seat, even pulpit and altar, would be full to overflowing. A gracious revival began. Over two hundred and fifty souls were converted. I received above two hundred and thirty names, numbers of which remain on the roll till the present time. On one Sabbath day there were ninety-six of these dear people called around the altar and received into full connection at one time, the largest number I have any knowledge of ever having been received at one time into the church up to that date. The scope of the revival was such that leading members in other churches desired their ministers to invite seekers to an anxious seat, or "mourners' bench," and they declining, were removed.

Thus four settled pastors were unsettled, simply because they would not unite in this glorious work. The work in the Methodist Episcopal Church went on. The town was shaken, and very many rejoice yet that they enjoyed the privileges of that meeting.

We had the new church walls up, roof on, spires partly finished, a grand Sunday school, several side appointments, and these hundreds of converts to look after. Our classes were of the Wesleyan type, full of fire and love. Conference came, and everybody was expecting my return to Birmingham. They were paying me a good salary. The work was really in its most important, if not most precarious, state. Conference met at Cambridge, Ohio. My wife accompanied me to Steubenville to visit friends. On our way we learned, to our surprise and consternation, that Bishop Jaynes had written from Kansas that Leavenworth City was left to be supplied, and that he desired my transfer and appointment to that charge. I could not have been more surprised if it had been proposed to have sent me to China. Bishop Simpson was sick nigh unto death. Bishop Baker presided.

The letter of Bishop Janes was sent to Bishop Baker, who, on the first day of conference invited me to his room, read the letter, and asked me what he should do in the case. I told him all about my Birmingham work, and said I could take no responsibility in the case. The matter was laid before the cabinet. Eight presiding elders were opposed, while D. P. Mitchell thought I ought to go. Rev. Sylvester Burt offered to go to Leavenworth for a year, and I was to follow. Rev. D. P. Mitchell offered to resign his office as presiding elder and go in my stead, but Bishop Baker said: "They have asked for Brother Fisher, and if I send any one I'll send him."

So it stood till the last hour of conference. Rev. S E. Babcock, who had taken me into the church when a boy, came to me and said the Bishop wanted me to go but would not send me without my consent. I told Brother Babcock to say to the Bishop just what he pleased. I would stand it.

It was at the last moment decided that I should go to Kansas.

Brother Lynch, with whom I stayed, said he suffered inexpressible agony over the matter. The people of Birmingham were inconsolable. Their disappointment was beyond imagining and sorrowful indeed to witness. When I preached my farewell sermon I do not think if my body had been before the people prepared for burial they would have lamented more than they did at my removal from them.

THE AUTHOR AT THIRTY

CHAPTER XVI.

WESTWARD, HO!

At an early day we embarked on the steamer "South America," Captain Shepherd commanding. She was advertised for the Upper Missouri River. There were no railroads west of the Mississippi River at that date, and the Missouri had been patrolled by pro-slavery minions to prevent free-state emigration. The journey necessitated nearly eighteen hundred miles of steamboat travel. The captain, other officers and crew and passengers were very kind to the preacher and his family, consisting now of my wife and three little boys, aged seven, five and two. Especially were the cabin boys attentive to the wants of our little fellows, and in the genial atmosphere much of the tedium of the trip was lifted and the run, though hazardous from Cairo to St. Louis, because of flood, was restful and enjoyable.

Owing somewhat to the frailty of our craft, which was heavily laden, our captain decided to go no farther than St. Louis and we were so fortunate as to drop our lines and "lay to" immediately in the rear or at the stern of the good steamer "Oglesby," a noble craft under the command of the son of a Methodist preacher who had introduced Methodism into Illinois. We were kindly offered special rates, and at once transferred from the "South America" to the "Oglesby," bound for Leavenworth City. The captain and crew gave us every needed attention to make our voyage pleasant, and with admirable success.

Here I was; I, an outspoken abolitionist, en route and nearly to Kansas in the year 1858! All along the voyage the difference in improvements, the evidence of a different civilization, as between Ohio and Virginia, Illinois and Kentucky, had been to me a most impressive phase of the advantage of freedom over slavery. I was sailing up the river to my future field more and more ready and primed to engage in the encounter already so long waged on that soil between liberty and bondage. Little did I dream how actively the struggle, like an octopus, was to draw me, with all who held Kansas dear, into its embrace!

When we arrived at Leavenworth we found a welcome from our future congregation in the persons of George S. Weaver and Jacob Lander, who took our boys in their arms, carried them safely ashore, and escorted us to a home with Brother and Sister Morris Roberts, old parishioners from McKeesport, and who —we always suspected—had much to do in our unexpected removal from Birmingham to Kansas.

A most encouraging instance of the solicitous affection which was to be my portion in my new home befell us immediately upon our arrival. An elect lady of seventy years or more—Mother Day—said to me heartily and simply as she grasped me by the hand: "Brother Fisher, ever since I heard you were coming I have been praying that God would be with you and bring you safely to us." Among other loved parishioners whom we had left behind was one Mother Garrison, as old and venerable a lady as this one, who had said just as we were leaving Birmingham, "Brother Fisher, I shall not cease to pray that the Lord will go with you and bring you safely to your destination."

Here had been the prayers of these two good old Christian mothers outspread over me for a journey of eighteen hundred miles, and I wept for joy at the thought of the answer to that prayer as a rainbow of promise fulfilled!

I had left the new church approaching completion. It would seat eight hundred or more people, the old church having accommodated six hundred souls. We left a grand congregation, large Sabbath school, good house to live in, with a competent salary, and probable increase; we had journeyed at our own expense eighteen hundred miles—to find twenty resident members, no missionary appropriation, not a foot of ground to build a church upon, not a dollar to build with. Yet I was expected to build a church and sustain my family on what the people would give.

My first sermon was to a congregation of less than thirty hearers, and that in a little shot-marked schoolhouse, seated with rude benches, and very untidy, indeed filthy, with Kansas soil. The whole condition of church affairs was so different from those we left that the first Sabbath of June, 1858, was absolutely the "bluest day" I had ever experienced. It was the date of my first sermon in Kansas. But as I preached the gospel of consolation tears started from many eyes. My heart was touched and my tears began to flow. I wept because it seemed to me that I had brought my wife and three dear boys away out to Kansas to starve them to death. It looked so that day. But I wept also because I knew Christ, whom I preached, was able to deliver all those who would put their trust in Him. And before the sermon ended I was convinced I was in a providential opening, as it evidently turned to the good of the church.

But we had to face difficulties. The "Town Company," being all pro-slavery men, had early resolved that the "Northern Methodist Church," as they called it, should not build a church in Leavenworth. We had no provision for such grounds, and my society, being so weak numerically and financially, had not bought a site. Hence we were barehanded and handicapped. To add to our trouble, six weeks after our arrival, and after I had obtained a good subscription to aid us in building a house of worship, a fire originating in the greenroom of the theater destroyed the whole business center of the city, including the business of the only four persons connected with our church upon whom we could depend for substantial help, namely, George H. Weaver, H. P. Johnson, R. Newland, and Rev. Stewart of Philadelphia. None of these recovered except Mr. Weaver, who after fourteen years of patient toil and great economy re-established a very prosperous business.

Our subscription was wrecked. The struggle we had because of poverty and abounding wickedness in the city was enough to discourage the most heroic. But our necessity was so absolute that we could not go back on our plans of work nor could we safely stand still. We were compelled to press on to success, or forfeit all we had gained. So committing our cause to the God of all grace, and confiding in Him, we pressed forward to the work. Renewing our effort we purchased a lot in the most central part of the city, still occupied in 1896, and raised our subscription to the highest point possible. By the request and direction of my official board I made a visit abroad, succeeded in raising some money and returned to cheer my brethren in the good work. A few months later I made a second visit, and much farther East, which resulted in the raising of considerable means, through great effort, wherewith to sufficiently complete the church for temporary occupancy. I spent several weeks in Philadelphia, Baltimore, New York and other cities and towns, while the building went slowly on.

I met with many very interesting and instructive incidents in this work, some of which were really encouraging, and their memories are thrilling and refreshing. I was generally well supplied with letters of introduction and endorsement by merchants and others in official position. I had especially the endorsement of Bishops Simpson and Ames. One letter I bore was to Mr. D. A. January, of St. Louis, from Nelson McCracken of Leavenworth. Mr. January was a Presbyterian elder. A traveling companion from Leavenworth was Rev. Mr. Backus, a Presbyterian minister, going East on a mission similar to my own. On the way down the river I became familiar with the passengers, made known the object of my trip, and circulated a subscription book for my church, When we arrived in St. Louis I stopped at a hotel where charges were light, while Mr. Backus went to an up-town hotel where charges were much higher.

Next morning—"the King's business demanding haste"—I went forth early with my letters of introduction to Mr. January. He was not in. The porter invited me to take a chair, gave me the morning paper, and I began to read. Presently a very affable gentleman came into the office. I arose and asked, "Do I address Mr. January?"

He extended his hand, and with a smile answered, "You do. Whom do I address?"

I replied, "H. D. Fisher, of Leavenworth, Kansas, a Methodist preacher; and I have the pleasure of bearing a letter of introduction from our mutual friend, Nelson McCracken."

He read the letter with evident satisfaction, and then asked: "What can I do for you?"

I told him in a few words what the object of my visit was, to obtain money to build a church, at the same time handing him my book in which my steamboat subscription was recorded. He took it, saying, "I am a Presbyterian, but I will help you what I can this morning."

He wrote his name, put down $20, and handed me a twenty dollar bill with many a good wish expressed for my success. I was in the act of bowing myself out of the office when in stepped Mr. Backus. We recognized each other and I was about to introduce him to my new acquaintance when the latter very kindly said, "I have met Mr. Backus before."

Without any ceremony Mr. Backus drew from his pocket a book, saying as he did so, "Mr. January, I have called to ask a subscription to help pay for a Presbyterian church in Leavenworth City."

Mr. January laughingly replied, "Why, I have just given Mr. Fisher twenty dollars. That is all I can give, and this should teach you not to let a Methodist preacher get ahead of you again."

I replied, "It is not Mr. Backus' fault. It was foreordained, and I was simply carrying out the orders. I am very glad they were in my favor."

When I arrived in Philadelphia, I found myself in a strange city, with but sixty-two and a half cents, having remitted my funds as fast as I collected them. I felt that time was everything, and learning that there was to be a family gathering, or kind of love feast or reunion at Cohocksink M. E. Church, of which Rev. Fernly was pastor, I determined to attend and enjoy the meeting. As it was an "Experience Meeting" I arose to speak of my Christian experience, and told the congregation that as a stranger I wished to bear my testimony; that I had been sent by Bishop Baker, at Bishop Jayne's request, from Pittsburg conference to the Kansas conference, and stationed at Leavenworth; that we had been wonderfully sustained by divine grace, and now I was here to raise money to help build a church.

Brother Fernly jumped up and said, "Come right forward, Brother, so the people can see you, and tell us all about matters in Kansas."

I gladly accepted the opportunity of describing just what we were trying to do.

At the close of the meeting Brother Fernly told the people to come up and give me all the help they could. He and another preacher began writing the names and amounts, but the people came so fast they quit writing and just put the money in a hat. To me this was a complete surprise, and made me almost shout for joy.

The amount was about sixty dollars, as many dollars as I had cents in the morning.

As I had letters of introduction to merchants down town I started to walk in the morning, hoping to see at least a few of them before night. A street car came along and my first impulse was to ride to save time. Then I thought if I did some one who has given their money to help will think, "Yes, he can ride at our expense." I walked on rapidly until seeing I was losing precious time I resolved to ride. So I ran and caught up with the car and stepped inside. As I did so a lady arose—that is unusual—and extended her hand and I gave her mine, when to my extreme embarrassment she held to me saying, "You are the brother from Kansas who was at the meeting. I was very much interested in your remarks and I hope you will get all the help you need." I thanked her for her good wishes and when she let go my hand she left a five dollar gold piece in it. I came very nearly shouting, only remembering in time that it would not do to shout in a street car in Philadelphia. Yet I dare say if it were to happen again I would shout—arrest or no arrest.

I went at once to the store of a Mr. Townsend, a Quaker, to whom I had letters. He gave me twenty dollars and I soon sent home a draft for one hundred dollars and was very happy.

The next marked surprise was in Hartford Avenue Church, Baltimore, of which Rev. G. W. Cooper, was pastor. Dr. D. W. Bartine and Rev. Alfred Cookman and I had gone down to Baltimore to aid Dr. Aquila Reese and Brother Cooper in protracted meetings. Brother Cooper said if I would preach for him I might state my case at the close of the sermon and let the people give voluntarily. Kansas was not a very savory name for Baltimoreans, but I preached and made a short statement of my case and of my visit East. Before I was through a solid looking old brother rose, hat in hand, and started for the door. I thought he was offended, and that the "fat was all in the fire." But just as I closed my remarks he stopped near the door, turned around and sang out: "Brother Cooper will take his hat. I've got mine, and we will stand at the doors and when you are dismissed you can drop into the hats what you wish to give Brother Fisher. Now, get out your pocket-books and give liberally."

Brother Cooper asked me to dismiss the company but my emotions overcame me and he pronounced the benediction and the people passed slowly out. Brother Cooper and I walked down the aisle. The old brother spread out his bandanna, and dumping the contents of the hats into it, said to us, "Now, come home with me and get dinner, and we will count the collection." We obeyed with pleasure, and after dinner found there was over sixty dollars. Father Thomas has ever had my sincerest thanks for this pleasant surprise. Doubtless when we meet in heaven we will talk it over.

On Sabbath evening I preached for Dr. Reese in the old Exeter Street Church. The sainted Cookman and Dr. Bartine had been assisting in his meetings, but up to this date there had been no particular signs of revival, except deep and growing seriousness. There was general curiosity awakened to hear a Kansas preacher. While I preached Dr. Reese's mother-in-law, a saintly woman of great faith, was praying, and would occasionally say audibly, "Lord, bless the sermon." The tide of feeling rose and spread, and as I closed Dr. Reese said to me: "Brother Fisher, invite mourners to the altar." I did so in a short, earnest exhortation. There were a lady and three daughters sitting midway in the church. The mother and two of the daughters were Episcopalians. The third one arose and very deliberately walked up the aisle, the tears streaming over her face. When she reached the altar railing she put out her hands to steady herself in the act of kneeling, and as she paused she looked up and cried piteously, "Lord, save or I perish!" Instantly a gleam of light covered her face, and she turned in the face of that vast congregation and cried aloud, "Glory to God, my sins are forgiven. Where is my father? I want him to come and be saved too."

The scene that followed is indescribable. Men wept like children; strong men bowed themselves in prayer. The congregation swayed like a forest under a whirlwind. Women shouted the praises of God. The altar was soon crowded with seekers of salvation, nearly every one of whom was happily converted before the meeting closed. It was a remarkable victory. Thus, while I was begging money for a Western church God was watering my soul and repaying others in spiritual benefits for what they bestowed upon us in the way of material help. I was learning rapidly the way of working in the vineyard.

Later on I visited a camp meeting near Dover, Delaware, and preached, making known my mission. While here a devout and venerable man who had come a long distance to attend the meeting came to me and gave me a dollar and seventy-five cents, saying he wished it were more but it was all he had and he wanted to give it to help plant the church in Kansas. I declined to take it, and pressed him to keep it to pay his way home. He replied, "The Lord has promised to provide, and he will take care of me." At night I preached again, and invited seekers to the mourners' bench. As I stood in the pulpit the good old brother who had given me his last penny came to me and opening his hand, said: "Look here, someone put that into my hand just now and disappeared so quickly I did not see who it was." There sure enough was double the amount he had given me. "Now," said he, "I know the Lord's promise is true," and he actually wanted to give me what he had just received. But, strange as it may appear, I declined it. I have often wondered if I did just right. I rather think I did.

I next visited and preached in Union Square M. E. Church, Baltimore. Rev. Brother Chapman was pastor. The church was large, and had galleries on both sides and front and accommodated a large audience. The house and galleries were filled. I was describing Our Lord's ascension, and the grand pronouncement of his benediction, "Peace I leave with you; my peace I give unto you; not as the world giveth, give I," while with outstretched hands he ascended and was lost to sight, amid the shout of angels and the brightness of the more excellent glory. The audience seemed to catch the inspiration of the Holy One, and almost simultaneously arose to their feet, while shout after shout rang through the large church. It was a most blessed time; many wept for joy in anticipation of seeing their ascended Lord in like manner descend in the last day.

I preached also at Shrewsbury camp meeting by request of Dr. Henry Slicer, and had among other noted hearers, Drs. Sargent, Reese and Littleton Morgan. My text was the tenth verse of the tenth chapter of Romans. This sermon was so well received that seven different Baltimorean pastors requested me to preach from this same text, saying, "Our people have heard of your preaching from the text and want to hear for themselves." I preached from that same text more than fifty times during my visit East.

After having spent more than six months of incessant toil and labor in preaching and begging, I at last made my way homeward to my wife and dear boys who had been well for the most of the time, but had had a very hard battle with poverty.

By the help I raised abroad and $1,000 I borrowed from Brother Fry, of Baltimore, on my own paper, we began pushing the church to completion as fast as possible. I found services had been suspended during my absence, the congregation scattered, and matters in a state of general disorganization, except the Sunday school; but we soon rallied, finished the lecture room, and gathered in the church and Sunday school to a new home.

The first service we held nine persons joined our ranks. We had the best Sabbath school in town, and Methodism became so strong and respectable that we held the controlling influence in the city, and greatly aided other churches to get a foothold.

There were a few colored persons in Leavenworth who affiliated with the Southern Methodist Church, but they were not permitted to commune when the whites held their sacramental service. Brother Pritchard, the pastor, announced that they would hold a special service for the "colored population" in the afternoon. This was so contrary to my feelings of Christian equality that I advised Uncle Moses White, his name and soul are white though his skin was very black, to come out and organize a church of their own people. He was a local preacher, but said they had no one to administer the sacrament, as he was not ordained. I told him to go on and organize, and if my services were needed I would cheerfully serve them until they had a minister of their own. They soon organized and at the ensuing conference held at Alton, Ill., the African M. E. Church sent them Rev. John M. Wilkerson, an unordained man. Their presiding elder lived at a great distance and they unanimously invited me to administer the ordinances. Great numbers of colored people were seeking homes in Kansas and their society grew very rapidly. They early resolved to build a substantial brick church, just one foot larger every way than the church I had built for the white people. And they accomplished their work. The two churches stand to-day—thirty-six years since erection—as monuments of the real grit and liberality of Christian people under trying circumstances. Brother Wilkerson and I had the pleasure of remaining to see the work in both departments flourishing, and still live to labor together in the gospel of peace.

I had gained much valuable information in Philadelphia, Baltimore, New York, and other cities, and had everywhere received from ministers and people the greatest degree of kindness and sympathy in my work as well as having been greatly aided by their liberality.

In my visits to the East I demonstrated the need of a "Church Extension Society" to encourage liberality, and save time and expenses of preachers whose presence and labors in their pastoral fields were much needed. On this subject I had very interesting interviews with Brother Long, who for many years afterward was Treasurer of the Church Extension Society. I wrote the Pittsburg Christian Advocate an article advocating the organization of such a society and offered a resolution in the General Conference of 1864 which resulted in the appointment of a committee to present a plan on this line, the outworking of which has been so fruitful in results.

The loan I obtained from Brother Fry of Baltimore of $1,000 was the beginning of our Loan Fund, which has become such an efficient source of help to church extension.

CHAPTER XVII.

DIFFICULTIES ATTENDING THE SETTLING OF KANSAS.

Every new country has had its attractions by which emigrants have been drawn thither, and its hardships through which they have had to struggle to make pioneer life successful.

The South has had its sugar, cotton and rice fields; but it had its bogs and swamps and cypress forests. The New England states had their granite hills and mountains and rigorous climate to impede progress; but they have their fruitful valleys, their living streams, whose swiftness furnish an abundance of cheap power for factories, their rich fisheries, and their northern part its immense pineries. The more western forests, while they had to be cleared, furnished timber for house, barn, fence, and fuel. But Kansas, in particular, was inviting mainly for the opportunity offered adventurous reformers to plant anew the seeds of a higher, broader and deeper civilization. Besides her rich and productive soil, her salubrious climate, her Italian skies and her indescribable sunsets, she was inviting to the pioneer as a central and pivotal state.

The early emigrant was confronted with unusual difficulties as he wended his way across her rolling surface to found for himself and family a home and to do battle for the glorious cause of freedom. Here he met the border-ruffian bushwhackers from Missouri and Arkansas; the little less uncivilized American Indians of the western plains; the terrible droughts and famine of 1860 and 1861; the hot winds from the southern sandy deserts, and here, above all places outside of Egypt, he suffered the indescribable annoyances and the losses incident to the devastating swarms of locusts known as the Kansas grasshoppers, which blighted the face of the earth as they swept in migratory tour from their habitat further north to their objective point further to the south and west.

It is no exaggeration to say that no pioneers in all this great country have suffered the disastrous series of drawbacks which have had to be met and overcome by the courageous and enduring Kansan, at least since the early days of Indian massacre and witchcraft in New England.

It may be well in passing to attempt a feeble description of the terrible drought which caused so much ruin and distress in 1860, just before Kansas was admitted to the Union of states. The pioneers of the eastern tiers of counties, for the western part of the territory was still unknown to civilization, had but recovered from the devastating effects of the border-ruffian contest which had been waged from 1855 to 1858 with more or less of continuance; the black cloud of civil war was threatening the entire country; in the very nature of things Kansas was destined to suffer seriously, in proportion to her resources, as this great cloud should burst upon her; her people were anxiously awaiting the coming of those awful events whose coming was as certain as is the rising and the setting of the sun, realizing that they were to suffer almost beyond endurance, yet not flinching from the contests before them. It would seem that the territorial population had had enough to contend against already, and that with the impending internecine struggle immediately ahead they might have been spared further tests of endurance and suffering. But it was not to be.

The spring of 1860 opened auspiciously. Fields were planted and the hardy pioneer went to his work of opening up new farming ground and planting new sod-crops with confidence that the fertile prairie would repay him for his toil and privations. But he was to be disappointed. As the young crops came along the rain fell not. The skies were as clear as the most beautiful Italian skies ever depicted by poet or painter. The sun shone upon beautiful Kansas with a generosity that would have given us the most bountiful harvests had not nature forgotten to turn on the water. But though the winds blew and the sun shone, and the sky was clear, and all nature looked gay enough in the spring and early summer, yet for seven long months we suffered the horrors of a desert drought. For four months consecutively there fell not a drop of rain. The country was blighted almost as if by a great prairie fire. The grass dried up; the leaves fell from the trees as if from the autumnal frosts; the ground opened with great yawnings, by which horses and cattle were often stumbled and injured; running streams went dry; the rivers became so low that steamers of even the lightest draught could navigate them with difficulty; the wells and cisterns were soon emptied, and people had to haul water for domestic purposes many miles in many instances; horses, cattle, and even the buffalo on the plains died from thirst, the blighting drought being destructive in the extreme upon every living thing. Hundreds upon hundreds of struggling pioneers were compelled to exist for months upon the most unsavory and unhealthful food, the result being that sickness and death added terror to the disaster.

It is impossible to depict the suffering and distress

incident to the terrible drought and awful famine of 1860. So widespread were they that thousands of brave pioneers were compelled to return overland to their former homes in order to keep from starving. A committee of the Kansas Conference of the Methodist Episcopal Church, in session in Atchison in March of 1861, reported that careful investigation showed that in October of the year previous there were not provisions enough in the territory, nor the means whereby to procure them, to preserve more than half the people from starvation, and that most of the population were being compelled to live on corn-bread and a little salt meat. This report was based upon the desire of the conference to ascertain, if possible, the status of affairs when emissaries were sent East the year before for contributions and provisions, in order that the Conference might properly express its appreciation of the assistance which had been given the territory during the drought and give its assurance to the charitable donors that the benefactions they had bestowed had reached their destination and had been properly distributed to actual sufferers. It is noteworthy that the report of the Conference was to the effect that in almost every instance relief had been judiciously distributed, with the result that the aid invoked by pen and pulpit had resulted in the saving of untold suffering and hundreds of human lives.

My visit to the East in the interests of church-building was in a measure transformed into a tour of the states for relief for the drought-sufferers. So severe was the situation that I sent for my family and they joined me in Ohio, spending a portion of the period covered by the drought with their Ohio friends and my wife's parents and mine. As they were compelled to flee from famine so were thousands of others. In fact, nearly everybody who could get away from their business and the disaster which stared them in the face left for the season, thus reducing the number who would otherwise have had to have relief. The generosity of eastern people who watched with intense interest the struggles of the Kansas pioneers was an open-handed generosity, and succor came to the distressed as fast as the steamers and the overland freight caravans could carry it. Senator Pomeroy especially distinguished himself, and won a sobriquet which ever after clung to him, by soliciting and sending a great many carloads of New England beans to the drought-stricken district. It was his splendid efforts toward bringing relief to his distressed neighbors, more than anything else, which made him United States Senator when Kansas was admitted to the Union. "Baked Beans" Pomeroy was a character in early Kansas history, the awful drought affording him an opportunity his generous nature took advantage of to assist the territorial pioneer at a time when assistance was demanded by the highest considerations of humanity.

Upon returning from Ohio in the fall of that disastrous year we were most plentifully supplied with provisions for the winter by our friends of the Pittsburg Conference and our immediate relatives and friends in Steubenville. Crates of cabbage, barrels of potatoes and apples, cases of ham and side meat, canned fruits, jells, jams, pickles and other edibles and delicacies were showered upon us for ourselves and friends until our freight assumed the proportions of that of a green-grocer. And as our boat swung loose from her moorings and we departed a second time for our then far, far-away Kansas field, our hearts went up in gratitude to those who had so bountifully supplied us, and to the "Giver of All Good" for His watchful care over

THE SETTLING OF KANSAS.   149

the people of Kansas during the awful struggle through which they had been called to pass.

The character of the farewell ovation tendered us as our good steamer left her wharf at Steubenville made it one never to be forgotten. The unsettled condition of the Union; the distance we had to travel; the uncertainty which existed in relation to the struggle that was impending between slavery and freedom; the ravages of drought and the blight and distress of famine, combined to make our second embarkation a memorable one. The steamer came down from Pittsburg on Sunday afternoon. I preached a farewell sermon that morning, and it was known all over the city that we should leave for our mission field that afternoon. When the time came all the religious people of the town and vicinity who could gather at the wharf were there gathered to bid us Godspeed. It was an occasion of solemnity. As we boarded the steamer and the gangplank was drawn in the prayers and tears and songs of a multitude were commingled. Shouts of hosannah and praise went up from hundreds of throats, and the songs of the people still ring in our ears, though this was nearly forty years ago. Our fellow passengers from up the river, the steamboat officers and employees, the people on the opposite shore of the river—all were intensely interested in the embarkation and the scenes attending it. At both ends of the line prayers were being offered for our safety and the growth and life of the cause which took us from the scenes of our boyhood and early ministerial life. Kansas was to be free. The Nation was to be free. The martyred Lincoln was to lay down his life. Hundreds of thousands of noble lives were to be sacrificed upon liberty's altar. A new and then far-away country was to be opened up to civilization. Great lines of railway were to span the continent and supplant the steamboat traffic to large degree. The journey of three weeks was within my lifetime to be reduced to within two days. The electric age was an unthought of thing; hardly had the age of steel come in. But the privations to be endured, the losses to be sustained, the dangers encountered and the labors to be performed were all to be compensated for by the goodness of a providence which was directing us and the glorious achievements of these forty years have fully compensated for all the struggles through which we have had to pass as we have labored on and struggled on and fought on and prayed on as God and the people have built up this splendid Christian commonwealth.

A short time prior to the return of my family from Kansas to Ohio, during the very height of the drought, there occurred at Leavenworth, which was then our home, one of those awful tornadoes which are known to characterize unusually long and severe dry weather. It was on the evening of the fourth of July. The day had been unusually hot, so that but little interest was taken in its celebration. The whole face of the earth was parched and burned as if by hot winds from Egypt. Not a drop of rain had fallen for months, and the people were suffering most terribly. As night came on there rose in the southwest a leaden-looking cloud and there came on an ominous stillness. For an hour not a breath of air seemed to stir, the heat and stillness becoming most oppressive. As nightfall became well established it became apparent that something unusual was about to happen. The horses and cattle were unusually restless, as if apprehensive; the fowls were slow in getting settled on their roosts; even the dogs and cats about the premises showed signs of impending danger, in manifestations of uneasiness and fear. The night

THE SETTLING OF KANSAS.

birds flitted swiftly across the lowering sky and the horizon quickly assumed an inky blackness. Out of the awful stillness came a sound as of a rushing torrent, and there soon sprang up fitful gushes of wind which showed that a storm was gathering. Almost before it was understood that possible danger lurked near the storm broke in mighty fury and spread wide its destruction. Houses were unroofed and blown down; the county jail was so badly damaged that prisoners were liberated, only to find death in the path of the tornado; trees were torn up by the roots and church spires and roofs were demolished; Three-Mile Creek became a raging torrent from a dry ravine in a few minutes, sweeping away a number of houses and drowning a dozen people; such little garden patches as had been nursed through the drought were destroyed by the wind and hail and rain; the inky blackness of the night, only relieved by the most vivid and blinding flashes of lightning, made the situation the more appalling and increased the terror of the already greatly alarmed people. It seemed as if out of drought and heat and famine had come another destroying power to finish the devastation that had been worked upon us. It was one of those quickly-come and quickly-go tornados which sweep through a narrow stretch of country working a harvest of destruction and death, but which fail to bring permanent relief from drought. And no sooner had the waters which fell from the sky swept off the dry ground into the river beds and been drunk up by the cracked and broken earth than was the full force of the blight again upon us. The storm which brought its rain was but a mockery; it had also brought death and damage, and had aroused the fears of the people lest more like destruction should come upon them; truly their lot was a hard one, and most truly do I say it was a courageous people who endured such hardships for the sake of home and life and liberty to this great nation.

During that awful tornado my wife and children were alone, and as they realized the danger my wife knelt with our three little boys near the kitchen door in prayer; she had chosen a spot in the garden to which they were to fly in case the house gave signs of falling in upon them, and had told the boys to cling to her and lie flat upon the ground, face downward, in the furrows between the lines of blackberry bushes which crossed the garden. Thrice her hand was on the doorknob to throw it open, that they might flee for safety. But they were spared; our house withstood the storm, and though terror-stricken and all but destroyed through fear no harm came unto us. The providence which had thus far carried us through the tribulations of pioneer-life had again come to our rescue, and my family were spared from disaster and death.

Only less destructive than the blight of 1860, because the conditions of the people had improved, were the grasshopper raids of 1865 and 1874. When the first scourge occurred we had but escaped from the horrors of the long civil war, during which Kansas had suffered as no other northern state had suffered. The boys-in-blue had returned to their homes and had just begun anew the peaceful pursuit of farming. The crops were in and growing finely, with a most excellent prospect for the young state, when out of the heavens, from their habitat in the far northwest, came clouds of the Egyptian locusts. They filled the sky, covered the earth, polluted the streams and wells, stopped trains by clogging the machinery of the locomotives and being crushed in such numbers as to render the tracks too slippery for the ready control of the engines; devoured fruit on the trees and ate onions and turnips out of the ground; blighted thousands upon thousands of acres of growing corn, eating blades, tassels, the young ears and the upper parts of the stalk, leaving only the deadened stalks like so many blackened broom-handles stuck up in the ground, and actually devoured whole fields of wheat, oats, rye and other small grain. The devastation of the grasshopper cannot be adequately portrayed. I have seen them in such numbers at the confluence of the Missouri and Kansas rivers, and moving in such masses, that men might have shoveled them into trains of freight cars the whole day long without having made a perceptible inroad upon them. They ate the lint off of pine fences and unpainted houses and barns, until these looked as if scraped with knives. They ate the meat off of peach stones as they hung on the trees, until whole orchards were destroyed and the trees looked as if their fruit had been boiled off the pits as the latter were still clinging to the stems. On my way to hold one of my quarterly meetings I met a cloud of hoppers so dense that they darkened the sun at noonday and beat like hail against me and my horse until I was compelled to turn aside till the cloud passed by.

This grasshopper scourge and the one of 1874 cost the state millions upon millions of dollars and thousands upon thousands of population. Whole counties among the more western settlements were depopulated, and again were the pioneers compelled to seek assistance from the East. It became necessary to send out emissaries to solicit contributions of food and clothing for a suffering people. On the principle that The Lord Loveth Whom He Chasteneth, the people of Kansas were divinely chosen in those dark days. Thousands of experimental farmers, men who had taken advantage of the Homestead Act to get for themselves and family farms for the living upon them, were compelled to leave their partially acquired properties and seek employment at former vocations. Thousands who had not the courage to withstand the struggles which confronted the early Kansan left the state for good. Others, more courageous, but who were not in position to stick it out, left temporarily, returning after a time to pick up where they left off and struggle anew for a permanent home. It took courage to withstand all the attacks which were made upon us in those early days, and the later-come Kansan can never be brought to understand what it required to be faithful and loyal to Kansas, to freedom, and to the church and schools of this beautiful state of today in those early days which tried men's souls. May God in His infinite goodness and wisdom spare them from all the inflictions through which we were made to pass that we might be purified and made the more perfectly to understand and appreciate His mercies as they come unto us.

CHAPTER XVIII.

FRONTIER EPISODES.

I remained three years pastor of the First Church in Leavenworth before the restrictive rule was changed. My third year was one of most remarkable agitation in the civil and social affairs of the city. Upon a certain occasion I had invited the preachers of the city to my house. When we met I proposed the discussion of the general question: "What are the hindrances to the spread of the gospel in Leavenworth?" This was adopted, and I divided the themes and appointed a brother to open the discussion of each topic, e. g.: Drunkenness, Gambling, Dancing, Profanity, Theater Going, Balls.

Each preacher was to preach on these specified topics, and then on each Monday night following a public discussion was to be had, in which laymen were invited to participate. The politicians soon saw that this was reformation and they called an anti-Sunday law meeting. I attended one at Wyman's Hall. At each of three corners in this hall they were selling beer. The other corner was ocupied by a band of music. The speaker, a young lawyer from Cleveland, delivered the most bitter tirade of abuse I ever heard against the Bible, churches, Christians, and the Sabbath. Col. Vaughan and others were to speak, but when they saw a company of Christians present they declined. The Germans had a very popular man among them named Fischer, who was engaged in selling beer and the hall echoed with calls of "Fischer, Fischer." Finally Brother Miller said to me, "Here is a chance to make a speech. Get up on this stool and give them the truth." They called again, "Fischer, Fischer," and I mounted the stool and began to address the crowd. They listened a moment and asked: "Who is this?" a little curly headed Jew replying, "The Methodist Preacher." With knives and revolvers they made a rush for me. Young men around me repelled them and said they should not harm me. I waved my hand, commanded silence, and told them I had a right to speak; I was a German; my father could not speak a word of English when he was a boy; that to prove to them that I was a German I would tell them my grandfather's name, it was Johannes Christofer Fischer." Whereupon they cheered and cried, "Go on, go on!" I gave them hot shot for a little while, till they began to cry out lustily, "Ausgespielen! Get out! Dry up!" and again fell to brandishing their knives and revolvers. I stood unmoved above the storm 'till it quieted, when I announced a meeting in Stockton's Hall for the following evening and invited them all to attend.

By morning we had the dry goods boxes and corners of stores covered with notices of the meeting, some of us working all night to accomplish this result. Saturday evening witnessed the most respectable and enthusiastic mass meeting ever held in the city. Appropriate addresses were made and law and order were vindicated. Revs. Mr. Baldridge, Stone, Pitzer, Parker, and I preached on the Sunday law the Sabbath preceding election day, and we exhorted the Christian women, as they could not vote, to pray that God would give us the victory.

I visited the Catholic Bishop, who kindly said: "My

people have need of the Sabbath for a day of worship and rest and I will instruct them so to vote."

Our mayor was a pro-slavery whiskyite and appointed the polls at inconvenient and out-of-the-way places. But Mr. Stone, the Episcopal Minister, doffed his surplice and gown, Mr. Baldridge put his trousers inside his boots, Brother Pitzer rolled up his trousers and put on a pair of rubbers, while I doffed what little ministerial dignity had hitherto embarrassed me—I have never seen it since—and we pitched in to win. And win we did.

The morning after election I met Jerry Clark, a high Episcopalian, who accosted me with, "Brother Fisher, you should have been down at the courthouse last night to have given Brother Stone a word of exhortation. We should have had a grand Methodist shout, for," said he, "thank God, we beat the rummies one hundred and sixty votes, and Mr. Stone staid right there till the last vote was counted!" He was a noble man of God and we loved him dearly.

The following Sabbath was pronounced the quietest enjoyed by Leavenworth since her first saloon was opened. The churches were filled and all moral influences had a chance thereafter.

About this time, while in Leavenworth, a colored man named Charley Fisher was claimed by heirs in New Orleans, and in order to take him away with as little noise as possible he was kidnapped, gagged, handcuffed, and taken to a bagnio and saloon in Missouri. His captors became drunk and sleepy with debauch, and he effected his escape by recrossing the Missouri amid ice, though manacled, in a skiff, and made his way to a cabin, where Mr. Justis Skeen lived. Mr. Skeen directed him where to look for a file, which he firmly placed in a crack in one of the logs and filed the fetters off his hands. He then returned to Leavenworth and was finally brought into court before the notorious Judge LeCompt, under a ruse, as a witness against Charley Shepherd and Jack Henderson, the men who had kidnapped him, the real object being to get him into the hands of a pro-slavery marshal. When dismissed from the witness-stand he was seized as a fugitive slave, taken under guard to the Planter's House, and locked in an upstairs room.

A rescue was planned. Twenty young men with muffled boots met mysteriously at midnight and by concert of action went to the room, which now constituted a prison, to rescue the man. But the plan miscarried, for the young man who was to bring an axe, with which to open the door, in the excitement forgot his axe and the alarm was given.

Next day the marshal changed the prisoner to another hotel, the "Mansion," fearing a repetition of the effort at rescue. Four of the young men boarded with me. The second night the knowledge of the whereabouts of Fisher was made known by a hotel waiter, who took him his supper. "To the rescue!" was passed from mouth to ear, with a determined tone, which meant that no axe should be forgotten this time. Nor was it! And for years I had that very axe for a memento. Afterward it was borrowed by a careless fellow who failed to return it.

Charley was rescued, taken to Judge Gardner's, held under a habeas corpus order, and in returning to the city under cover of a sham fight, escaped and fled toward Lawrence. He lost his way, hid all night in a shock of corn, and next night came to my house. My wife gave him a coverlet and directed him to hide in the weeds until she could send me word to prayer meeting that a refugee was needing our assistance. I arranged for Brother Clayton to pray. I told him to take his time, and he prayed loud and long, while I gave the rescuers word to rally, and when prayer ended I found a company of willing ones at my house. We concealed the poor fellow, hunted like a wild beast, until the next day, when my wife and Mrs. Weaver dressed him in women's clothes, but unthinkingly gave him a pair of my hose. When I was a young preacher nearly all the young women of Ohio knitted their own and their brothers' stockings and socks, and as I was popular among them they had made me presents of many pairs. Indeed, I had enough given me to last me for fourteen years after I married. Among others was a beautiful pair with my initials in red in the tops. These were the ones my wife gave to the black fellow and these he wore away. After his departure it became a source of great alarm to her lest he should be captured through the initialed socks and she and Mrs. Weaver be discovered as having helped a fugitive slave to escape. Happily no such result followed.

We sent him off under escort of three trusty rescuers, in open daylight in the presence of the marshal's posse of sixty men, under the guise of a wedding party from the country, landed him in Lawrence, and his pursuers were never the wiser. He subsequently fell into their hands on his way to Canada, was taken to New Orleans, remained there till the rebellion broke out, then working his way to Vicksburg, was there when it fell into Gen. Grant's hands, when he again come North. At the close of the war he made his way to Kansas, reporting himself to my wife and Mrs. Weaver in great demonstration of gratitude for their interest in his escape.

CHAPTER XIX.

AN UBIQUITOUS CHAPLAIN.

At the close of my ministerial term in Leavenworth I was stationed at Lawrence. We were soon at our new post of duty, and though the church was small and the society weak it was a pleasant field. After spending four months of very active effort I had erected for my family a very substantial brick house. Our boys were anxious to help, though yet quite young. So, to save material and secure perfectly cemented walls, I arranged that the boys should wet every brick that went into the walls in tubs of water. The wisdom of this will be seen in the chapter on "Quantrell's Raid." At the expiration of four months I moved my family into their home. The next day I was appointed Chaplain of the Fifth Kansas Cavalry by Gen. James H. Lane, and approved by the officers of the regiment, Col. H. P. Johnson commanding.

War had fairly commenced. The battle at Wilson's Creek had taken place, Gen. Lyon had fallen, and the Union forces had been defeated. Large army stores had been sent to Fort Scott as a basis of supplies for Lyon's army. These supplies became a tempting object for Sterling Price, Gen. Raines and Gen. Slack. Gov. Calib Jackson of Missouri was anxious that Price should capture them and his army was sent to Fort Scott. Gen. Lane was ordered to Fort Scott and directed to repel Price's army. He hastily collected his brigade, in a half equipped condition, and sent word for the militia of the state to rally and help repel the approaching enemy, with an army eighteen thousand strong. The work of equipment was quickly and imperfectly effected. Among these equipments was the locally noted "Old Sacramento" belonging to Col. Moonlight—a howitzer that might have been carried on the shoulder and which had been taken in the Mexican war.

We were ordered on a forced march. The cavalrymen were mounted on brood mares, farm horses and ponies, with sabres, muskets, revolvers, double-barreled shotguns and Sharp's rifles. There were sixteen hundred all told on a forced march of one hundred miles, to meet a disciplined army of eighteen thousand men, many of whom had been on what to them was a victorious field at Wilson's Creek!

I rode to Lawrence, on the way to bid my family farewell. I was simply a chaplain, but I took the authority to hire every wagon I could find to carry the infantry, whom I knew would be foot-sore and weary, to the scene of conflict. When the commander came next day he approved the timely forethought and contracts for the wagons, publicly thanked me, and took charge of them. We hurried on, the wagons greatly relieving the already foot-sore infantry. When we reached Fort Scott we went into camp and prepared for the defense of the military stores. Price's army finally approached. Citizens were coming in, many unarmed, from all the country round. We drew ammunition and equipage. I opened the cases of Springfield rifles and bayonets and gave them to men on horseback who rode off with them like rails lying across their saddles. It was a serious time, but into it crept now and again the grotesque and laughable, the ludicrous as well as the solemn.

General Lane finally ordered his advance guard,

under Colonels Montgomery, Weir and Johnson, with Colonel Moonlight's howitzer, to hold the rebels in check at Dry Wood, a creek ten miles to the east of Fort Scott; for nearer and nearer had come the rebel army. The detail proceeded to this duty in fine spirit, while the general and officers engaged themselves in getting all available forces in the field in good shape. Our men met the enemy, dismounted, and from the tall prairie grass poured deadly shot from their Sharp's rifles into Price's advancing columns. Moonlight began to give play to his little gun and the first shell burst in the midst of Captain Bledsoe's battery, killing three gunners, upsetting two guns and seriously wounding Captain Bledsoe. One or two more shells went screaming from Moonlight's unerring piece into the rebel column. The hiss and whirr of the Sharp's rifle balls sent rider and horse to the grass, and in less than an hour after the first shot was fired the rebel army was in full retreat, and the rebel General Slack afterwards had to report to Governor Calib Jackson that when he came up with his division he found his friends, Generals Price and Raines, in rapid retreat, amounting almost to a panic. Less than three hundred and eighty Kansas troops were in the fight, but it was the acme of patriotic eloquence. It was action.

The superior force of the enemy was known to General Lane, and apprehending that his forces were known by the rebels he naturally supposed they would return, renew their march on Fort Scott, capture the military stores and endanger the whole border of Kansas. So he ordered the immediate removal of all the stores to a new post, which he selected, and called Fort Lincoln. It was a busy time. Mrs. Col. H. P. Johnson, myself and two teamsters, struck our regimental tents and camp, loaded our wagons, and had everything in readiness to move out as soon as the command returned from the field. We first busied ourselves feeding the hungry soldiers, without reference to the regiment to which they belonged. The whole night and part of the next day were occupied in moving the military camp and stores. General Lane was ubiquitous, everywhere directing the hasty and difficult work. Believing, as he did that the enemy would come and take possession of the evacuated fort, he ordered a detail of eight men, gave me a box of matches and placed me in charge, commanding that if the enemy came up, to fire the post and town and burn it rather than let it fall into their hands.

It was a strange sight, and one over which I have often mused, to see a Methodist preacher, with revolver in one hand and axe in the other, preparing fagots and placing them in the houses where they would do the speediest work, watching for an approaching enemy as a signal to the men detailed to fire the buildings which afterward sheltered us. The enemy, however, avoided the Kansas line and marched to the capture of Colonel Mulligan, at Lexington, Mo., after which they returned to Springfield.

The Sabbath following Dr. W. R. Davis preached for my regiment while I drew from the stores clothing for our entire regiments as our old quartermaster had not yet got familiar with his work and because my general seemed to have an idea that my services in an emergency were as valuable as an ordinary sermon. The previous Sabbath I had organized a "Camp Church," on a liberal Evangelical basis which I have reason to believe was the first camp church of the war. The day Dr. Davis preached for us quite a number joined the church. This camp church lasted through the war, and some of its members are Christians to this day.

When we left Fort Lincoln we marched to Barnsville to prevent the rebel army from coming to Kansas after having taken Lexington. Here our commissary stores were in great danger, and General Lane sent for me to act as commissariat—a new role for a chaplain. I requested each company in the brigade to send a detail of eight men and an orderly and in less than an hour each had its portion of the stores and had been made responsible for its care. As it was their means of subsistence they were ready to protect it or fight. We soon had every pound under most efficient guard, and so distributed that it could be safely moved in the company and regimental wagons.

When we reached the "Old Indian Mission" the general issued an order directing that I repair as early as possible to Quincy, Illinois, and other points east and bring out companies, regiments and brigades to join the army of the border, instructing us to apply to Capt. Insley at Quincy, and Capt. Prince, commanding at Fort Leavenworth for all needed transportation for men and horses, as well as money to outfit these commands.

I started on this unusual mission and was detained a day or two at Leavenworth awaiting orders from Washington when the sad news reached me that my Colonel, H. P. Johnson, who had been a local preacher in my charge in Leavenworth, had been killed in an engagement at Morristown, Missouri. His wife was at Leavenworth. She was an intimate friend, and upon Capt. Prince's advice and her persuasion I awaited the arrival of Col. Johnson's remains, attended the funeral, preached the sermon, and then went to Lawrence to visit my family, having learned that I would meet General Lane there.

In the meantime the Illinois troops were being mustered for the Mississippi Valley. Since Price's army was making all possible haste to Arkansas leaving the army of General Fremont to be reinforced by troops from the West, via Kansas City. Our command was soon marching via Osceola to Springfield, Missouri. The Osage River was a difficult stream to cross at Osceola. There was only a miserable old scow with a chain made of iron rods reaching from bank to bank. No quartermaster or wagonmaster would venture to cross a team on the rickety boat. Colonel Ritchie had succeeded to the command of our regiment. I accompanied him and General Lane to see if we could by any possibility get the command over. We went down to the river where I examined the boat and told the general if he would detail six men from each company I would take the train over. We pulled the boat out of water, made some necessary repairs and then launched her, provided with a half a dozen battery buckets to bail out the water. I took command, and we took over a light wagon and four mules. We ferried the wagons and animals belonging to my regiment first; then the general's wagon, the staff-wagons and the artillery. When this was done Captain Haskell, quartermaster of the Third Regiment, relieved me, seeing I had demonstrated the possibility of crossing the river. (After the war I was introduced by General Lane in the United States Senate chamber to a number of senators as "the chaplain who saved the day and his brigade at Osceola.")

We joined Fremont's command at Springfield, and remained in camp until General David Hunter took command and relieved Fremont. While encamped here we were short of rations. Colonel Ritchie, myself and about thirty men were sent on a foraging mission. We took possession of Isam's Mills and sent the men to the farms, and they threshed the wheat and brought it to the mills, where we ground it into flour and sent it to camp, thus supplying the wants of our army. While camped at Springfield and, on our return march, via Lamar, our camp was the center of attraction to multitudes of "contrabands" and refugees, so that they cumbered our camp and movements, and became at last so numerous as to threaten our subsistence.

On the march to Lamar General Lane sent an orderly to notify me that he wished to see me as we marched. I rode to the head of the column and was at once asked by him:

"Chaplain, what can we do to relieve the army of these contrabands, without exposing them to their enemies?"

My advice was that they be sent to Kansas and provided with labor and homes to help save the crop and provide fuel, as most of the men were in the army. When we went into camp the general issued an order that all the contrabands and refugees should be reported to headquarters, and ready to move by eight o'clock next morning. The following order was issued:

"Chaplains Fisher, Moore and Fish:—You are hereby ordered and directed to take charge of the contrabands and refugees in camp and proceed with them to Kansas, finding homes and employment for them, and dividing the property among them to the best of your judgment.

  (Signed)   J. H. LANE,
   Commanding the Army of the Border.
"T. J. ANDERSON, Adjutant General."

Next morning early there was a stir in the camp. Fourteen men were detailed as an escort to save us from falling into the hands of the guerrillas. We had a wagon load of almost useless guns. I picked out about thirty negroes and armed them, the first negroes armed during the rebellion. We divided this company, and also the white escort, and placed half as an advance guard with orders to "scout well," and the other half as a rear guard with orders to keep well up, and by no means to allow a surprise. Such a caravan had not moved since the days of Moses. It was a nondescript emigration. We traveled day and night, not stopping to cook, only eating what cold food might chance to be on hand. Once we came upon a little herd of cattle of which the boys shot three, and while they were yet kicking the flesh was cut from their bodies and hastily broiled, while other portions were put in the wagons for use when we were secure in camp.

When we reached Kansas I halted the command, drew them up in a line and, raising myself to my full height on my war horse commanded silence, and there under the open heavens, on the sacred soil of freedom, in the name of the Constitution of the United States, the Declaration of Independence, and by authority of General James H. Lane, I proclaimed that they were "forever free."

Their mouths flew open and such a shout went up as was never heard. Men and women who had been sighing for liberty during many long unrequited years of toil now felt and knew they were free. They jumped, cried, sang and laughed for joy. These were the first slaves formally set free. It occurred in September, 1861, long before Mr. Lincoln's proclamation had been issued. I made my proclamation effective by giving to everyone of them a new name. Many of them still live to confirm the story of their emancipation.

A frosty-headed old negress of eighty years stepped out of line and shouted: "Chillen, heah me! I'se been tellin' you dese many a yeah de yeah of jubilee'd come, and Glory to Gawd! de yeah of jubilee am come!"

When we arrived at Fort Scott we began hiring the negroes to any who would agree to take care of them and pay them for their labor. We changed their names from the old plantation names to those of Northern significancy, to prevent the possibility of their being returned to slavery in case the war should be a failure. This was more than a year before the immortal Lincoln issued his proclamation. It was a remarkable experience, a never-to-be-forgotten opportunity of useful work. Almost all those brought out of bondage did well. Many of them came with nothing but their plantation outfits, and these worn almost threadbare. Now they own lands, horses and cattle and are rearing their families with good educational and religious advantages.

Upon reaching Lawrence—I had been talking religion and morals all the way up—I announced that I would preach to the emancipated contrabands in the Methodist Church. The house was full. I preached, Rev. I. T. Ferrell exhorted, and then I invited them to join the church. Twenty-six joined that night, others the next night, and they finally organized a church which has done and is doing a vast amount of good.

I next visited Leavenworth, where I met Rev. John M. Wilkinson and advised him to go to Lawrence and take charge of the colored members, now numbering about sixty, knowing they would be happier and more contented in a society by themselves. Rev. L. B. Dennis was perfectly willing to have them thus organized, for though he was a radical anti-slavery man, he understood the situation and appreciated the desirability of the proposed change. When these people had joined the Church, we had to give them new names. We called one "Elizabeth Dennis," for the elder's wife. Her son, Rev. Baxter Davis, protested, saying, "Oh, no! That's my mother's name." But the name had been given the former slave, and by it she was ever afterwards known.

Brother Wilkinson organized them, and the society has grown and built a fine brick Church of imposing dimensions. The organization during those troublous times, and since, has done a vast amount of good.

The jubilee of the First Methodist Episcopal Church of Lawrence was held last October. At that time it was my pleasure and very great privilege to preach to a large congregation of colored people in the African M. E. Church thus planted, and in the audience were some of the number whom I had brought out of slavery.

I count this among the incidents of my life which go to make up a record of which I shall not be ashamed in the last great day.

CHAPTER XX.

THE CAMP CHURCH—CAMPAIGNING IN ARKANSAS.

Upon our return to our commands we found plenty to do. The Fifth Kansas Cavalry went into winter quarters in Camp Denver, in Kansas. My colored help, "Nels," and his brother and I built a log house of rails, stopping the crevices with hay, covering all with a large tarpaulin, thus making a tent that would accommodate two hundred people. I had this for my camp church. We had instrumental and vocal music and I preached often to the boys. Finally the paymaster did not make his appearance and the men became almost mutinous, for they had not received any pay for about five months. They held a mass meeting in my camp church and requested the colonel to appoint the chaplain to visit General Hunter at Fort Leavenworth and secure payment of the troops. Orderly Samuel Cargo was requested to accompany the chaplain. Accordingly I was appointed and received military orders to proceed to Leavenworth and secure the immediate payment of the men. I obeyed and was very kindly received by General Hunter, who directed Paymaster Adams to proceed with all reasonable dispatch to pay the troops. Orderly Cargo returned with the pleasing intelligence that the paymaster was coming. General Hunter extended my leave of absence, and I made a visit to my home, finding my family well and contented, though "wishing for the war to cease."

When I returned to camp they had converted my church into a paymaster's tent. Then, when the men got their pay some of them became drunk and disorderly and the colonel converted it into a guardhouse. When they had sent the disorderly ones up they seemed very much ashamed to think they were put under the eyes of the chaplain. Afterward I was requested by a number of the soldiers to take their money to their families, which I was enabled to do by the commander giving me a leave of absence for that purpose.

Besides frequently preaching to the command I read and explained the army regulations, which seemed to be of great help to the men in fully understanding the details and purposes of military discipline.

The second term of our service was under the command of Colonel Powell Clayton. He was emphatically a military man. Our regiment was connected with General Curtis' command, and ordered to Helena to reinforce General Grant bfore Vicksburg. The regiment was at Rolla when General Curtis penetrated the fastnesses and swamps of Arkansas, and we marched to unite with him at Batesville. A party of us were left at Rolla to bring on the quartermaster's stores and ammunition. As soon as we could get mules we began the march to overtake the command. The rebel army had been driven before Curtis and his men, but a large body of guerrillas hung upon the skirts of his army, and Confederate General Hindman had been stationed at Desark with thirteen hundred men to take in any Union soldiers who might turn their attention to Little Rock. Our party consisted of eighty men, some of whom had just come out of the hospital at Rolla. We met the noted guerrilla chief, Coleman, and surprised his advance guard, whereupon the rebel party fled precipitously.

We were under the necessity of marching night and day, only camping one Saturday night when completely worn out, at five o'clock a. m. breaking camp and starting again on our way to Black River. Captain Morse had charge of the advance. I was riding in a covered buggy, caring for Lieut. Trego, who was very ill. We were immediately behind the advance guard. Just as we were reaching the top of a hill and as day was fully upon us we beheld at the foot of the hill three hundred rebel soldiers marching to surprise us in camp. Captain Morse gave orders to draw sabres and charge at full speed. Our command was coming up. The word rang back, "The rebels are here!" and our men put spurs to horse and came rushing on as fast as they could. Meanwhile I put the whip to my horses and down the hill I went, amid the dust raised by Morse's men, while the rattle and bang of my callash-top buggy made the rebels think there was a "pack of flying artillery" coming. Our men yelled like savages. When they struck the head of the rebel column they killed eleven and scattered the whole force. I never before saw such breaking through the brushes and over fences. It was well for Lieut. Trego and me that they ran, for we never could have gotten out of the scrimmage in our buggy had they made a stand.

We were blockaded the next day, but an exhibition of bravery was our only possible hope, so our men charged the blockade, and after cutting through pressed on in hope of overtaking the main command.

At Black River we were compelled to cross on a

frail boat, which was pulled over by hand, by a rope suspended from side to side from trees. When we had about half the train ferried across the stream we were surprised and attacked by three hundred Texas rangers under command of General Johnstone, who had been promoted for meritorious conduct at the battles of Pittsburg Landing and Corinth. The attack was a complete surprise, and must have resulted in overwhelming disaster to us if the enemy had dismounted. But they were over-confident and rushed upon our dismounted men, who took to trees and fence, and from behind these and banks of sand and other barricades poured a deadly fire into the "Secesh" and their horses. Their commander was killed early in the attack. Seventeen rebels were left dead on the plateau at the ferry, and the repulse became complete in less than an hour.

During this time, with the help of comrades Thompson, Harrington and Winship, I was employed in bringing over the rest of our men, running the old scow of a boat across the river under a shower of bullets, some of them whizzing into the gunwale, others whizzing about our heads. As we reached out on the rope a bullet passed under my arm and struck Winship in the thick part of his shoulder. He dropped by my side, but we soon had him on shore. The boat was filled in a trice, and run as by steam to the side where the fighting was going on, and the men sprang to the fray with a yell, let loose a volley upon the swaying rebels and rushed upon them with such deadly purpose that they turned and fled.

Some of our men were in the river bathing when the cry of "Secesh! Secesh!" was raised. They scrambled out of the water and as the rebels ran mounted their horses, graciously attired in cartridge box, with gun in hand, and followed the retreating foe until his rout was complete. We at once finished the task of crossing the river and that night bivouaced on the further bank. The next morning came with a long march ahead, and our quartermaster proposed to abandon the train.

"Never!" said I, and "Never!" cried the boys. "We will go in with the train and colors up or we won't go in at all. We'll fight for the train as we have done all the way through."

So we lightened it up as much as we could and went on our way. We had lost but one man, and he by drowning. The poor fellow had been ill and was too weak to stem the current.

Pressing on as rapidly as possible we sent word to General Curtis asking for relief. We were nearly out of provisions and likely to be annihilated at any moment. Our first messengers fell into the hands of the enemy, but the second ones sent got through the lines with our message. Curtis sent word that he could not spare a regiment and that a company would do no good, suggesting that we had better abandon the train, separate, travel at night and make all haste to concentrate at Helena. But we determined to remain together and take the train in rather than abandon it and then sneak in like cowards.

At Cache River we were so fortunate as to come up on three or four head of cattle, which we soon dispatched and appropriated to our urgent needs. After a dinner consisting almost entirely of fresh beef we broke camp, crossed the Cache and burned the bridge behind us. Before it fell there were thirteen hundred rebels in sight; but the bridge went down, the stream was impassable, and they were compelled to fall back to Desark while we went marching on.

We were out fifteen days and nights before we were able to join our command. The march was full of privations and dangers, all of which the men bore uncomplainingly, and upon our arrival at Helena we were in as good condition as might be expected after so trying an experience.

The camps at Helena, as before at Lamar, were over-run with contrabands seeking freedom. In addition to my duties as chaplain I was postmaster for the regiment, and, with Chaplains Foreman and Newland, was appointed Superintendent of Contrabands. The blacks came in upon us by the thousands, requiring the exhibition of great care and patience for their handling. Here my church building experiences served us well. We built a large though rude church which answered for both church and school purposes. I preached the dedicatory sermon and we opened a school with Orderly Benfield as teacher. A Mr. Leech also taught in the Episcopal Church. I believe these were the first free schools in the state of Arkansas, where all colors and classes attended together.

Upon their return trip from taking supplies to General Grant at Vicksburg the steamers J. J. Simons, War Eagle, Emma and Katie White were put under my control at one and the same time, and by military orders I took large numbers of contrabands to St. Louis and Leavenworth, and scattered them throughout Missouri, Illinois, Iowa and Kansas, sending some of them as far as Ohio. One of the steamers had a crew all of whom were sympathizers with the rebel cause, and when we were ready to start General Prentiss called the captain of the boat to one side, and also a military captain who was to accompany us, and said to them:

"I am sending Chaplain Fisher in charge of these people. I want you to obey orders strictly, and follow his commands to the letter. We must not allow these boats to fall into the hands of the enemy. Render him all aid you possibly can.

Then, turning to the military commander, he said to him: "Captain, I wish you would see that Chaplain Fisher's orders are obeyed, and if any officer or man on the boat should disobey them put him in irons and deliver him to the military authorities at St. Louis."

After we were under way I told the mate that if he desired any help at the wood yard or in coaling up to let me know and I would detail as many men as he wished, so as to save time and avoid danger of capture. We forbade all persons except the engineers going back of the boilers. I had orderlies with me, and placed four men in the pilot house and four on the forecastle, to prevent being betrayed by the pilot or commander.

After supplying the mate with a detail of sixty men to help wood up Orderly Want came to the cabin and said to me that there was trouble below and he wanted me to come down. I went with him and found the mate and a deck-hand back among the refugees cursing them in the most violent manner, and the poor people in utter alarm.

I asked what was the matter, and he turned upon me and with an oath told me to mind my own business.

I replied, "That is what I am here for; and now, sir, I want you to leave here immediately. I don't allow any one back of the boilers."

He refused to go. I called the orderly in charge of

the soldiers on the forecastle to bring his men and told them to fix bayonets and surround the man. I took out my watch and told him he had just five minutes to get out of that, or we would let daylight through him. He stood defiantly until I told him he had just one minute left and ordered the soldiers to advance.

He weakened and said to me, "Chaplain, take them away; I'll go, and I'll not trouble you any more."

I then told him again if he wanted a detail at any time to let me know and I would have it ready, and that if he and his men would obey orders there would be no trouble. After that we got along without difficulty and I reported the whole party safely at St. Louis.

CHAPTER XXI.

THE SAM GATY—A NARROW ESCAPE.

I was also ordered to take a large party to Leavenworth and find homes for them. The steamers Magenta and Sam Gaty were loading for Fort Benton. I put a part of the company on the Magenta in care of Orderly Want, who was with me in this work for eighteen months. The rest I put on the Sam Gaty, intending to go in charge of them myself. Just as the cable was cast and the last gang-plank was being drawn in I was impressed that I had better go via rail and prepare for the reception of the party. I gave my papers to Mr. Wilson, an orderly, went up to the office, obtained railroad transportation, and reached Leavenworth in time to receive the Magenta. The Sam Gaty was detained by a broken shaft at Herman, Missouri, and when she reached Napoleon on Sunday evening a band of guerrillas, having been notified that I was on her, captured the boat. Orderly Wilson lay down by the cylinder timbers and the women covered him with their cooking utensils and clothing. The guerrillas took the black men off to the beach and made the mate hold a light while they shot them. When the order to fire was given many of the blacks fell and lay as though dead. Nine were killed and several wounded. Seven women were shot but none killed. Then they instituted search for me and would not be satisfied that I was not on board till they had killed three men in my stead.

Meantime I was about to preach a sermon in the

Methodist church in Leavenworth when the provost marshal came up and notified me that he had received word that the Gaty was captured and all on board had been killed. I requested him to telegraph to Liberty and learn the facts. He returned as I closed my sermon and reported that some had escaped and hailed a boat and were coming up and that the Gaty would be in on Monday.

Her arrival baffles description! Such a scene was never before nor since witnessed on the levee at Leavenworth. Hundreds had assembled at the sound of the steamboat's whistle. When she was safely moored Captain Sours, commandant, came ashore, and in the presence of the crowd threw his arms around me and wept for joy. "Oh, Chaplain," he cried, "I am so glad you were not on my boat; the guerrillas had fagots lighted three times to burn her if you were not surrendered, and they took three men out of their beds, one at a time, and killed them, thinking they had you. I protested from the first that you were not on board, but they said they had word from St. Louis that you were and they were bound to get you."

The blacks cried like children, and asked me, "Why did you leave us? We could have escaped if you had been with us."

The guerrillas had taken eighteen of the boys and girls and run them away into Missouri, scattering them among sympathizer's families. There was soon organized a rescue party of loyal boys in blue who scoured the Missouri country near Napoleon and recovered all the children but one, a boy named Jackson. And even he escaped his captors and came to Leavenworth, where, by our help, he found his mother, to the joy of us all.

The whole party were promptly provided with homes in good families. Orderly Wilson was so crushed by the events of the trip and his exposure so broke his health that he did not return to his company, but in due time was honorably discharged from service.

CHAPTER XXII.

THE QUANTRELL MASSACRE.

Having returned to my regiment I was detailed in the early part of August to take charge of a large number of sick and wounded soldiers, with orders to take them to the hospital at St. Louis. There were nearly one hundred men, with sixteen nurses, Surgeon White and several assistant surgeons and hospital stewards to care for the sick and wounded. I was also ordered by Colonel Powell Clayton to proceed to Leavenworth and contract with a surgeon to join the regiment at once, as our regimental surgeon, Dr. A. J. Huntoon, was sick and on furlough in Pennsylvania.

After seeing that the party under my care were safely placed in the hospitals at St. Louis I proceeded to perform the second part of my duty. At Leavenworth I contracted with Dr. Carpenter to go South immediately and join the Fifth Kansas Cavalry for surgeon's duty at Helena. I was then ill, due to exposure on the trip, and having been seized with quinsy, to which I had long been subject, repaired to my family at Lawrence, a very sick man, reaching home about the middle of August. It thus happened that I was there, an invalid, at the time of the most fearful and barbarous occurrence of the War of the Rebellion, the massacre and pillage of Lawrence by Quantrell and his murderous band.

For a long time rumors had been afloat that it was

the intention of the Missouri guerrillas to sack Lawrence and slaughter her citizens. More than once guards had been placed on all the roads leading into town. The cry of "Wolf" had been raised too often. The people had served as pickets and had been frightened so many times, each time to learn that the alarm had been false, that they had come to look upon the danger of a raid upon their town as not even remotely possible, and had become accustomed and indifferent to alarms of this character. Thus it happened that when Quantrell came at last, with hellish and dire destruction, the guards had all been withdrawn and the town was asleep to danger.

The unnatural and barbarous state of affairs engendered by war was terribly emphasized on Kansas soil, where the anti-slavery people were exposed to the malignant hate of an enemy in the throes of defeat, whose schemes of revenge took form in arson, robbery, pillage and murder wherever defenceless bordertowns promised hope of success to these murderous marauders. How deadly their purpose, how sweeping in destruction were these guerrilla raids many a Kansas town was called upon to bear testimony to. But of them all none were made to suffer and mourn as Lawrence was made to suffer and mourn. The black cloud of darkest woe was her mantle. The citadel of free-state thought and sentiment, beautiful in situation, easy of approach, presenting avenues of escape to the hills of Missouri because of her contiguity to the border line, an object of supremest hate and fellest design to the desperate bandits who roamed the country and gloated in the opportunities which war afforded, their leader embittered toward the town for its ostracism of him for crimes he had committed within her limits, Lawrence easily fell a prey to the vicious products of a fratricidal war and furnished the historian the records from which to pen the darkest deed inflicted upon a city and people during all the dark days of a needless conflict.

Quantrell was the chief of border murderers and leader of the most desperate band of highwaymen ever organized for pillage and death in all this country. In him were represented courage and cowardice; successful leadership, intrigue, cunning, desperation, revenge and hate, all to a marked degree. A brief retrospect of his life will bear testimony against him for the evils he accomplished.

Wm. C. Quantrell was born in Canal Dover, Ohio, in 1837. His father was a tinner by trade, a schoolteacher by profession. Under his direction the son was given a fairly good education. Quantrell junior came to Kansas in 1857, locating near Stanton, Miami County. In his new surroundings the baser motives of his character came quickly to light. He initiated himself into his new home by appropriating unto himself a yoke of oxen from a man who had befriended him. Concealing them in a deep, unfrequented ravine, and there lariating them with a log chain, he carried stolen fodder to them and in so doing betrayed himself —the trail he made in going to and fro leading to the finding of the cattle. He made his escape to the mountains and was next heard of in Salt Lake City.

After a few months he returned from the West and located in Lawrence under the alias of Charley Hart. Here he taught school for a brief term, but his associates were low and he was shortly connected with them in an inter-state thievery of no small pretensions. This consisted in the liberation of slaves and mules from Missouri and horses from Kansas, to be returned to their respective owners when reward of sufficient amount to justify the transaction was offered. The Lawrence officials at length became aware of this brigandage and broke it up, ordering the soi-disant Charley Hart and his associates out of the state. This so embittered him against the town that the enfevered guerrilla chief, as he afterwards became, was imbued with the spirit of revenge and the determination took possession of him to give vent to it in destruction and death when his moment should come.

Upon being driven from Lawrence he settled in the Sni Hills, in Missouri. This locality is perhaps the most picturesque and romantic in all that Southwestern section. Its geography is characterized by the Big and Little Blue rivers, as also by the Sni, by mountains and hills, dark ravines and impassable gulches, deep defiles and precipitous canyons, and open glades of limited extent, much of the country seldom if ever penetrated by man or domestic brute, almost unknown to the sunlight of heaven, a typical home for demons of darkness, destruction and death. It was here that Quantrell made his rendezvous and guerrilla headquarters.

His lieutenants embraced all the desperate characters who were Missouri's disgrace during the border-ruffian period, while the war between the states was going on, and for many years to follow. There were among them Bill Hickman, Joe Maddox, the Younger boys, the Jameses, Bill Anderson, Tuck Hill, Woot Hill, Bill Hulse, Jim Hinds, Ben Broomfield, Dick Yeager, Tom Maupin, Ben Morrow, Sid Creek, Fletch Taylor, Jim Little, Col. John Holt, Col. Boaz Roberts, and Sim Whitsett, all of whom were men after Quantrell's image, skilled in daring, cunning and murder, all men with grievances—grievances against Kansas, the United States and their fellow men. They all thirsted for revenge. And they all slaked their thirst in blood.

At a meeting of these chieftains and men on the banks of the Blackwater at the house of one sympathizer by the name of Pardee, the raid on Lawrence was determined upon, consummately planned and the details carefully worked out. In this council Dick Yeager made a speech, now passed into history, where he deftly outlined the massacre. Quantrell was on his feet in an instant to say that he had anticipated the plan and already had spies in the town, one of whom lived at the Eldridge House as a cattle-speculator and occasionally opened a bottle of wine at the same table with General Lane. When the motley conclave broke up Lawrence's doom had been sealed. The date for the raid had been settled upon as the 20th of August, 1863.

Meanwhile, as each setting sun brought the fateful day one step nearer life went hopefully on in Lawrence, where men passed to their daily occupations, unwitting of the fact that upon their heads prices had been set and that they, of all Kansas, would be called upon to bear the heaviest woe of the war.

The town in those days was spread over a fair site on the South side of the Kansas river and had held its own with growing beauty and prosperity since its founding in 1854 as the home of a New England colony, one of whose constituents, Amos Lawrence, had given it his name. Off to the West lay Mount Oread, in after years to be the home of the magnificent buildings comprising the University of Kansas, but in those eventful days covered with breastworks and rifle pits of freedom's defenders.

THE QUANTRELL MASSACRE.

The beautiful streets, stretching away at right angles and parallel with the river on the North front, the substantial dwellings, the enterprising stores, the bustling little market, had all that long August day been alert with the sturdy life of the town, and when at last the twilight came it enfolded a weary people, who slept all too well despite the war and rumors of war which kept Kansas electric in those dark days. So that when the sun came up in his slow August grandeur on the morning of the 21st the people yet slept—many of them for the last time on earth.

The destruction of Lawrence is directly attributable to two main reasons, with all their dependent chains of circumstances.

The first of these was to be found in the utterly unprotected condition of the town, as indeed of the whole border, because of the absence of all able-bodied men the state could spare at the seats of war, and because, too, of the censurable indifference of those in municipal authority in Lawrence to the dangers of the time. Warnings had been so frequent that the ears of the officials had grown deaf to threat or entreaty. They had no guards about the city, no pickets, no signals, no rallying point.

The second causative influence was in the method of guerrilla attack. Sure-footed, noiseless, quick, treacherous, these border fiends won many a victory before their dazed contestants recovered from the first bewildering alarm. Their spies were everywhere at work, and they kept themselves well posted on all weak and defenceless points in the enemies' ranks. An old Mrs. L——., of Kansas City, was the spy who furnished the necessary information and map of Lawrence. On her map she had marked all objectionable houses, and this map Quantrell and his men had studied zealously in her parlor while Union men scoured the country for them. So that while the people slept on that fatal morning Quantrell and his men came upon them with a full and fiendish knowledge of their helplessness and an intimate conversance with their situation.

The line of march was up out of the Southeast across the line into Kansas between Aubury and Shawneetown, thence in orderly fashion over the open prairies and small streams toward the village of Franklin, four miles to the Southeast. As they came they floated over their column the stars and stripes of the United States, to avert the suspicion of any who might cross their path. They halted briefly in Franklin to await word from their scouting spies, who were to report a favorable opportunity for attack, emphasizing there their plan and determination to kill Jim Lane, Chaplain Fisher and Col. Eldridge. Favorable word being brought them out of Lawrence the column moved on. There were three hundred all told, one hundred and fifty of whom were Quantrell's tried and trusted guerrillas and one hundred and fifty of whom were picked from Price's most desperate Texas rangers.

As they neared the town the stars and stripes were lowered and out over the heads of the column shot the black folds of the Quantrell flag, flaunting the name of the leader, inwrought in red upon it by a woman's hand.

And where all this while were the out-lying troops? Why did not Fort Anthony send the warning? Why did not some early riser shout an alarm? Were people to be slaughtered like dogs? Was that awful holocaust to be permitted while the heavens smiled on and never a sound reached the ears of the sleepers? Alas! the troops at Fort Aubury had been woefully intimidated and, bereft of their senses, could only wait in fear and trembling for the end to come. Three times men who happened to be already up and about attempted to give an alarm, but three times unerring bullets laid them low with death-groans on their lips.

Lawrence had a population of nearly twelve hundred people. It was accounted the loveliest town in the state. Mount Oread, lying to the West, rose several hundred feet above the level of the main residence and business portion. Seven miles to the Southeast lay Blue Mound, plainly in view. Directly South lay the Waukarusa flats, or bottom lands. The river coursed directly Eastward on the North, the road to the Missouri line following close by its banks. To the Southeast, from which direction the guerrillas came, there lay a beautiful stretch of farming country, just being opened to cultivation. There was here and there a farm yielding a bountiful crop, but the settlements were scattered and few. The main wagon-travel to and from Lawrence was from the Northeast, from Leavenworth, and directly to the South, through Prairie City and Baldwin to the Southern part of the state. Hence the guerrillas were enabled to come in upon us undisturbed. Recruiting stations had been established at various points, among them one at Lawrence, and the cowardly ruffians were easily able to avert suspicion by floating the stars and stripes above them.

Entering the town from the Southeast they marched in regular order until the center of the residence portion had been reached. Here they broke into a main body and squads of four, six and eight, the larger body galloping furiously down Massachusetts street to the business section, the smaller squads riding as fast as their horses could carry them to the various parts of the town assigned them for individual action. Some flew to the extreme Western limit, the residence of General Lane and other prominent citizens. Others galloped swiftly to the Southwest, skirting Mount Oread and the Southern edge of town. The river front needed but little guarding, yet here, too, pickets were quickly stationed. As the affrighted people flew for safety, no matter what the direction, they were confronted by squads of guerrillas so stationed as to cut off escape. A cordon of death had been thrown around us while we slept.

Fairly within the city the work of death and destruction was begun. With demoniac yells the scoundrels flew hither and yon, wherever a man was to be seen, shooting him down like a dog. Men were called from their beds and murdered before the eyes of wives and children on their doorsteps. Tears, entreaties, prayers availed nothing. The fiends of hell were among us and under the demands of their revengeful black leader they satiated their thirst for blood with fiendish delight.

The lurid glare of burning houses joined with the oncoming sun to shed more light upon the awful scene. The torch was applied to every house that had been marked on the traitoress' map. Everything that could not be carried away as booty was doomed to destruction. Every business house on Massachusetts street save one was burned to the ground. No home that was picked out as the home of a soldier's family or that of a Union man was left if it could be burned.

Not only was the torch applied for the destruction of stores and homes, but in many instances the bullet-pierced bodies of their owners were consigned to the flames, in individual instances before life was extinct. Such scenes of barbarity have never been witnessed, even in the days of war, in recent centuries, except among the most degraded tribes of earth.

Particularly atrocious were the murders of Senator Thorp, Dr. Griswold and Editor Trask. Together with Mr. Baker they, with their families, were boarding in the Northern part of the town. The guerrillas called them to the doorway, and assuring them and their wives that they were only to be taken down town to a rendezvous at which the citizens had been gathered, that the danger to the raiders might be lessened as they did their work of robbery and arson, they were marched to the front side-walk and as their wives bade them adieu were commanded to front face, and before the eyes of the women and children on the porch but thirty feet away they were shot in their tracks. The entreaties of wives and mothers and children went for naught. Shot after shot was fired into their prostrate forms until life was extinguished in all but Mr. Baker. Though pierced by seventeen bullets his splendid constitution saved him and he lives to-day.

Equally atrocious was the murder of Judge Carpenter. In delicate health he had not joined the army of the frontier, but he sympathized earnestly with the Union cause and served us nobly in many ways. His judicial utterances were always on the side of the right, and thus he became an object of hatred to the ruffian element. Called from his home in early morn he saw the danger and attempted to escape by running around his house, hoping to get out by a side gate and away to some place of safety. They chased him, and when his wife saw he was certain to be caught she flew to his side and threw her arms around him, enfolding him in her skirts. The murderous guerrillas tried to wrest him away from her, failing in which they forcibly held her to one side and shot him down in her arms. She fell with him and again they tore her partially from him and finished their crime by repeatedly turning their revolvers upon him while still she clung to him and begged for mercy and his life.

Most terrible was the fate of a Mr. D. D. Palmer, an inoffensive man who happened to be in his gun-shop when the murderous band came upon him. Having become satiated with ordinary blood-shed they shot him and an assistant, then fired the shop, tied the hands of the men and threw them into the burning building which, being of wood, burned fast and furiously. The wounded men arose and struggled to the door to be kicked back into the flames! When the fire had at last burned the cords from their wrists they again fought their way to the door and begged for mercy. Demoniac yells of revengeful delight came from their tormentors for an answer, and death, slow but awfully sure, was their release!

One hundred and fifty-four of the best business houses and dwellings of Lawrence were burned to the ground. The value of the property destroyed was estimated at one and one-half million dollars. Two-thirds of the people were homeless. Many of them had not a suit of clothing left and but few had a dollar in money. That night nearly an hundred widows and two hundred fatherless children sat wailing in the streets. One hundred and eighty-five men had been killed. Shorn of her pride and beauty and sons the city wept in sack-cloth and sat in ashes—a Phoenix who should one day rise again. Desolation like a pall hung over every home. There was nought doing but burial. The hearse was the only trafficker.

Many a good name and fair is on the list of the lamented dead who were left bleeding on the streets of Lawrence on that terrible day of the raid. A partial list of them is appended. These men and the others slain deserve to have their names inscribed upon the pages of the history of Kansas and the Union. They fell martyrs to a noble cause. Upon the sacred soil of Lawrence, whose individual history is more intimately interwoven with the history of the struggle for the emancipation of the Negro race than that of any other city in the Union, there should be erected a monument to these men, commemorative of the destruction of their town, the burning of their homes, and their murder, which shall tell the history of this awful crime to generations to come. Lawrence stands as the Thermopylae of Kansas and freedom.

LIST OF THE MASSACRED.

Albach, George
Allen, E.
Alwes, George.
Anderson, John.
Allison, D. C.
Argel, Jas.
Allen, Clay (colored).
Bell, Capt. Geo. W.
Bowen Samuel.
Brechteshaner, James.
Brant, E.
Burt, George.
Burnes, Dennis.
Burns, Michael.
Carpenter, Judge Louis.
Coats, George.
Collamore, G. W. Mayor.
Crane, John L.
Clona, Charles.
Cooper, James.
Coleman, L. D.
Cornell, I.
Dix, Ralph.
Dix, Stephen.
Dyer, Uncle Frank.
Dulinsky, Sylvester.
Eheles, August.
Eldridge, Jas.
Ellis Frank (colored).
Evans, John.

Englar, Carl.
Englesman, Samuel.
Fitch, Edward P.
Fillmore, Lemuel.
Frawley, John.
Frank, Joseph.
Fritch, S. H.
Giebal, Anthony.
Gentry, Levy.
Green, John.
Gates, Levy.
Gill, John.
Griswold, Dr. J. P.
Griswold, Watt.
Gregg, Geo.
Hay, Chester.
Hoge, Calvin.
Holmes, Nathan.
Johnson, M.
Johnson, Ben.
Jones, Samuel.
Kimball, Fred.
Keefe, Pat.
Klaus, Wen.
Klaus, Fred.
Kleffer, W. M. R.
Lawrie, John.
Lawrie, William.
Leonard, Christopher.
Lambert, Noe.
Little, John.
Limbach, Henry.
Laner, Christian.
Longley, Otis.
Loomis, Rich.
Lowe, Joseph.
McClelland, Amos.
McFadden, J.
Martin, Robt.
Murphy, Dennis.
Martha, Samuel.
Martin, Michael.
Meeky, M.
McFarland ——
Nathan, W.
Oldham, Anthony (col'd).
Oerhie, Jno.
Oneil, Jas.
Palmer, Charles.
Palmer, Daniel W.
Perine, James.
Pope, Geo.
Pollock, J.
Purrington, David H.
Roach, Jacob.
Reedmiller, A.
Reynolds, Samuel.
Range, Geo.
Range, Samuel.
Speer, John M.
Snyder, Rev. S. S.
Stewart, Henry.
Smith, Charles.
Schwab, John.
Sanger, Geo. H.
Sargent, G. H.
Stonestreet, Benj.
Stone, Nathan.
Swan, L. L.
Thorp, S. M.

Trask, Josiah C.
Turk, David.
Wise, Louis.
Williamson, John.
Zimmerman, John.
Woods, James.
Waugh, Addison.

The following were "Unmustered Recruits" who were killed in their tents unarmed:

Anderson, C.
Allen, Chas. R.
Cooper, Jas. F.
Green, John R.
Griswold, Walter B. S.
Walderman, Aaron.
Markel, David.
Markel, Lewis.
Markel, Samuel.
Parker, Ashbury.
Parker, Isaac.
Riggs, Chas. F.
Speer, Robt.
Watson, John.
Waugh, Wm. A.
Wilson, Jas.
Woods, Andrew.

Of a company of twenty-three recruits, of the ages of from eighteen to twenty years, only five escaped with their lives.

Note.—There is some doubt about the orthography of Quantrell's name. So far as I am able to learn, it has always been spelled as I have spelled it. In later years an "i" has taken the place of the "e" in the last syllable. The pronunciation has always been "Quantrell."

CHAPTER XXIII.

THE STORY OF MY ESCAPE.

The most miraculous incident in my eventful life is my escape from death at the hands of the guerrillas at the time of the Quantrell raid. There were many narrow escapes experienced by our citizens on that awful morning, but none of which I have knowledge is more strikingly illustrative of the dangers and terrors of the situation, nor of the fortitude and courage and resourcefulness under the most trying ordeals of a heroine having faith in herself, faith in her God and devotion to her husband and family. Could I but remove self from the recital of this occurrence I would freely proclaim that of all the individual incidents of the war none is more deserving of record, none more pregnant with heroism, none more truly illustrative of the bravery of the gentler sex when called upon to face the most exacting trials of life.

I had been ill and was wakeful through the night. About four o'clock in the morning I was awakened by the sound of horses' hoofs directly in front of my dwelling on the Northwest corner of the public park in the Southern part of the town. Arising hastily I partly dressed and went to the door opening to the east on our upper piazza and saw three horsemen riding rapidly out of town to the South. I felt that some calamity was impending and said to my wife that I was afraid something terrible was going to happen. She replied that I was ill and nervous, that there had been a railroad meeting the night before and that some of the countrymen who had been in attendance were doubtless going out early to their work on their farms. Thus assured I felt easier and lay down again, though troubled in mind and still fearful that the presence of those horsemen and their rapid ride to the Southward boded no good. It was so near getting-up time that I did not fully undress, but lay on the side of the bed with trousers on.

A half hour later my wife decided to get up, remarking that she had planned to take the older boys and go wild grape gathering that day, and that she believed she would get breakfast and start early that a full day might be put in in the woods. She arose, commenced dressing and called the children that it was time to get up. Dawn was just streaking the eastern horizon, and she went to the front windows to raise the curtain to let in the light. As she looked out Southeastwardly she was attracted by a body of troops entering the outskirts of the town. She looked attentively for a minute and turning quickly exclaimed:

"Pa, get up! There is a company of soldiers coming into town. I believe it is Quantrell and his men!"

I bounded to the door just in time to see them shoot down Rev. Mr. Snyder as he sat milking his cow in front of his house, and was confirmed in my wife's fears that Quantrell was upon us. As I watched the raiders for a minute they began to break into squads and fly to different parts of the town, shooting right and left as a man would appear in sight, and calling men to their front doors in their night dresses to kill them at sight.

I did not stop to dress further, except to throw on a shirt and put on my shoes, and thus arrayed I ran

THE STORY OF MY ESCAPE.

down stairs, out of the house to the stable and turned loose on the common back of our lot a blooded horse and a pony we had in the barn, thinking them less likely to be stolen if loose upon the prairie than if tied in the stable.

By this time my boys, William and Edmund, aged respectively twelve and ten years, were dressed, as was also our son Joseph, aged seven. My wife had Frank, six months old, in her arms and Josie by her side, and begged earnestly that with the older boys I should take to Mount Oread lying a quarter of a mile to the West and try to get to the bushes beyond it. So we started up the prairie to the foot of the hills, running together, Mrs. Fisher remaining behind with the younger children.

As I ran I felt all the time that I was going away from the only place of safety. I was weak from my illness and knew that I could not run far nor fast. Furthermore, upon glancing up the hill I could see pickets stationed every hundred yards or so, so that it would be impossible for me to get through their line alive. The boys were smaller and could dart through the hazel and sumach bushes skirting the hill, and they ran on while I decided to go back to the house.

Willie fell in with a school fellow named Robbie Martin, an older and larger boy, and they ran together. Robbie's mother had made him a suit of clothing out of his father's old soldier clothes, and as the boys ran together near one of the pickets he was attracted by the uniform and gave them chase, killing young Martin right by my boy's side, his brains and blood spattering in Willie's face, frightening him almost to death and so terrorizing him that he has never fully recovered his nervous vigor.

Edmund got separated from his brother in their flight and caught up with Freddie Leonard, a boy a year or more older than he, the two running together. They succeeded in evading the pickets, though shot at from a distance a number of times, and sought refuge in the town cemetery two and a half miles out. After their first terror had somewhat subsided they became frightened at being in a graveyard and sought a place of hiding in a patch of cotton being grown by an enterprising German farmer a little way from the cemetery. From this they could see the smoke from the burning town and hear the firing, and so terrorized were they that it was well on toward the middle of the afternoon before they dared venture to get a sip of water or to return toward the town.

After leaving my boys as they ran I made my way back into my yard through a rear gate and down the garden walk into the kitchen and on into the cellar. Our house was a two-story brick, with a one-story stone kitchen built on later. The entrance to the cellar was through the kitchen, consequently I was able to enter it without going through the main part of the house. My wife heard me, however, and asked if it was I who had gone down stairs. I replied in the affirmative, whereupon she expressed her fear that I had done wrong, telling me that the guerrillas were killing everybody they could find to shoot at and that she was afraid they would find and kill me too. I told her of the pickets on the hill and of how weak I found I was as I tried to run, and that under the circumstances there was nothing to do but to come back and take my chances.

"Well, trust in the Lord and pray that he may save you. I will pray also, and do all I can for you," she

THE STORY OF MY ESCAPE.

replied, as she left the cellar way and went to the front part of the house to look after Josie and the baby.

She had hardly got to the front part of the house when four of the murderous villains rode up to the front gate, dismounted and demanded admittance. I was lying just beneath the front hall, parallel with it and near the front door, and could hear every word they said.

Accosting my wife with oaths they inquired, "Is your husband about the house?"

"Do you think," she replied, "that he would be fool enough to stay about the house and you killing everybody you can? No, sir; he left with the little boys when you first came into town."

With an oath one of them contradicted her, and to her astonishment and mine replied, "I know a d——d sight better; he's in the cellar; where is it?"

"It is not very gentlemanly for you to doubt the word of a lady," she said, "and besides, I don't want you to swear in the presence of my children. The cellar is open, if you think he is there go look for yourselves."

The men walked right over where I was lying, through the dining room into the kitchen and to the cellar doorway. There was no other entrance for light and it looked very dark down the steps, so one of them turned to her and remarked, "It is too dark for us to go down there without a light; get us a candle."

"We don't burn candles," she replied.

"What do you burn for a light if you don't burn candles?"

"We burn oil—in a lamp," was her answer.

They demanded a lamp and my wife, believing the only way to save me was to throw them off the track, freely gave it to them. As the man after taking it from her attempted to light it he turned the wick down into the bowl and turned to her to ask her assistance. She looked at it and told him he had ruined it, that it would take half an hour at least to get it so it would burn.

This diverted them for the time and they set about ransacking the house, appropriating unto themselves everything they could find of value and many articles that were new to them but which possessed no value. Finally one of them said to her, "Haven't you another lamp in this house?"

"Yes," she replied, "but it is up stairs."

She was ordered to go and get it, but protested that she could not carry the baby and suggested that one of them must go and get the lamp or hold the baby while she went for it.

One of their number took Frank from her arms and walked the floor with him, cooing to him to keep him quiet while his mother went for the lamp, perhaps wondering the while whether the father whose life they were seeking had eyes like the baby's eyes and what would become of the child if they took his life.

I heard my wife come down the front stairs and knew that in her hand she held the lighted lamp with which they were to search for me, and was almost persuaded to save them the trouble by emerging from the cellar and surrendering myself into their hands. Just then, however, I heard the man to whom she handed the lamp say:

"Come on, now, cock your revolvers and kill at sight."

This determined my action and I gave up the thought of surrendering, knowing that it meant certain death. As I reached this conclusion they began to descend the stairway into the cellar and my life hung as by a thread.

The body of our house was twenty by thirty feet in dimension. The cellar was but eight by fourteen feet, occupying the middle part of the space beneath the house. It had been dug just deep enough and large enough to accommodate our immediate necessities, it having been our intention to complete it later. The dirt which had been excavated had been thrown up on the bank between the limits of the cellar and the foundation walls of the house, more on one side than the other. When I entered I crawled upon the bank on that side of the excavation and lay behind the bank of dirt thus carelessly thrown up. I lay flat upon my back, and as my face was deeper than wide I turned my head on the flat, also, and lay as close to the earth as I possibly could. My left foot shook so that I was compelled to place my right foot upon it to keep it still.

Just as I got as snugly in position as was possible the scoundrels entered. There were three of them, one having remained behind to guard the house against approach. The ceiling was low, and as the man who held the lamp in one hand, a cocked revolver in the other, stepped to the floor he was compelled to stoop to keep from striking his head against the joists. In stooping he brought the lighted lamp directly under his face, and the heat and glare caused him to hold it to one side, the side on which I was lying within a few feet of him. This threw the shadow of the bank of dirt over me and they did not see me. My wife had so completely thrown them off of their guard that their search was not thorough, else I would not be here to tell the story. I could see them plainly, could even have reached over and touched the leader on the shoulder. But they did not see me and I was saved.

"The shadow of the Almighty was over me," and under his wings He protected me. My heart stood still. I did not breathe. Every act of my life came before me like a panorama. I lived but did not live. I died but did not die. In God's goodness and mercy the hour of my departure had not yet come. I was naked and helpless before my own conscience and could see eternity as plainly as noonday. "This poor man cried and the Lord heard him and delivered him from all his enemies." Blessed be the name of the Lord, he saved me when salvation seemed impossible, when death was at hand, when deliverance had ceased to be hoped for!

During this fearful ordeal the agony of my wife's soul can readily be imagined. As the guerrillas took the lamp from her and went to the cellar doorway she passed quickly to the front part of the house, pressed the baby to one ear and her hand to the other to deaden the noise of the fatal shots she now expected to hear and to drown my death groans. Her agony was intense. Her soul was tried to the uttermost. Her heart-strings were almost rended asunder; and especially since she had almost become convinced that her courageous assurance had not misled the villains and that in part upon her pure hands might rest my blood. If it was an awful moment for me, what must it not have been for her? As I calmly consider what she must have passed through during the minutes those murderous men were seeking my life I am filled with admiration for her courage, her fortitude, her confidence in God. It is one of the grandest exhibitions of womanly devotion and hope of which there is record. Had she swerved in the least degree, had she allowed her emotions to overcome her, had she allowed her fears to be seen, all would have been lost. God never blessed man with a nobler wife than mine, nor one possessed of greater courage and resourcefulness in time of trouble. To God and His servant, my wife, I owe my life, my all.

Finding themselves baffled in their pursuit of the hated pioneer preacher whose life they had so often sought, one of the men said to the others with an oath, "The woman told the truth. The rascal has escaped," and they turned and left the cellar.

When they were gone I found that the suspense had been most awful and that it had left me as one dead. It was a physical effort to return to life, and it was a moment before I fully realized that whether in or out of the body the Lord had marvellously saved me thus far.

When those cold-hearted villains went up into the dining room my wife's confidence and courage returned and she took the lamp from one of them, extinguished the flame, and said to him:

"You will believe me, now, I hope. I told you my husband had gone an hour ago. You needn't suppose that any one is going to be fool enough to remain around and be shot down if he can get away."

He uttered a muttered oath, continued the search for valuables and ordered the house fired, as it was one that was doomed to go. After the fire had been started up stairs they left one of their number to stand guard, the others riding off to further deviltry.

"Madam," said the one who remained, "if there is anything you wish to save I'll help you save it."

"Turn in and help me put out the fire," she replied, as she struggled to stamp and smother it out in various places.

"It would cost me my life to do that," he replied, "but I can help you save your stuff if you want me to."

"If you can't help me put out the fire," she said, "just get on your horse and ride off, telling them that it was burning when you left and I'll soon put it out myself."

"I will do so," he said, "but it will do you no good, for this is one of the marked houses and is bound to go."

He mounted his horse and rode off, cautioning my wife to save what she could as the house would surely be burned. She thinks he was the one to whom she handed the baby when she went for the lamp and that this confidence in him and the child's cooing had touched his heart.

My wife carried water up stairs and extinguished the flames, and having flooded the floors and beds thoroughly came again to the cellar door.

"Pa," said she, "those men who were hunting you set fire to the house in several places and left, but I have put the fire all out so you have no need of being afraid; I must go now and attend to Frank for he is crying for me. But I am afraid another party may come and find you yet and kill you, and I want to know, if they should, are you ready to die? That knowledge would be better to us than all besides."

I told her how I felt, and she said, "Continue to pray and trust in the Lord, and I'll do all I can to save you; I must go now."

She left me and it seemed like a long time until she returned. Lying on the ground, as I was, I could hear the horses' feet and the roar of the burning town, the noise of the falling houses, the shouts of the human demons and the screams of the dying. It seemed indeed as if pandemonium reigned and that a whirlwind of destruction was sweeping over the city. Imagine, if possible, my relief when I heard the voice of my wife as she came near, talking loudly to the children that I might know it was she.

They had scarcely reached the parlor when three other of the murderers came rushing into the hall inquiring, "Madam, are you a widow?"

"Not unless you men have found my husband outside and have killed him," said she. "He left the house with our little boys when you first came to town. There has been a party of your men here already and they hunted all through the house and in the cellar for him, but, thank God, they did not find him."

"I am d——d glad of it," replied the impulsive leader.

They did not visit the cellar, my wife had so completely thrown them off the track. But when they saw the house had been fired by their comrades and that the fire had been extinguished, and having drank whisky freely before coming, they were very angry and swore that the house must be burned, "as it is one that was marked to be destroyed."

This second band broke the window shutters and chairs and book-case into fuel, made kindling wood of the furniture, and fired the house more effectually than before. Then two of the number left. The other one, now drunk and murderous, remained with revolver in hand and swore he would kill my wife if she attempted to go up stairs and put out the fire. She slammed the door in his face and began drawing water out of the well, filling buckets, tubs and pans. When the fire had driven this fiend out of the hall and into the street she saw that fire from the main building had ignited the kitchen roof, and realizing that through the kitchen was my only way of escape she climbed upon the cook stove and dashed water on the under side of the board roof, then drew a table near outside, set a stand upon that, and putting pans and buckets of water on the roof climbed up and threw the water upon it, thus saving the kitchen.

But she saw another danger. The roof of the main building projected over the kitchen, and the burning cornice was about to fall. So she got down, filled her buckets and pans anew and again climbed to the roof and after dashing a pan of water over her dress to keep the fire from lighting her clothes stood with the roaring fire in front of her until the flaming cornice fell at her feet. Then she dashed water on it where it was nailed together at the crest, and stamping it apart tumbled it off the kitchen and threw the rest of the water on the roof.

Then came still a new danger. The small windows in the rear wall of the main building were on fire and might fall outward on the kitchen and yet set it on fire. So she called to Joseph, our seven year old boy, to give her a stick of cord wood and with this she punched the windows into the burning building. She had saved her kitchen, and through it had saved me!

The main building was built of brick, which had been saturated by the boys dipping them in tubs of water as the masons laid them in the walls, so the cementing together was perfect. Hence the walls stood when all the lumber was burned out. I was lying on the bank of earth just under the door that led to the kitchen, when the whole upper story of the house fell to the floor immediately over me.

HUGH FRANCIS C. FISHER, M. D.

My wife then began pouring water through the kitchen door on the floor beyond, but the heat and flames became so intense that she had to draw the door shut to prevent them from setting fire to the kitchen. The lower floor burned through, fell into the cellar and burned to within a yard or so of where I was lying. I expected to be cremated alive, when suddenly I saw a little stream of water trickling through a knot-hole in the floor. I then realized what an unconquerable fight my wife was making for my life. Soon a Mrs. Shugro, a neighbor, came to where she was working close to where I lay and said to her, "Mrs. Fisher, what are you trying to save that piece of floor for? It won't be worth anything."

"I don't care, I am going to save it if I can for a memento. Bring me more water." Then addressing the woman in a lower tone she said to her, "Mrs. Shugro, I have a secret to tell you. By the Virgin Mary and all the Saints"—she was a Catholic—"will you keep it?"

"I will."

"Mr. Fisher is under that floor."

The woman raised her hands and was about to scream when my wife said to her, "Don't speak a word, for they are all around here watching for him."

"What are you going to do to save him?"

"I'll have him come up the cellar-way and crawl under that piece of carpet, and we will hide him in the garden under yonder little bush, covering it with the carpet."

Then she came down into the cellar and said to me, "You must come out of there or burn alive; I can't keep the fire back any longer. I am afraid they will find you outside and kill you, after all; but stand here till I look outside and when you come up to the level of the floor crouch down as low as possible, crawl under the carpet and follow me out into the garden to the little bush overgrown with morning-glory vines, lay flat on the ground under the bush, and I'll throw the carpet over it and you."

She looked out and finding the coast clear told me to follow her. As I came up the stairs she dropped a dress over my head and shoulders. I gathered it about my body, crouched close to the floor, crawled along as close to her and the ground as I could, part of the time tramping on the carpet she was dragging from her shoulders, and followed her to the bush. Here I lay flat upon the ground and wormed myself under the little bush while my wife and Mrs. Shugro threw the carpet over it. When this was done and the women turned away there were four guerrillas by the fence, not eighty feet away, with guns in their hands, standing looking at the women.

"Mrs. Shugro," called my wife, loudly, "Let's throw those chairs and things on top of this carpet. What's the use of saving anything from that old burning house and then have them burn up outside?"

We have three of those chairs yet as heirlooms.

They piled the chairs and everything of the kind on the carpet, while the bush kept them from exposing me. I was almost famished for a drink, and at one time as my wife came near I whispered to her that I wanted a drink of water.

Josie, who was close by, heard me and said to his mother, "Pa is here somewhere; I heard him speak."

His mother replied, "Why Josie, your papa went away with the boys when the men first came to town. You go up to the stable and bring me the rake."

When the little fellow had gone she came close, tucked the carpet around the bush and warned me not to speak again for my life. I obeyed and laid there until after eleven o'clock, when the band of murderers had all left town.

When I came out of hiding I was all but dead. I had gone into the cellar before five o'clock and had been under intense mental strain and had been four times in imminent danger of death in those six hours of most terrible and indescribable experience, all of which my wife had passed in agony and heroic effort to save her husband. When I came out from under the carpet and bush our house and all we owned in it were in ashes.

Willie came back after a little while and told of Robby Martin and his terrible death, of others who were killed in the prairie, of how he ran past the picket after they had killed his little comrade and joined Mrs. Solomon and her children for safety, and how, bye and bye, another party of the guerrillas had come to them and asked who they were, threatening to kill the boys. When asked whose boy he was he said he was Mrs. Solomon's boy; and he told us how his heart was almost broken at the thought of having denied being my son; but he knew they hated me because I was a chaplain in the army.

Upon recovering our self-control we went down town to find that more than one hundred and eighty of our citizens had been killed and many of them burned until they could not be recognized. The whole business part of our town was in ashes. Eighty widows and two hundred and fifty children were in indescribable grief!

Crushed and grief stricken we returned to our own desolation, and remained about the ashes of our home until four o'clock. Edmund had not returned, and my wife had became almost frantic by this time, fearing he had been killed and was lying on the prairie uncared for, or perhaps wounded and bleeding to death. She left her babe with a neighbor, and taking an old sheet and table cloth saved from the fire ran in search of him, calling to everybody she could see asking for her boy. After traversing nearly a mile she saw him and Freddie Leonard coming toward her, and he, seeing his mother, rushed to her. She joyfully threw away the sheet and table cloth which she had carried to bind up his wounds, and ran to meet her new found boy. As they came near each other, he called out to her in fright and anguish,

"O, Ma, is Pa or Willie killed?"

"No, thank God," his mother answered, "we are all alive."

As they came down the garden walk I took the babe in my arms and William and Josie by my side and we met mother and Edmund in the garden under the shadow of a little peach tree, and there I put my arm around my wife and we all knelt on the ground and sent up to our Father in Heaven a volume of thanksgiving and praise. None but those who have passed through like dangers and have experienced like deliverance can conceive the gratitude to God that springs up within the heart. We realized that the Angel of the Lord encampeth around about them that fear him and keep his commandments and delivereth them.

The question has often been asked of my wife, "Mrs. Fisher, how could you keep you courage and confidence and plan and do so much to save your husband?" And always her reply has been, "The Lord helped me. Has he not said, 'Call upon me in the day of trouble; I will deliver thee and thou shalt glorify me'?"

THE OLD WINDMILL AT LAWRENCE.

This quaint old structure stands upon a hill overlooking Lawrence. It is the only one of its kind and size in the United States, and is an object of interest to thousands of visitors who annually visit the Historic City. It is a landmark which is cherished by the citizens of the town, more especially by the old residents. It was built in 1863, the year of the raid, at a cost of $9,700, by twelve skilled workmen brought over from Sweden for the purpose. It is of true Holland style, and is an unusually large windmill. The foundation is forty feet across, the revolving cap in the dome being twenty feet in diameter. The arms are forty feet in length, the sails, or wing boards, being ten feet in width. With the wind blowing at twenty miles an hour the capacity of the mill was eighty horse power. It is four stories high, and was originally used for grinding wheat and corn. Later it was used as a machine shop, for the manufacture of farm implements. It made its last run in July, 1885. It has been purchased by the Associated Charities of Lawrence, and will eventually be made a museum and place

CHAPTER XXIV.

THE DAWN OF PEACE.

Quantrell learned that Colonel Plumb was on his march from Kansas City, and fled the town, going directly south through Prairie City, making his way to his retreat in the Sni Hills. General Lane gathered all the men he could to follow him, but his men were poorly armed and poorly mounted. When Plumb found the guerrillas retreating toward him he countermarched and fell in between Quantrell's men and Lane's citizen band. It was expected that troops at Paola would intercept the retreating murderers, but they safely escaped to their rendezvous on the head waters of the Little Blue.

Later, after I had returned to my regiment, I was told by men who were captured on the Fourth of July when the rebel army was defeated and when General Grant captured Vicksburg, that as they were marched to Little Rock the rebels consoled themselves that Lawrence had been destroyed and that "Jim Lane and that nigger-freeing chaplain, Parson Fisher," had been killed. General Price had given sanction to the massacre by sending one hundred and fifty Texas rangers of the worst type to aid Quantrell in destroying the town, whose destruction would have taken place earlier but for the vigilance then shown in guarding it.

Our friends in Leavenworth heard that I was killed

and sent a deputation of men with a hack to get my body and family to take me to Leavenworth to bury my remains. Learning of my marvelous escape others came with money and supplies, among them Brothers Geo. E. Smith, John Best, Ralston and Rev. D. P. Mitchell. Kind friends in Pennsylvania and Ohio also sent us relief, which came most timely, for we were left without a suit of clothing for any of us or a bed to sleep on, a pillow to rest our heads upon or a quilt or blanket or coverlet to sleep under.

Lawrence had been from the first the center of free-state sentiment in Kansas, and as such was the apple of the eye of New England and an object of hatred to the pro-slavery party. It is not surprising, therefore, that the raid and massacre helped arouse the loyal North to a resolve that the rebellion should be curbed, in spite of the fact that just about this time the war for the preservation of the Union had been declared a failure in convocations held in Chicago. The reaction set in, the army was reinforced, the rebellion was crushed and peace restored.

For two weeks we slept in our hay-loft, in the hay, without pillows or covering, and ate our meals under the shadow of a tree in the garden. The first week after the raid, while the fire was still smouldering, I hired carpenters and contracted for lumber to rebuild my house, for the walls stood like walls of iron. We cut trees in the woods, loaded them from the stump, and they never touched the ground until the joists were laid down at the door. In a short time the roof was on and the plasterers were at work completing the house for occupancy. It still stands, a monumental reminder of what was and what is.

Before we were allowed to finally settle in peace,

however, our community was subjected to several severe and rousing scares. On the evening of the 23d, while my wife and I were sitting in scanty attire in the shadow of our stable, our boys having retired to their beds in the hay, we heard an unusual noise at Mr. O'Connor's, a neighbor's close by. With others, a very dear friend of ours, a chaplain and colonel in the army, Dr. D., on coming to Lawrence on Saturday had taken occasion to censure the people for having allowed Quantrell's band to raid the town and had said with some gusto, "If we had been here we could have driven them out of town with stones and brickbats." Their other professions of courage were likewise somewhat remarkable, until those who had been in the fray felt almost as if there need have been no fray had these brave men been at hand. But on Sunday evening, when Dr. D. and others were planning to form a party to follow Quantrell to the ends of the earth and punish him, word came into the town that he and his murderous band were returning to make complete work of their destruction in killing men, women and children. The doctor was taking supper with a friend, where two or three of his party were with him. Mr. O'Connor was at home. Attracted by the noise, I ran to learn the occasion of the excitement.

There were Mrs. O'Connor and another lady in the "hack," O'Connor had hitched two wild horses to it, with no bridle on the horses and was tearing around like mad, hunting the bridles.

"What is the matter?" I asked. "Run for your life, Mr. Fisher," says he, "Quantrell is coming back and will kill all of us."

I ran to the stable where my wife and children were; we got the boys out of the hayloft and my wife and boys ran to the Catholic church near by, while I started down town to get a gun, hoping to help to defend the remainder of the town. When my wife and little boys reached the Catholic church the men were all advised to go to the country. They started on a run to where Dr. D. and his party were at supper. Our second boy outran the rest, and rushing in upon the company cried out, "Run to the country, Quantrell is coming back to kill every body!"

Just at that moment my wife rushed into the door with the babe in one arm and the other hand waving in the air.

"Take your children and run for your lives," she cried, "Quantrell is coming!"

The party of men did not wait for explanation, nor for wife nor for children, nor for hat nor revolver, but flew out the back door and up the hill, my wife and boys after them. Before she was half way up the hill they had crossed its top, and she saw them not again until the next day. She and the oldest son with the babe, none of them half-clad, spent the live-long night in a drenching rain and a chilling northerner in a corn field.

The alarm proved to be false, but it vacated the town. Men dressed in women's clothes crossed the ferry to escape danger. The stampede was most effectual. I remained down town until we were assured that it was a false alarm, when I went to the hay-loft to seek a little needed rest. Joseph, meantime, had become lost from his mother and brothers, and remained in the Catholic church. In the morning the little fellow came to the stable where I was sleeping and called piteously for his mother. I awoke to a profound impression that my wife had run to the country, and through fright and sheer exhaustion had perished in the darkness of that stormy night. I took the dear little fellow and cuddled him in the workplace in the hay where I had been sleeping and then ran here and there and everywhere, frantic with alarm, almost beside myself, hunting for my wife. I climbed on fences and called, while the hollow air seemed to mock my agony. I inquired of every one I met. I got men to guide me on horseback, while I struck out in the direction I finally heard my wife had gone the night before, and after driving a mile or more, met her and Mrs. Cherry, with the children, coming home through the wind, in the sorriest plight imaginable. I wept with delight to find them unharmed.

The moral effect of that night on the inhabitants of Lawrence, I have often thought, was more profound than the raid itself, yet it was only made possible by the horrible massacre which preceded it. May Heaven in mercy forbid the nation should ever again have occasion to record such a crime!

In 1882, while I was visiting the Southwest Kansas Conference at Chanute, a most thrilling circumstance took place. On Sabbath morning a conference lovefeast was held in the Methodist church. There was a large company of laymen, as well as the whole body of the members of conference present. Many testimonies to the saving power of divine grace were given, and a delightful spirit of liberty prevailed. About the middle of the service I arose near the front part of the church and related briefly part of my Christian experience. As I sat down a brother arose in the back part of the congregation and in a loud and triumphant tone cried out, "Glory to God, that I have lived to meet and hear Dr. Fisher tell his experience. His miraculous escape from Lawrence from Quantrell's band led to my conversion and call to the ministry."

Every body turned to see who was speaking when the gentleman continued, "I'll tell you how it occurred. In August, 1863, I was employed in the government service as a teamster and we were ordered to Ft. Smith, Arkansas, with government supplies. We reached the north bank of the Kaw river on the afternoon of the day that Quantrell's massacre occurred. After we had cared for our teams we crossed the river and went up into the city and viewed the ruins while the fire was yet burning and the dead remained unburied. I was acquainted with John Shugro and his wife, and they and myself were Catholics. I called upon them at their home on the lot adjoining Dr. Fisher's home, which had been destroyed. Mrs. Shugro told me about Dr. Fisher's miraculous escape, and said it was all in answer to Mrs. Fisher, who said the Lord had heard her prayer and helped her save her husband. I held that surely the Lord would not hear and answer a heretic's prayer, but Mrs. Shugro insisted that it was true. Then I said to her, 'If the Lord hears heretic's prayers we ought to cease persecuting them.' My friend still repeated that the Lord did hear Mrs. Fisher's prayer and saved her husband, for no human being could have saved him from the fire and murderers. The next day we proceeded on our journey South, and all the way I felt that I was a sinner, and there was no priest to confess to, and I repeatedly thought, 'If the Lord heard a heretic pray and saved her husband certainly he would hear me pray,' as there was no priest to confess to. Finally, after we had started to return to Ft. Leavenworth I became so deeply convicted of my sins that I was very unhappy, and one evening after I attended to my team I went away off from the camp—in the woods—and fell on my knees and cried, 'O, Lord, if thou canst hear and an-

METHODIST EPISCOPAL CHURCH AT ATCHISON.

swer a heretic's prayer, hear my prayer and save me;' and I kept on praying until the Lord did hear my prayer and saved me. I am here to tell you that Dr. Fisher's deliverance from death was the cause of my salvation, and I am glad I live to tell him how good the Lord has been to me. He called me to preach the gospel, and I am now a member of this conference."

The conference and multitude were thrilled with joy, and many came to me and said tearfully, "Dr. Fisher, you could well afford to pass through the fire to save a Roman Catholic and make a good Methodist preacher out of him."

Truly, the Lord does hear and answer prayer!

Among the important events occurring while living in Lawrence was the coming of our fourth son, Hugh Francis, whose birth occurred on the eighth of February, 1863. He was six months old at the time of Quantrell's massacre. It was he who was held in arms by one of the guerrillas seeking his father's life while his mother bravely went to get the lamp for them to use while searching for me. Frank was with us through our varied experiences in the far West, related further on, and served during my life as agent of the American Bible Society as a colporteurer, doing efficient work among the Mormons and mountaineers. He subsequently studied medicine with his brother in Texas, graduating from medical college in Chicago. Later he took up the special study of Ophthalmology, graduating in 1890 from the New York Ophthalmic College and Hospital, since which time he has pursued this special study. He has practiced for some years in the South, but has recently returned to our immediate neighborhood and located in Kansas City that he may be near us in our closing years. He has long been an active worker in the church and Sabbath school, and has attained a satisfactory reputation as a competent specialist in his department of medical work. Several college positions have been tendered him, one of which he has accepted. We have reason to believe that a useful and efficient life will be his for many years to come, and that not only in the profession but in the church he will be able to do great good unto his fellow men.

While residing in Lawrence we adopted an orphaned child, a bright little girl named Jennie Arthur, whose parents died while she was very young and whose first foster-parents followed soon after her adoption by them. Jennie became a part of our family and grew up to sensible womanhood under our roof. In the winter of 1870-71 she was happily married in Atchison, during my pastorate in that city, to Mr. Porter Hazeltine, a successful hardware merchant of Columbus, Kansas. This happy marriage resulted in the rearing of a family of several children, two of whom are now married and already installed in motherhood. Mr. Hazeltine has prospered steadily in business, and has been able to give to our foster-daughter all the comforts of life, and to provide well for his family through all the troublous years that Kansas has seen. We enjoy our relationship to this good family as though they were of our own flesh and blood.

CHAPTER XXV.

A PRESIDING ELDER.

Soon after the raid I returned South to join my regiment and was made superintendent of contrabands. But as I was almost at once ordered on detached service by General Halleck, to report to General Curtis at St. Louis for duty in New England as agent of the Western Sanitary Commission, I spent the fall of 1863-4 in this field with headquarters in Boston, where Governor Andrew, Amos Lawrence, and other noted men became my advisers. I lectured throughout Massachusetts and Maine, aiding in filling in the quota of some of these states and raising supplies for the Sanitary Commission and Freedmen's Bureau. While in Boston we bought a whole cargo captured off Cape Hatteras, that was intended for the rebel army, and sent the supplies to the contrabands of the South. I had the privilege of lecturing to immense audiences in the Old South Church, and in Tremont Temple, Boston, and also in the city halls of Portland and Charleston. In February, 1864, I returned to St. Louis via Philadelphia, where I preached for Dr. Bartien, in Old Green Street Church, from "Behold, I will shake all nations, and the desire of all nations shall come, and I will fill this house with My glory, saith the Lord of Hosts."

I was shortly commissioned to visit the middle states in the interests which took me to New England. Dr. Mitchell of New York was ordered to meet me in Philadelphia and arrange the plan of appointments for me to lecture. My conference met in Leavenworth. Bishop Baker, who transferred me from the Pittsburg to the Kansas conference, presided, and appointed me presiding elder of the Baldwin District. I was also elected first delegate to the general conference, which was to meet in May in Philadelphia.

I was ordered to the East by military authority and to report to headquarters every week. I also had to report to my colonel in the South monthly, as to where I was and what engaged in; and to report to Mr. James Yatesman, secretary of the Sanitary Commission at St. Louis, weekly. I was also superintendent of contrabands and refugees for Kansas and Arkansas, providing for thousands of them coming monthly to Kansas. My district was large, but I made it the basis of distributing the contrabands and refugees. At one and the same time I was Chaplain of the Fifth Kansas Volunteers, Presiding Elder of Baldwin City District, Agent of the Western Sanitary Commission, Superintendent of Contrabands for two states, Delegate to General Conference, and the director of an immense work in the middle states. I worked day and night, and received congratulations upon my success from Gen. Curtis, Mr. Yatesman and my own conference and regiment. Dr. Mitchell made my appointments wisely, so I could fill most of them and yet be in my place at the sessions of the general conference. Frequently, while in Philadelphia, I was called on to preach that memorable "Shaking Sermon," as it was called by Dr. Bartien's people.

During the session of the general conference the first decisive battle of the Wilderness was fought. When the news reached the seat of conference an impromptu meeting was held on the steps and in front of Union Chapel. Dr. Granville Moody, who had created a great sensation in the conference a few days before, made a characteristic patriotic speech—a marvel in its way. This was a glad day, as it was a turning point in the life of the Union. The Bishop said publicly, "Now we have hope of preserving the Union, since that wonderful, silent man proposes to 'fight it out on this line if it takes all summer.'"

The general conference at this session extended the term of ministerial service to three years. I had served Leavenworth Station three years. Bishop Ames could not reach our conference, the people had declared an emergency, and we had a bishop pro tem who did not ignore that seeming emergency.

I had advocated in Philadelphia, in 1859, and by letters to the Pittsburg Christian Advocate of August, 1859, the organization of a Church Extension Society. Mr. Long, who has served the society as treasurer, and I, as early as March, 1859, consulted on this important matter, and in 1864 I offered a resolution, which was referred to a committee, proposing the organization of such society. The plan prepared by Dr. Kynett and the committee was adopted, and some time later the society was organized and has been of immense benefit.

When general conference closed I remained but a short time in the Eastern and Middle states, but after reporting to Mr. Yatesman in St. Louis called upon General Curtis and went into active work within the bounds of my district in the interests of the refugees and contrabands. My district extended Eastwardly to the Missouri state line and West as far as white men lived, toward Mexico.

Life had many ludicrous phases, even amid solemn circumstances. The Saturday after the Kansas Conference adjourned I started for Baldwin City to hold my first quarterly meeting as presiding elder. It was a beautiful morning. Baldwin is the seat of Baker University and a great center for church dignitaries. I harnessed one of my faithful army friends and servants to my buggy, and with Bible, hymn-book and Discipline in my gripsack, whip and bucket provided, started to my first quarterly meeting. I traveled blithely and joyfully three or four miles until I reached the Wakurusa river, the Indian name meaning "Hip-Deep." As I went down the steep bank and entered the stream to my dismay and discomfiture my front axle broke, the right front wheel rolled into the water, and I came nigh plunging out of the buggy into the stream. I had on my best suit, but rolled up my trousers, got out, and, wading in mud boot-top deep, got the buggy to one side, unhitched my horse, fished the wheel out of the mud and water and laid it on the side of the road. Then folding up the lap-robe to use as a saddle, with whip, bucket and gripsack I mounted on top of the harness and blanket and seizing the bridle reined my faithful steed to a keen trot, still on my way to quarterly meeting. I was so occupied with the thought of the mishap that for several minutes it did not enter my head what a ludicrous thing it would be to go riding into town in that plight. At last the sun, breaking through a rift of the cloud, threw my shadow fair on the roadside, showing me my outfit and noble steed in a distinctly fantastic photograph. Appreciating at once my ludicrous situation I laughed outright at my plight and the sight of the new presiding elder going to his first quarterly meeting. But I was both "called and chosen," so on I rode laughing, though heartily wishing I was not a presiding elder. I soon gave up the wish, however, for having reached a farm house I was kindly furnished with saddle and bridle, and leaving my unique outfit journeyed on, reaching my appointment in due time.

While holding a quarterly meeting in Olathe, as the preacher and myself were walking toward a little church in which we held a love-feast at 9 A. M. and preached at 11, we noticed two men riding into town leisurely. When the love-feast opened they sat in their saddles in front of the door awhile, then rode away. We learned afterward they were noticed during the day riding saunteringly in different parts of the town, and late in the evening in the Southeastern part. We had a great attendance, for the preacher had been diligent in announcing my presence at the meeting, clear out to the Missouri line. The two men spoken of inquired of some citizens where the Methodists were holding their meeting, and if Elder Fisher was in town, and where he stopped. They were heavily armed, but as this was usual it attracted little or no attention. In the evening the attendance was so great that not more than half the people who came could get into the house. The Congregational preacher, who held services in Francis Hall, sent an invitation to us to occupy the hall. We accepted the invitation and while we sang a hymn some brethren lighted up and we transferred the crowd to the hall. It was entered by stairs and platforms on the outside. The people left their horses and wagons hitched near the church. The hall was soon filled, and many had to stand on the platform. Services began, and in the midst of my discourse I could hear from without voices, as if horsemen were trying to make their horses stand steady. I hesitated to call attention to this, knowing that many had left their teams at the church, a little way off and that it would arouse their fear that something might be wrong or that there might be trouble among the horses.

I was preaching earnestly and had straightened up and stood squarely in one position for a moment, when, "Whang!" went a gun, "Crash!" went the window South of me, and the audience screamed as a bullet flattened against the opposite wall and fell into a lady's lap. Instantly there was heard the patter of running horses' feet; a few men ran quickly down stairs, but could only hear men in the distance riding swiftly away in the darkness of the night. I stood unmoved, and said to my congregation calmly, "I am not hurt." The splinters of glass fell all over the platform where I stood, and the ball ranged from where it entered the glass to where it struck the wall in a line not a foot from my head. I took up the thread of my sermon, finished it and dismissed my audience, several of whom were army officers. One was a United States detective, and after examining all the facts he gave it as his opinion that the bullet was intended for me and only failed of its deadly aim because the would-be murderer did not take into account that firing through glass at an angle would deflect the ball. The ground outside showed that the horses, after the shot, had been spurred to their utmost speed. This gave occasion to my being cartooned in the Police Gazette as "Parson Fisher being shot at in the pulpit in Olathe."

I look upon the incident as one of God's great providences toward me, and as I pen these lines feel that my life has been spared for a purpose and ask, "Lord, what wilt thou have me do? Show me, that I may do it with my might."

Subsequently I became the pastor in Olathe for two years of hundreds who were present in the congregation and remembered the assault upon my life, presumably by ex-members of Quantrell's guerrillas.

During the term of my presiding eldership I held responsible positions, as president of the board of trustees of Baker University, regent of the State University, president of the State Temperance Society, and member of the state central committee of the republican party. The board of regents requested me to spend as much time as possible in Topeka, attending the sessions of the legislature, to aid in securing appropriations for the erection of university buildings and the maintenance of the faculty. I arranged my district work accordingly, and spent several weeks in the capital holding quarterly meetings on contiguous charges. I also gave part of my time and attention to temperance enactments.

A bill was submitted by a representative from Jefferson county which provided that no person should be granted a liquor license by municipal or county authority until he had obtained on petition a majority of the names of all persons, male and female, over twenty-one years of age, in the ward or precinct where he proposed to engage in the sale of intoxicants. The rum power fought this bill bitterly. When it came to its passage, seeing they could not defeat it, they tried a checkmate move by amending the bill to read that it should not take effect until published in the Leavenworth Bulletin, intending to pigeon-hole the law until the Leavenworth city council and other councils should issue batches of licenses to run a year, thus making the law of no effect. The law passed, was engrossed and a copy was made and mailed by Mr. Barker, secretary of the state, to the editor of the Bulletin. The ice was running thick in the Kansas river and there was no bridge except at Lawrence, twenty-eight miles below. The council-men of Leavenworth who were at Topeka were telegraphed to come home immediately as there was not a quorum present. They chartered a stage and started at midnight, ran down to Lawrence, crossed the river on the bridge and took cars for home to hold a council meeting that night, thinking thus to head off the law. In the morning the man whose duty it was to put the mail containing the law on the train failed to cross the river on account of the ice and returned the mail to the office. I early learned of his failure and of the departure of the Leavenworth councilmen who had so opposed the law, and, hurrying to the home of the secretary of state awoke him and requested an order on the postmaster for the copy intended for the Bulletin, which he wrote for me without hesitancy.

Thus provided, I hurried to the postoffice, where the postmaster had just arrived who quickly opened the mail pouch and gave me the desired paper. I hastened to the telegraph office and sat by the side of the operator until the last word of the act was sent to the editor by wire, who, when he received the law thought it was sufficiently important to be published promptly as it had been sent by telegraph; so he put his whole force to work and when the councilmen from Topeka arrived at the depot at Leavenworth the news boys were selling the paper, calling out, "Here's your Leavenworth Bulletin, with the new dram-shop law in it!" The councilmen swore and "tore the ground" in anger and chagrin. One of them, a Dutchman, said to the rest: "I tole you whot; dot is de work of dot meddlesome Mettodist breacher." They did not have a council meeting that night. We beat them by acting on the impulse of the moment, not knowing their plans. The Lord led us in our efforts to restrain wickedness. The designs of evil men were brought to naught, and law was triumphant.

During my presidency of the temperance society there occurred a very interesting convention in Topeka. I drew up and presented the first resolution ever offered to a convention in any state memorializing the legislature of the state of Kansas to submit the question of legal prohibition by constitutional amendment and enactment to a vote of the people. Col. Lines, of Wabaunsee county, then pension agent, seconded my resolution in an able speech. But it was opposed by Hon. Geo. T. Anthony, Benjamin Kincaid and others. All the women in the convention voted for the resolution, but it failed by a small vote.

I then took my resolution, flaunted it in the face of the enemy and said to them, "Gentlemen, we nail this proposition to the mast-head of the good ship Temperance, and we will never strike our colors till Kansas is redeemed, and the national constitution is amended, forever prohibiting the manufacture, importation and sale of intoxicating liquors as a beverage!"

Our dram-shop act was very efficient until amended, giving cities of the first and second class the privilege of dispensing with the petition. This change facilitated the movement of prohibition, for the rural districts bore the burden imposed by the cities' debauch and drunkenness.

CHAPTER XXVI.

OPPORTUNITIES FOR POLITICAL PREFERMENT.

A seat in the United States Senate has always been looked upon as one of as great honor and dignity as a place on the bench of the United States Court. Each state, irrespective of population and wealth, by virtue of being a sovereign state and a member of the national sisterhood, is entitled to two seats in the United States Senate. It has always been, or should always have been, the ambition of the states to select their choicest men to occupy these posts of dignity and honor; and it has always been, or should always have been, if it has not, the one great object of a United States Senator to fill with fidelity the exalted position to which he has been chosen by his state.

Until the admission of California into the sisterhood of commonwealths there had always been an earnest effort on the part of the slaveholding states to control the nation by keeping the balance of power in the Senate and on the Supreme Bench. The admission of the Golden State gave that balance to the anti-slavery party and made the securement of Kansas to the pro-slavery cause an end greatly to be desired. But when Kansas was admitted to statehood on the twenty-ninth of January, 1861, the die was cast and slavery was doomed. The Legislature convened in joint session on March 26th, 1861, and elected Samuel C. Pomeroy, of Atchison, and General James H. Lane, of Lawrence, as senators to represent the young Spartan state at

Washington in the upper branch of Congress. These honorable senators occupied their seats with great distinction, and in various relations of importance with President Lincoln and his war secretary, Edwin M. Stanton, serving their state with fidelity and zeal through the trying period of our great civil war.

But, with senatorial duties and quasi-military service Gen. Lane was so untiring and zealous that at length his strength gave way and his iron constitution showed signs of breaking down. It was while thus overworked and undone by the grave responsibilities of those early Kansas years that, in an unfortunate moment, he yielded to the temptation of President Johnson of the growing patronage of his adopted state and voted against the measures of Seward and Sumner and Chase, against all his former free-states friends and the Civil Rights Bill, which engrossed the attention of the Nation at that time, thereby alienating himself from his party and his warm personal friends and ardent admirers in Kansas and over the Union. The knowledge of this alienation was more than he could bear, and the additional burden so told upon him that his strength gave completely away and he was brought home to recuperate. As he learned the disappointment of his Kansas supporters and friends his despondency became even greater, so completely overwhelming him that he sought relief in death by his own hands, suiciding while out driving for his physical well-being in an ambulance at the military post at Fort Leavenworth.

I was immediately called to Leavenworth by telegram and spent his dying hours with my old commander and his family, administering such comfort to them as was possible under the sad circumstances by which they were confronted, and upon his death was most earnestly urged by his widow and family and by their immediate friends and a large number of leading citizens of Kansas as his successor. So extensive was this sentiment that I was soon summoned to Topeka by Gov. Crawford and tendered the appointment. The vacancy developed any number of candidates. One public man offered to place the sum of fifty thousand dollars at the disposal of the chief executive for the position. Another wept and prayed, and almost went to the opposite extremes and cursed and raged when not chosen.

When I received the message from the governor that he desired my presence my wife and I went to our private room and laid the matter before God in prayer, praying that He might guide me aright in making a decision. I was then Presiding Elder of the Baldwin City District, which began at the Missouri line and extended westward into New Mexico as far as civilization went. This was a church work of great importance, and needed careful attention. I felt that I could not abandon it without heavenly guidance, and when I started to Topeka was undecided what course to pursue.

Upon reaching the governor's private office he announced his intention of appointing me to the vacant senatorship. I explained to him my relations to the church and the importance of my eldership to the work of my district, and declined to accept the appointment if it carried with it my retirement from the ministry to which I had been called of God. This left the matter open, and after a lengthy conference it was agreed that I should return to Lawrence and consult with my family. Early next day I received another telegram from the governor to repair to Topeka at once, as he had determined upon naming me for the vacancy. Again we entered the chamber of prayer and laid the cause before our Maker and again I reached the conclusion not to accept the senatorship if thereby I was compelled to lay down my license to preach the gospel. Twice during the war I had refused to accept a colonelcy at this expense, and now, with a seat in the United States senate laid before me I still felt that my call from God was of greater importance than any earthly call that might be made upon me and decided accordingly, urging upon the governor to appoint some one else. He finally yielded to my request, and named Major E. G. Ross.

This is a matter which has often given me the deepest concern. I have been perplexed time and again to know if I did the right thing and at the right time. The remarkable struggle among men for senatorial honors from then till now makes me sometimes feel that I made the mistake of my life; but when I contemplate the bitterness and wreckage that have strewn the senatorial seas I am led to think that I did for the best, and I sometimes deem my escape from the maelstrom of politics almost as remarkable as my escape from the murderous hands of Quantrell and his men. Without particularizing, I need not go beyond the confines of Kansas, my own beloved state, to point out senatorial wreckage from the like of which I may well thank my heavenly Father that I have been delivered.

> "There is a Providence
> That shapes our ends,
> Rough hew them
> As we may."

Following close upon this senatorial possibility another political honor was tendered me and also declined. At the state convention of the Republican party, at that time overwhelmingly dominant in Kansas, Gov. Crawford and his friends decided upon my name as their candidate for the state superintendency of Public Instruction. The caucus had entered upon its work and there was no organized opposition. The nomination meant the election. But at this critical juncture my brother presiding elders, Revs. D. P. Mitchell and W. R. Davis, deeming my services more necessary to the church than to the state, urged me to decline and remain on the District. We three presiding elders prayed over the matter as my wife and I had done over the senatorship, seeking the direction of God that I might be directed aright. As in the other case so in this; it was decided that my work was in the church rather than in politics, and I declined to allow my name to go before the convention. Rev. Peter McVicar, of the Episcopal Church, was chosen and elected by a large majority, as was the entire Republican ticket. I remained presiding elder of my enormously large district for the full term of four years, and when my time was up was assigned the pastorate at Atchison.

At that time I was a member of the State Central Committee of the Republican party and a Regent of the State University. My record in these positions has been written. And "That which has been written has been written."

As I review these moments of political opportunity and grow worldly in my reveries I am led to think I acted most unwisely in declining to go to the senate, and almost as unwisely in declining the nomination for the superintendency of Public Instruction for Kansas. Military, political and educational preferment have great charms for most men, and I am not unmindful of their advantages and emoluments. But as I view this subject from a Christian viewpoint and as one believing fully in the Divine Call to the work of the Christian Ministry, and as I recall how by keeping out of politics I have been enabled to do my part toward laying a broad and deep foundation for the grand Christian commonwealth which has risen from those early days of territorial and infant statehood, I look upon my decision with satisfaction and believe I was in each instance directed by the author of good to those who trust Him.

I might have attained honor; but I might have obtained dishonor.

I might have gained riches; but how many men might have laid it up against me that I obtained them by dishonesty in political life.

I might have obtained the gratitude of some who have not been my friends by having obtained positions for them; but I would have lost the opportunity of being identified as I have been with the growth of our church, school, temperance, social and national interests.

I have thought to title this book "How I Hit it and How I Missed It," weaving into my story circumstances and opportunities like these to justify the title. Perhaps I missed it in not engaging in a political instead of a spiritual life. But when the last great day shall have come and the great Book of Life shall be opened I am more inclined to believe that it will be accorded that instead of having missed anything by the declinations of worldly honor it shall be inscribed that it is just here that I have attained that full fruition that comes to them who serve the Lord.

CHAPTER XXVII.

CHURCH BUILDING AT ATCHISON.

When my term as presiding elder had ended I was stationed by Bishop Thompson in Atchison. I had here dedicated a frame church in 1859. It was illy located, however, being at one side of the town, on a hill and out of the way. It had always been difficult to secure a congregation. The house had been neglected and was delapidated; the west foundation had careened so as to draw the sill from under the joists, and had left the floor teetering as people walked upon it, so that house, as well as congregation, was in danger of collapse. Old indebtedness and alienations of friendships existed, and the outlook was anything but encouraging.

Knowing that church debts are always damaging to church growth I resolved, with the aid of the Ladies' Society, to revive the church, pay the debts, repair the house and try to secure a congregation that would demand and build a new church in reasonable time. We raised about five hundred dollars, with great difficulty, and when the old church was repaired and beautified we had a re-opening which became the harbinger of promise and success. This done we began the work of upbuilding in good earnest and courage. The people though poor had a mind to work.

In this charge I had two typical families—one poor but pious, the other rich and worldly-minded. In these two homes wealth and fashion contrasted severely with piety and devotion. Brother B. had great wealth, had been a member of the church for years, but had never learned to pray or speak in meetings. Brother D. was powerful in prayer and rich in experience, very industrious, as was his wife, economical, cultured and frugal, their intelligence contrasting favorably with the family of affluence, who were gay and vain, attending parties, balls and theaters occasionally. None of Brother B.'s children were Christians, nor were any members of the church, while Brother D.'s whole family were both and constant in their attendance on class and prayer meeting. Brother B. said to me often, "Parson, you must do the praying; I'll do my share of paying. I can't pray. I never learned how;" while Brother D. often said, "I'll help all I can both financially and spiritually, for I have resolved with Joshua that 'As for me and my house, we will serve the Lord!'" Both these families filled their chosen niches, but the contrast was so manifest that it was often the subject of remark, and none could fail to see the advantage of piety and devotion and the superior value of Brother D. to the church. We often wished and prayed that the rich brother would couple with his wealth and influence the piety and zeal which were manifested in the poor man, so as to become a blessing to the church. Now that they and the writer are getting near the close of life, Brother D, still poor in the world's goods, is still growing rich toward God in faith and good works*

The building of a new church involves a great strain

---

*Since the above was written Brother D. has reaped his reward, while Brother B. is self-satisfied in possession of his millions, which he must soon leave to others.

on minister and people, under almost any circumstances, and in Kansas in early days this was peculiarly true. Yet we pressed the work, with the reasonable co-operation of the members and friends of the church, to a state of satisfactory completion, and before my pastorate ended moved our growing Sabbath school and congregation into much more commodious and convenient quarters in the basement of the new building, taking possession with rejoicing and praise to God. This was a great achievement, as we were now centrally located. Methodism took a new start and a broader sweep of usefulness, and became and remains a leading factor in reformatory and saving agencies in that growing community. The church and Sabbath school have grown very largely in influence and members since then.

I spent a very pleasant pastorate, a three years term, in Atchison, during which time we enjoyed a visit from my wife's aged mother and my equally aged and much respected step-mother, whose society our children and the members of the church greatly enjoyed. They were objects of interest on account of their plain style of dress and bordered caps, which were severely in contrast with western fashions. Their visit to us was a great benefit to us.

We had in our society here the widow and blind daughter of the martyred Rev. Anthony Bewly, who was massacred in Bonham, Texas, for his loyalty to his church and country. His bones were left to bleach on the roof of a shed, in the rays of a tropical sun. A more prudent and conservative man and minister could not have been found. He died a hero and a martyr for the cause of Christ and humanity. Mother Bewly and her daughter still live within the bounds of the conference of which their husband and father was a member at the time of his death.

While living in Atchison we were led by the advice of physicians and our own knowledge of his condition to place our oldest son on a farm to avert nervous break-down superinduced by the terror caused by the massacre at Lawrence. Two of my wife's brothers, practical farmers, had come out from Ohio and bought adjacent lands in Atchison County. I bought with them and built and the married brother's family moved into my house on the home farm. William was placed with them, and here in good part regained his health.

The summer after placing him with his uncle and family I went to the farm on a visit and was out in the field with him when he was partially overcome by the heat. I sent him to the house and took his place behind the plow, while he sought rest. His aunt and four children were with him in the house, when, almost without warning, a Kansas cyclone came sweeping across the country and struck the house with all its mighty force before the inmates could flee for safety. The structure was lifted from its foundation as if it were a straw, carrried fully twenty feet, perhaps more, into the air, and thrown with such violence to the ground as to completely demolish it. My sister-in-law and the cook-stove were thrown through a small window together. The stove was full of fire, as it was baking day, and the live embers were scattered in every direction. My boy was dashed feet foremost out of the house, while the children were hurled amid the general wreckage like so many pigmies. Every one in it was more or less bruised, but, although the house was completely destroyed, by the Grace of God none of them were seriously hurt.

As an incident illustrating what strange things may happen in occurrences like this let me recite one which is difficult of belief. Joseph, our third son, had been saving hen's eggs and duck's eggs to set in due time. He had placed them in boxes above the window of the second story, and though the house was torn into fragments and the roof carried away down in the orchard a small section of the house, with the window and the eggs, was let down amid the wreck so gently that not an egg was broken.

The storm destroyed fifteen houses in its mad career. No lives were lost, as it occurred in the day time. One school house, with the teacher and children on the floor in their spelling class, was picked up by the wind, turned face about on the foundation, and set down so gently that not a child was hurt nor a light of glass broken in the windows. I soon got the women and children from the debris and put them in a field close by till the storm was over and help arrived. Our house took fire in many places, but we saved the broken mass from burning by applying handfulls of mud wherever we discovered a flame. By adding new lumber and utilizing the broken timbers as best we could we soon rebuilt and reoccupied.

The storm was one of astonishing vagaries and pranks, and the escape of my son and family who were in the house at the time of its instantaneous destruction was almost miraculous. We had been burned out of our home in Lawrence, and now another house which all contemplated as a future home had been destroyed by a cyclone! But out of all "The Lord had brought us by His love, and still He doth His grace afford, and hides our life above."

At the close of a three years' pastorate in Atchison

I was sent to Ottawa, which divided my family into four bands, and now, after more than twenty years, we have never been home together at one time. Our oldest son, above alluded to, was too young to leave alone on the farm and his health too precarious to abandon him to the care of others. So my wife, acting on her motherly instincts, decided to go to the farm with him while I should build a new parsonage in Ottawa, and to remain until she should think it best to join me in my new field. Our second son, who was reading medicine under the preceptorship of Dr. Johnson, removed to Lawrence to prepare for a second course of lectures under the direction of our former family physicians, Drs. Richard and Samuel Huson. Our adopted daughter had married Mr. D. P. Hazeltine and removed to Columbus, Kansas.

The new church at Ottawa was built by Rev. J. F. Nesley, the lower story dedicated by the author several years before, and I was now expected to finish the upper story. I went to my work, proceeded to finish the church, and build the parsonage and prepare to move into it. At this juncture I was importuned to resign the charge and take the financial agency of Baker University, which was deeply indebted and liable to be lost to the Church. The indebtedness amounted to $20,000, and the notes and bonds had matured, with no provision for their payment. On my way to Lawrence to take out a power of attorney to legally transact the college business I met the lawyer, Hon. J. K. Goodin, on his way to the bankrupt court, with the papers all perfected to throw the University into bankruptcy. He developed his plans to me and knowing the legal status of the whole business from my long association with the university and educational society I turned a short but legal and just corner on him by telling him that if the creditors would but give us time I would pay every dollar ever received from them. If not, I would prove that their claim was groundless and worthless. I knew the mortgage had been given under mistaken views by men who had no authority to issue it, and I was prepared to establish the title vested in the educational board, the bonds and mortgages having been issued by an entirely different body of men. I knew the county records would show this to be the case.

The result was that time was given, and though the state was new, our people poor, and churches and parsonages were to be built, yet we succeeded by various expedients in paying over $11,000 of indebtedness and raising what was considered by the trustees a valid subscription of over $13,000 during my agency of eighteen months.

I then resigned and others took the agency. The subscription was not collected, for various reasons, and the residue of debt mostly remained unpaid until suit was brought, while Rev. J. M. Sullivan was agent. In the meantime I was in Montana, and received word that the case was in court and would come to trial soon with a prospect of the loss of the university, after all that had been done to save it. I immediately wrote Brother Sullivan informing him of the legal status of the bonded indebtedness. He was absent but his wife received my letter two days before the case came up and sent it by Dr. Read and Brother Walter to the court where, when it was received by Brother Sullivan and the attorney for the university, it enabled them to save $5,000 and gain time to pay all the debt actually due, thus saving this great interest to the Methodist church.

"Through difficulties to success," has been the

motto of the university, and none rejoice more in the results than I do. Many sacrifices were made for this great interest both by ministers of Kansas and lay members of both sexes. May God bless them all.

CHAPTER XXVIII.

THE LORD GAVE AND THE LORD TAKETH AWAY— BLESSED BE THE NAME OF THE LORD.

At the close of my agency I was stationed at Olathe, Johnson County. Our oldest son married April 15, 1873; our second son was practicing his profession in Wichita, and my wife and two youngest sons removed from the farm to Olathe, where we were destined to experience the greatest sorrow of our eventful lives. The charge was a pleasant one, the people kind, and the society in a good condition. But rum had a strong-hold and infidelity and spiritualism were thoroughly intrenched. With others, we engaged to break this triple alliance of evil. The struggle was a bitter one, but by a combined effort upon the part of all Christian churches in lyceum and pulpit the enemy was routed, horse, foot and dragoon. The infidel club was broken up, the spiritualists were put to flight by the electric light of gospel truth, and the rum power, though in city ordinances backed by the common council and mayor, was undone. We drew the mayor into public debate and, though seconded by Mr. Winans, a noted lawyer, Rev. Mr. Clark and myself met them in open discussion, and with the aid of the "Woman's Crusade" cleared the county of the saloon, never to return. This was really the beginning of prohibition in that part of the state.

But the defeated "rummies" had my wife arrested on complaint of a miserable old ex-saloon-keeper, and

THE LORD TAKETH AWAY.   243

held under bond for six weeks. The ladies signed her bond and would not allow a man to sign with them. Several lawyers in the state volunteered their services to defend her. Hon. J. P. St. John, afterward governor, was her chief defender and the case was dismissed, it being understood that it was designed merely as a "bluff" to the temperance people, and especially to the Methodist preacher and his wife. But the triumph of right and truth was complete and the Lord and the people gained a great victory.

I have said this was a time of great and sore trial. Our oldest son, John William, had remained on the farm where he had gone to escape the terrible results of nervous prostration on account of the Quantrell raid. Our second son, Charles Edmund, had gone into the practice of medicine and surgery in Wichita. Joseph, our third son, had spent most of the spring and summer on the farm, but in September, with several young companions, had entered Baker University, intending to fit himself for a useful life. He had been a Christian from his earliest childhood and never allowed an opportunity to pass without recording his testimony to the love of the Savior for a little boy. The boys on the farm worked hard and had fine prospects, but lost heavily by the grasshopper plague. The doctor son was young but successful, though his work was among homesteaders, and as they lost all by the grasshoppers he lost fifteen hundred dollars. My leading members were farmers, and when the grasshoppers struck Johnson county my salary dropped five hundred dollars in forty-eight hours. My farmer boy lost all his crop—not getting an ordinary wagon-box-full from one hundred and thirty acres of cultivated land. I had to stand the loss of at least $5,000 and back my sons in their enterprises, beside all the sacrifice I had made for the university.

But these things were as nothing compared with the great sorrow that came to our home in the death of Joseph, our third son. He was nearly eighteen years of age, attending the university, full of hope and promise, but was stricken down of two days' sickness at home, in the full possession of all his faculties, and a clear consciousness of the divine favors. Among his last utterances were these: "I am trusting in God, mother. I am passing through the gates washed in Jesus' blood." And just as he ceased breathing, as he reclined upon his mother's breast, he said audibly: "Lord Jesus receive my spirit."

There appeared a bright and shining way, right from the chamber where he fell asleep into eternal life. We wept in bitter sorrow, sorely, sorely bereaved, yet rejoicing in that our dear boy was saved by faith in the Lord Jesus Christ. One of our little flock is safely at home in heaven. We all believed he was the best prepared to go, and resolved to follow in his footsteps. It was a terrible blow to us, but we were wonderfully sustained by grace and the hope of heaven.

To add to the sorrows of that day, as if all before were not enough, misguided and jealous men began waging persecution and unjust, as well as unfounded complaints against me, growing out of my management of college affairs. When the case was set for trial at conference and their main witness was put upon the stand he broke down so utterly that they plead for the privilege of withdrawing all "charges, specifications and accusations" against me. This my friends advised me to consent to and it was done. Then the conference unanimously passed the following endorsement:

"Whereas, Rev. H. D. Fisher, D. D., has been in connection with this conference about seventeen years, laboring with acceptability in all the various fields of labor assigned him, and

"Whereas, The Bishop having transferred him to the Pittsburg conference by his own request, therefore be it

"Resolved, That we highly appreciate the labor and counsel of Brother Fisher while he has been with us, and should he at any subsequent period desire to return, we will welcome him among us again."

The members of a former charge, McKeesport, had petitioned my return on account of sympathy with us over the death of Joseph, who was born in that city, and because they had spent a pleasant and prosperous term under my pastorate. This led to my transfer to Bishop Merrill and the above action. They kindly provided funds to meet my moving expenses from Kansas to McKeesport, and a committee from the society met me at Alliance, Ohio, where the Pittsburg conference was in session.

I left Manhattan on Monday morning, March 15, 1874, at 9 o'clock to pack our goods. I met my wife at Nortonville, reached Alliance Friday night, and appeared in conference Saturday morning, where I was introduced and recognized as a member of the conference. But the committee and people of McKeesport and myself were doomed to disappointment. The conference was crowded. Some churches were demanding special transfers, and there was a great fever in the "body ecclesiastic" over my return, lest my transfer should be an innovation on the established rules of a ring, which had relegated to the rear those who had been away doing heroic work for the Master in other fields, that they might serve a second probation.

Even this would not have thwarted the people's wishes had it not been that Dr. O. H. Hartshorn, president of Mount Union college, had been wishing for a financial agent for the college. Dr. Samuel Wakefield, my former presiding elder, was chairman of the educational committee. They and Bishop Bowman, who knew of my successful agency in Kansas, united to influence me to become financial secretary of Mount Union College. Dr. Hartshorn's request prevailed with the cabinet and bishop, and I was appointed agent, the very thing I did not want. However, I addressed myself with zeal to my new work. My relations with the president, faculty, students and patrons were pleasant. They were uniformly courteous, but my experience with the debt on Baker University rendered it desirable to me to return to the pastorate.

After some months in this relation to Mount Union College, by request of the Women's Home Missionary Society of Cincinnati, by Mrs. Clark, its president, I was transferred by the authority of Bishop Foster from the Pittsburg conference, and made superintendent of the Home Missionary Society of that city. Here I was associated with one of the most devoted bands of Christian women on this or any other continent. The field was broad and difficult, but white unto the harvest. Laborers were few and untrained. The property of the mission was embarrassed by debt, and the Methodist people discouraged by reason of former failures in this most difficult work. But we were blessed with a good degree of revival, and a number of very clear conversions in the mission churches and at the city alms-houses. The work was so broad, diversified and pressing that I could not, even with the help at hand, accomplish all I found necessary to do. The Jesuitical and oppressive "Reagan Laws" had for several years previous kept protestant missionaries and preachers from successful visits to the inmates of the prison, alms-houses and infirmaries. Though they had been repealed, the missionaries of Cincinnati had not yet asserted their rights and privileges under the new law. Backed by my noble band of Christian workers, I presented myself at the various penal and charitable institutions and found hearty welcome. In the city work-house were three hundred men, and in the wards for women many a miserable female convict. These were of the lowest vagrant classes—ninety-five per cent incarcerated through the blight of rum. Here was a vast opportunity but for our poverty as a society, which precluded the work of reform after the expiration of the terms of imprisonment, for then those who gave good evidence of sincere desire for reformation of life were doomed to go back to their homes and haunts of vice.

Mission work from house to house among the poor demanded constant charity. We had large congregations in the market houses and a great field for useful work in a part of the city called expressively, "Over the Rhine," or German Cincinnati.

Strange to recount, the very activity and successes achieved kindled jealousies and antagonism among the local clergymen, with some very honorable exceptions. Those approving afterward filled honorable offices in the church. One became missionary secretary another book agent at Cincinnati, another editor of the Western Christian Advocate, the last of the four becoming secretary of the Educational Society of the M. E. Church. The opposition resulted in a decrease of funds to support the mission work, but we went forward, still reaching results which were very satisfactory. I preached frequently in Findley market place to great companies of Germans who never went to church, who only attended here out of curiosity. I was aided by a Brother Miller, a German preacher, who usuallly re-preached my sermon in German, and we were constantly aided by Brother and Sister Thompson and my wife, who led the singing, a feature the Germans all loved to enjoy.

In Raper chapel Brother Thompson had a large Sabbath school, composed entirely of German children. They at first were as wild as Texas cattle. Once in the midst of the lesson they were seized with a spirit of stampede, and out they went, pell-mell, over the tops of the pews, girls, boys and all alike, as a flock of sheep over a fence. But by the patient work of Brother and Sister Thompson and others an orderly Sabbath school was created which did much good.

Among the adults we often found the infidelity of the continent most positively established. Mr. E. G., a German butcher, whom Mrs. Fisher and I visited to converse with about his spiritual welfare, said: "I don't believe that I have any more soul than that brisket!" striking a large butcher knife into a quarter of beef lying on a block. Said he, "When I die I want a big funeral, with two or three brass bands to play music over my grave, for that will be the end of me."

At High Street we had a very good Sunday school, composed largely of what were called "Street Arabs." It was marvelous what active students they were, and how they improved. Many of them were transformed into active temperance workers, making this a fruitful mission field.

The closing night of 1875 and the morning of 1876, was a remarkable "watch night" occasion. I aided in three watch night meetings and preached in as many different churches, first visiting Finley church, where I preached to a great audience at 8:30 P. M. I then went to Christie Chapel, where Rev. Runyon was pastor, and at 10 o'clock preached to a larger congregation than the first. From thence I went to Trinity, where Dr. Earl Cranston was pastor, and preached to the largest congregation of the night, closing my sermon just in time to join with the devout worshipers in singing the "Covenant hymn," ushering in the New Year with prayer and praise. Thus ended the hundred years of American independence, and thus began the second century of our national history with us.

Many of my Sabbaths were the occasions of from five to seven sermons a day, made possible by availing myself of rapid transit to reach distant points in the field. My wife, who was always a good Bible student, became a remarkably efficient Bible reader, and did effective work in holding meetings and explaining the Scriptures. Some most disgusting scenes were witnessed, caused by rum, but we had the opposite scenes to cheer us in our good work. Some of the happiest Christians we ever knew were aged people in the city hospitals and Home for the Friendless; souls who were chastened by adversity, whose only happiness comes from simple, hearty trust in the divine promises, realizing that Godliness is profitable unto all things, and that Godliness with contentment is great gain.

At a meeting in one of the city hospitals two adults came forward in the midst of my sermon, uninvited, and knelt at the altar and were gloriously converted while I continued to preach. At Mears' chapel a German Catholic girl was converted while Mrs. Fisher was leading the meeting.

In the fall of 1877 I was solicited to take charge of the First M. E. Church in Omaha, Nebraska. The society had been rent by dissensions so that a large number of the members and one-third of the Sabbath school had withdrawn to establish a rival church. The old charge had an unfinished building and a bonded debt, with an accumulated interest of forty-seven thousand dollars due. The bishops had advised the society to give up the property and disband. They were depressed and poor but promised, through the presiding elder, Rev. H. T. Davis, that if I would accept the pastoral charge they would give me a salary of fifteen hundred dollars. I was receiving from the Woman's Home Missionary Society $1,800 per annum, and the day I resigned to accept the Omaha charge, three elect ladies, Mrs. Clark, Mrs. Simpkins and Mrs. Whetstone, all officers of the society, offered to add a hundred dollars apiece, making my salary $2,100, if I would remain superintendent of the mission work. But the distress at Omaha appealed with peculiar force and I resigned, and really lost in salary $800 the first year, going out "not knowing whither I went." I had heard the call and believed it to be of God and responded to it.

CHAPTER XXIX.

WEST AGAIN.

My removal was without incident of interest and my arrival a disappointment, in that the presiding elder, whom we expected would remain and by his presence, counsel and prayers be of great advantage to us, had summarily and unexpectedly removed to Lincoln. We were met at the depot by a committee of reception who were looking for a sleek, kid-gloved, city preacher and overlooked me until I had taken a seat in the bus for the hotel. Brother W., one of the committee, a lawyer, concluded that they had invited the wrong man. But when the Sabbath was over he related the joke on himself and said: "We made no mistake; you will do."

In a short time we succeeded in satisfying the creditors and liquidating the bonded debt by giving up all the church property. We sold out, "pole, hook and line," preached a farewell sermon to the old church and the old trustees, moved out of the building into a rented hall, and struck for liberty and a new church.

With judicious changes and readjustment in the composition of the official board and board of trustees we secured more adaptability and efficiency of service. The only remaining church prowess that was left was a modicum of spirituality retained by a few members. There was a band of noble-spirited women who were ready for every good work, whose aid was invoked, utilized and became potent for good under the leadership of the pastor's wife in visiting the sick, the erring, the poor and the neglected.

We popularized our service in the new hall, and with re-organized choir and unity restored began building from the foundation. We took steps to build a large, cheap, plain church for the masses. In taking a subscription a stranger arose and said if we would give him three months time he would give us twenty-five dollars. He did not know where it was to come from, as he had no employment; but, trusting in God, he would give that sum. We gladly received his subscription and commended him to the people. Two weeks afterward he came to the parsonage and said to me: "Dr. Fisher, I believe I promised to give twenty-five dollars to the new church in three months. I have called to pay it. When I subscribed I did not have employment, nor did I have any idea where it was to come from. But I prayed God to open my way. I found paying employment, and this morning I went to the post office and found a letter from a man in Indiana, who had owed me seventy dollars for more than eleven years? I had given up all hope of getting a cent from him, for I had heard no word from him for five years. In his letter he said: 'Ten or fifteen days ago I felt I ought to pay you, and as I am now prosperous and you have been so kind in waiting I here enclose a draft for the money I owe you with interest added, all amounting to nearly $100.' God put it into his heart to pay me. I want to pay the twenty-five dollars I subscribed and here is twenty-five dollars more I want to give as a thank-offering, and now I have nearly fifty dollars more than I ever expected from that source. I verily believe it all came because I trusted God to provide a way for me to pay my subscription."

He was happy in giving; so was I in receiving.

Through great labor and sacrifice we purchased a lot on Davenport street, between Seventeenth and Eighteenth streets, built a church and parsonage and had a superior Sabbath school and congregation. And before my pastorate ended we built a beautiful suburban church, also.

Engrossed as we were we yet found time to begin a crusade against the saloons, gambling hells and brothels, and with the aid of Col. Jameson and John B. Finch so aroused the city that the patronage of the saloons fell off to such an extent that the saloonists prayed the city council to refund a part of their licenses.

During my residence in Omaha a terrible calamity happened, by which five men lost their lives. The Grand Central hotel, costing $150,000, burned down through the carelessness of a drunken carpenter who was repairing the cupalo. The fire marshal, Charlie Hofner, was a saloonkeeper. When the fire broke out, notwithstanding his responsibility, he left his post of duty and went to his saloon and carried whisky by the jug-full and gave it to the firemen. Mayor Wilber ordered the saloon closed, but as they were near the fire where thousands gathered Hofner and others defied the officials. The firemen became frenzied with whisky, smoke and excitement, and five of them went down with the burning building and lost their lives.

There had been sent from our city a valuable young woman as a Christian nurse, to the yellow fever stricken south. She had died a martyr to her devotion to the sick. This, with the great fire, and the loss of those five valuable lives, produced a profound sensation.

I seized upon it as a fit season to preach upon the causes of the yellow fever in the south and the "Burning of the Grand Central." Our doctor son was serving as a volunteer physician in the epidemic at Chattanooga and we were deeply interested in the South's affliction. I took bold ground, and charged the local disaster to the besotted condition of the community where a saloonkeeper could be entrusted with the marshalship of the fire department. "And," said I, "a city whose fire marshal was guilty of such conduct when such immense responsibility rested upon him, who would carry whisky to men who would drink while on duty with such a fire raging, could expect nothing less than the destruction of life and property and no man's life or property is safe under such a condition of affairs."

This raised a cry of rage among the drinking class. The whole city was in a ferment. Some censured, others praised me. The city council removed Hofner and elected a Mr. Gallagher to his place, and the department elected J. W. Nichols, one of my stewards, as president of the Consolidated Fire Companies and elected four others of my best young men to important positions.

A few weeks later the department, by unanimous vote, requested me to preach a sermon to them, which I most cheerfully did, the mayor, city council and almost the entire fire department being present in a vast audience. My text was the "Burning Bush" and its lessons.

The reform was complete, the memory of which liveth after many years, even to the present day. Banquets given by the firemen had formerly been occasions of more or less debauch and drunkenness. But this was changed. Intoxicants were tabooed and coffee took their place. A beautiful steam fire engine was bought in Boston, and on its arrival at Omaha there was a great parade and banquet at Creighton's hall. Mr. Craig, Omaha's greatest brewer, sent a note offering to supply the firemen and their friends with all the beer they could use. Mr. Iler, the great distiller, did the same. Both offers were politely declined, on the grounds of public interests and because the ladies had proffered to furnish choice coffee instead. Mayor Wilber informed me that a banquet held in North Omaha by the department, which was attended by the city council, the first to discard rum, was the most enjoyable ever held by the boys, many of whom said they did not know a banquet could be made a success without liquor; but that this was the best one they had ever held.

Here we had ample opportunity to discover the perverted and erroneous views of some professors of Christianity as to the scope of the duties of the church.

> "Rescue the perishing,
> Care for the dying,
> Snatch them in pity
> From death and the grave."

This is evidently a duty too long and too generally neglected by the church of Christ. For this He established His kingdom among men—that the lost might be found and sinners saved. A peculiar case presented in Omaha as an illustration.

A young man of fine musical ability, member of a popular club and of the Protestant Episcopal choir, the son of a local preacher in Iowa, though maintaining the appearance of respectability, had yet been leading an abandoned life. He finally married a woman of like morals, took boarding with a very respectable family, who were charitable, and did all they could to help these young people to a better life. The sickness of their hostess, however, necessitated her removal to another state for medical treatment. Thus the couple were compelled to seek another boarding place. They were denied entertainment in homes and boarding houses where before marriage the young man, though known to be a debauchee, had been a welcome and popular visitor. It looked as if his effort to reform was doomed to failure, and that he and his wife would be driven to live and associate with the very class from whom they were seeking to escape. Appeals were made at the parsonage for the sheltering wing of Christian sympathy to cover them from the storm of persecution. After exhausting every expedient to find a home for them, without success, my wife resolved, rather than have them go back to associations which promised ruin, to take them to her own fireside. Some of the officials of the church said if we took that couple into the parsonage we might as well shut up the church, for the people would not approve it.

To this my wife replied, "If the church has not religion enough to countenance an effort to save sinners my husband will find a pulpit at the corner of a street and seek to save the children of Christian families."

She took the couple in. The church was not closed for want of hearers—it was too small to accommodate the crowd. The Lord helped us. The couple remained several months, and then, by my wife's aid, set up housekeeping for themselves, living happily together, saved from a life of shame.

Our new church was dedicated by Mrs. Van Cott, who had many friends in Omaha. Subsequently we were visited by Bishops Andrews, Merrill and Gilbert Haven, who was an old-time friend. He, his son and daughter visited us as guests at the parsonage. All these bishops knew of the very embarrassing conditions under which Methodism had been laboring in Omaha for years previous, and when they witnessed the changed condition of the society their surprise was unbounded.

Bishop Haven said to the congregation, "It is marvelous indeed!" and to me, "Where did you get all this? We have kown of the state of things in Omaha for years before you came. Some said Methodism was dead there and ought to be buried. But when I learned you had gone to Omaha I told my friends 'that means resurrection,' and so it did." The Bishop preached for us, and told the congregation that the bishops had regarded the case as practically hopeless and it was the man from Kansas who in the economy of grace had brought them resurrection.

Bishop Merrill also preached for us on his way to Utah to hold their conference, and as they needed a man for Salt Lake City church and as my time in Omaha was up, he requested me to try the grip of my faith on that difficult field.

CHAPTER XXX.

PASTORAL EXPERIENCES IN SALT LAKE CITY.

My predecessor in the Utah work, Dr. McEldowney, was a splendid preacher, but had failed, as had others, to get a hold on the influences that go to make up a successful church in the land of so-called "Saints," especially lacking also a following among the ex-preachers, local and otherwise. The church, Sunday school and day school were at very low ebb and were disbanding.

Upon our arrival we were received in a most cordial manner with a public reception. The Sabbath school numbered twenty-six. The congregation had an average attendance of thirty-five. Prayer meeting, class meetings and day schools had been disbanded and the scholars of the latter enrolled in the Presbyterian and Congregational schools. The resuscitation of the day school, called Salt Lake Seminary, was vigorously opposed by the officers of the church, including the superintendent of the mission. A debt of over $1,500 was in court awaiting judgment and foreclosure. The school furniture was being sold to satisfy debts for janitorship and other expenses. The board of trustees were out of harmony with Dr. McCabe, who had so nobly stood by that enterprise for years and who was carrying a large debt incurred in the same interest.

The church cost $60,000 and was a beautiful one, but owing to the altitude (though the accoustic measurements were perfect) the echo was so great that it was very difficult to preach in it. Indeed, it was rendered almost useless. The Rev. C. C. Stratton, who built it could not preach in it at all. Dr. McCabe, Joseph Cook, Bishop Simpson and others who had tried to address vast audiences failed to be heard and appreciated because of the echo. My voice was strong and flexible, and as I had had early experience with the echo from a Virginia cliff opposite my boyhood home on the Ohio, with the skillful criticism of my wife I overcame the echo, so that I could soon be heard with ease. My congregations increased and ere long Sabbath school reached an average of ninety-nine for months in succession.

To help along the cause my wife, who had been a successful teacher in earlier life in Ohio and Pennsylvania, took up a day school, commencing with eight little children, and without patronage or encouragement from the officers of the church or mission-help held on until she had an enrollment of fifty-two with a regular attendance of fifty.

We found, however, that Bishop Merrill's fears were well-founded, that in church matters we would fail to command financial support sufficient to make needed repairs, and to warm the large auditorium in winter. We were literally driven by cold weather out of the beautiful auditorium into a rather uninviting basement lecture room, our congregation decreased, and this inaugurated defeat of our cherished plan.

We held on, however, and adopted an "art loan" by which to raise money to relieve the case in court. By this expedient and through Dr. McCabe's efficient help we were enabled to take the case out of court the day before judgment would have been rendered, thus saving the church from this disgrace and financial loss. Interested parties stood ready to buy and crowd a transfer of that beautiful and costly house of worship from Methodism to themselves.

We had good helpers in our Herculean task, but had to expend a great amount of toil to overcome influences which should have been with us for good. The lack of a parsonage justified us in occupying the spacious parlors of the church as a home. This still left ample room for school purposes, as the lower story afforded several well-lighted and large, well arranged, recitation room. Living in the church parlors, in such close proximity to the convenient school-rooms, my wife was enabled to give due attention to her domestic duties and church work, and in addition thereto organized an evening school for Chinamen. Over sixty "Heathen Chinee" availed themseves of the opportunity to learn to read. She had at one time a class in the Sabbath school of twenty-six Chinese boys. One of them, Lee Chung, was a Christian, and learned rapidly to sing and read the Bible. He bought an organ and afterwards taught the boys to sing.

Joe Fong, Charlie Hop, Joe Waugh, Fong Wong, and Sam Sing were among the most devoted and diligent to learn. But the pronunciation of words bothered them. The "R" is "L" with them. Robin-Red-Breast is "lobin-led-blest." Joe Fong, in trying this over and over and over, said, "Oh, Mrs. Fishee, too muchee wordee." They showed great interest in learning Scripture verses, and in learning to sing such hymns as "Sowing in the morning," and "There is a fountain filled with blood."

On the last visit I made to Salt Lake City I visited

the Chinese boys' class which had been organized by Mrs. Fisher, and which, upon her leaving Utah, had been taken in charge by a Miss Wakefield and removed to the Congregational church. To my surprise I there found Lee Chung, who was now able to play the organ and teach music. He had a large placard with the notes of the tune and Chinese characters representing the hymn they were singing, and to my great delight he led and the Chinese boys sang melodiously in their native language. Then they sang in English, and this was their song:

"There is a fountain filled with blood."

It was a matter of regret to me that the work so nobly begun by Mrs. Fisher should have to be turned from our Methodist school into other hands, for it was full of promise. The day school of white children had been turned over to the Missionary Society, and Prof. Theopholis Hilton was sent out to take charge of it. The Woman's Home Missionary Society, aided by local generosity, provided a home for the school, which has grown to be a considerable influence for good.

CHAPTER XXXI.

BIBLE WORK AMONG THE MORMONS.

Upon the earnest solicitation of Bishop Wiley I next became the superintendent of the American Bible Society's work for Utah, Idaho and Montana. My official board at Salt Lake gave me a six weeks' leave of absence, and I immediately repaired to Montana and organized the canvass of that vast region in Bible distribution. I was pastor of the Salt Lake Church and Bible superintendent at the same time. But soon after my return from Montana I was relieved of the pastorate to devote my entire time to the Bible work.

My first visit to the great North was by cars to Beaver Head and Red Rock, thence in a barbarous vehicle called a "jerkey" to Virginia City or Alder Gulch, where millions of gold had been found, thence to Bozeman, thence to Helena and Missoula and to Deer Lodge and Butte, holding public meetings and organizing county Bible Societies. I had no hope of organizing more than two, possibly three, auxiliaries in Utah, as there were but two centers of any considerable number of Gentiles and in these very few Christians.

I re-organized in Salt Lake City and made a new organization in Ogden. I also arranged with Rev. George E. Jayne, our Methodist missionary in Provo, to hold a Bible meeting in his mission chapel. When I visited him he told me he had not enough members to fill the offices of a small society, and if a collection was called for we could not raise more than from seven to ten dollars, and his family would have to give the half of that.

After full consultation I concluded to go to Springville, six miles away, to interest Rev. Leonard, a Presbyterian missionary, and get some of his members to act as officers of the proposed organization and join in collections to help procure Bibles to supply the distribution in that county. I had made it a rule in all my extended travels to try never to be left by the cars; but when Brother Jayne and I arrived at the depot the train was moving away grandly, nearly a mile on its way to Springville.

I said to Brother Jayne, "This is providential." To this he naively replied, "I don't see much providence in being left." But I had already and immediately formed my plans. "Who is president of the Mormon Stake, and where does he live?" I asked.

"Bishop Smoot; he lives in a large brick house on the second street North.

I told him I was going up to see the president and try to get the privilege of speaking to the Mormons in the Tabernacle on the Sabbath, and of inviting them to the Bible meeting in his church. I wanted him to go with me, but he scouted such an idea as ridiculous, saying just a few Sabbaths before they had denounced all missionaries as devils and interlopers, not to be tolerated but to be shunned and avoided.

Now it happened that this same Bishop Smoot was at one time, early in Kansas, a partner with Majors, Russell & Co., in an overland transportation company. Mr. Majors was a Presbyterian and secured Bibles to supply the many drivers of their numerous and immense trains so they could read at camping time and on Sabbath, as they made the tedious journey to California. Mr. Smoot, for convenience, located in Salt Lake City, went into partnership with Brigham Young in the distillery business, bringing grain from the interior of California to Salt Lake City, and selling the whisky they distilled to the emigrants, miners and Mormons. He joined the Mormon church, and Brigham endowed him with an installment of three wives with whom to begin housekeeping. He had acquired great wealth, influence and more wives. When I called upon him, upon my ringing the door-bell, "President Smoot" made his appearance at the door in half dress, for he was in the midst of his toilet. He very politely invited me into a spacious parlor, where three of his wives were helping him dress. One buttoned his collar, another adjusted his suspenders, while a third brought him a necktie and handed him his nicely polished shoes.

Meantime I had been seated, when he asked me in a very polite manner if he could serve me in any way. I handed him my commission, remarking that I was superintendent of the American Bible Society's work. He immediately replied, "I am glad you have come. Our people are greatly in need of Bibles. I know all about that society, and will gladly do all I can to aid you in your work. What can I do to help you?"

I made known my wish, and he said he was getting ready to go to Salt Lake City for the Sabbath, but for me to go to Bishop Jones who would make all arrangements necessary.

Those arrangements were soon perfected. I was invited to come to the Tabernacle at ten o'clock next morning, and assured that, notwithstanding there were to be two returned missionaries present to make their reports, I should have all the time I wished, as the Bishop would instruct them to make short reports.

When I returned and told Brother Jayne what the arrangement was he protested that they were insincere, and if I went to the Tabernacle would repudiate the arrangement and insult me publicly. I told him that I believed it the clearest indication of Providence that I had met for years.

Sabbath morning came, a calm, clear, bright day. I went at the time appointed to the Tabernacle. The people were gathering in troops from near and afar. As I came to the gate I was met by Bishop West, who requested me to follow him, as Bishop Jones had directed him to meet me and accompany me to the vestry, there to meet the bishops and officers of the church. I was ushered into the vestry with no little ceremony. Here I met twenty dignitaries of the church, great, pompous, fat old polygamists except one. They eyed me closely and seemed to take my measure. I felt—well didn't know quite how to feel. I was never in such presence before, but I passed my commission around, took my seat, and scrutinized the crowd. I was in strange company, but I was there for a purpose, and under divine leading.

The service opened with singing, followed with prayer and singing again. Bishop Jones, acting president of the Stake, presiding, announced that there were two returned missionaries present who would make short addresses and reports and come next Sabbath and finish their reports, as Rev. Dr. Fisher, superintendent of the American Bible Society, was present and would address the people at length, and he wished him to have all the time he desired as he wanted them all to have the great pleasure of hearing him.

The missionaries gave a running account of their travels, labors and persecutions, and dwelt especially on Joseph Smith's being a prophet and a martyr, and on polygamy as a divine institution and a chief element of religion, exhorting them all to go into polygamy and to live their religion. I won't attempt to describe my feelings as I sat in the pulpit and heard all this, and witnessed how the people drank in every word. I was indescribably disgusted.

Finally I was introduced. The house was crowded. Every eye was fixed upon me. Every ear was intent to hear. Such a spectacle had never been witnessed by these people. A Methodist preacher occupying the pulpit of the Mormon Tabernacle in Provo!

I commenced by stating to the audience that I had been introduced as the superintendent of the American Bible Society, and I supposed they wished to know what that society was and what it proposed to do. "It is non-sectarian and non-political. It is composed of representative men from all denominations. Christian men and women and churches give of their money by thousands of dollars to print the Bible—not for the Presbyterians, Methodists or Baptists alone, but for everybody to read. It is printed in all languages, and many Bibles are printed with parallel columns, so that German parents can read it in their own language while their children can read the same truth from the same page in the English language. It is the Bible for North and for South, for East and for West, and for the whole wide world."

I had remarkable liberty in speaking, and as I described how my mother, who was long since in heaven, taught me to read the Bible, the adults were carried back to home and mother and Bible, long before they had learned of "Joe Smith" and the Book of

Mormon, and they wept like children. Aged elders, who had been Mormons for years, told me they had never seen such heart-felt emotion in the Mormon church.

I attended a number of their ward Sunday schools and addressed them on the necessity of the Bible in the Sunday school. As the hour drew near for the Bible meeting in the Methodist mission chapel Brother Jayne felt that there would be but few in attendance, and no Mormons, but I told him all the chairs from his house and study had better be brought in. He laughed at my confidence, but when the hour arrived the people arrived also and filled the house to overflow.

Bishops, elders and people came. Two Mormon bishops made addresses. Rev. Jayne and myself also made addresses, and then organized a county Bible Society. We elected a Mormon, Bishop Haygood, president, and the Methodist Missionary corresponding secretary. We took a collection amounting to sixty dollars, and the next morning the president gave his check for forty dollars. We sent one hundred dollars to the Bible house at New York, and requested a donation of one hundred dollars worth of Bibles, which was granted, and soon we received two hundred dollars worth.

When they came I was sent for and went to Provo, where we held a mass meeting in the Tabernacle. President Smoot presided, Rev. Mr. Smith, a Methodist preacher, offered prayer, and made a speech. Professor Measure, president of Brigham Young College, also made a speech and said: "All the religion I ever had or ever knew I learned out of the Bible, long before I ever heard there was a Mormon church on earth." Rev. Jayne made an address from the same pulpit with President Smoot and so did I. It was a wonder to all the people that their bishops, who had recently from the same pulpit denounced all preachers as impostors, hypocrites and devils, should join with us in this work. The Bible was distributed broadcast, and read by these crude people with great delight.

The proceedings of these meetings were written up by Brother Jayne and sent to the official papers of the church, and to gentile organs in the territory. As a result my way was open to every Mormon pulpit in the territory, even the great Salt Lake Tabernacle, where I addressed more than a thousand Mormon priests at once.

My next meeting was held in Logan, in the Presbyterian Mission Church. Rev. Mr. Park was missionary. Bishop Preston was president of the "Stake." The temple for Cache Valley was in process of erection. When I called upon the president to arrange for a meeting in his tabernacle he asked about my plan of organization. I told him I wished to address his people in the tabernacle, as I had done in the tabernacle at Provo, and in the evening hold a union meeting in Mr. Park's mission church and organize a board of Presbyterians, Mormons and others.

He replied that it looked very much as if I wanted to get them "mixed up."

"Well," said I, "You Latter Day Saints are going to heaven, and as we Gentiles want to go there too I thought it would be well to get acquainted beforehand."

He laughed very heartily over the idea of gentiles getting to heaven, both he and his bishop thought well of the suggestion and arranged for a meeting next day.

Brother Park, like Brother Jayne, was unbelieving, and reluctantly accompanied me to the tabernacle and, to his astonishment, was invited into the pulpit with me, where I had the unusual liberty of addressing the vast congregation.

I then visited the Episcopal Sabbath school and all of the Mormon Sabbath schools, and in the evening held a Bible meeting, organizing a county Bible Society, as at Provo. The board was composed of Presbyterians, Mormons, Episcopalians, and one outsider. The work in Cache Valley was carried forward by Mr. Fredrickson, in a remarkably successful manner, until the whole valley was supplied with the Bible.

Very soon after my visit to Logan I visited Ogden and held a great meeting in the tabernacle, presided over by Bishop Perrie, president of the Ogden Stake. The large, old-fashioned pulpit contained about a dozen of the dignitaries of the church. Here I had my usual liberty of speech. I was portraying the excellencies and superiority of the Bible as the divine revelation, incomparable in its adaptation to the wants of men, and said: "When Wycliff translated the Holy Bible into the English language and gave it to the common people it was as if he had lifted the roofs off their houses and let the sunlight of heaven in upon them. It had lifted them up into a higher civilization and given them the leadership in intelligence and literature for the whole race of mankind. The queen had sent a beautiful copy of the Bible to a foreign prince, with this expressive and truthful message, through the minister: 'Tell your prince this is the cause of England's great prosperity.' And when Luther translated the Bible into the German language he liberated the German people from the Roman yoke, broke the temporal power of the pope, and not only made Germany free but raised her to a place in the front rank of the influential and educational nations; and that Bible will live and triumph while the world remains!"

At the close of my address several of the bishops spoke in very approving terms of my discourse. Then, before we left the pulpit, President Perrie said, "Dr. Fisher, if you will allow me, I want to say I most heartily approve of all your statements about the excellency of the Bible and what it has accomplished; but as you are going into Idaho and Montana I want to suggest that if there are Papists in your audiences they won't want your Bible if it uproots Romanism and destroys the temporal power of the pope." I thanked him for his suggestion of caution.

Bishop Balentine, who was the county superintendent of the Mormon Sabbath schools, invited me to dine with him. Bishop Perrie urged me to go, saying, "Balentine is a good liver; and, besides, he will take you to all the Sunday schools and you can address them after dinner."

I consented, and on the way home the bishop took me by the arm and said very confidentially, "I tell you, Dr. Perrie is sharp. He don't care a great deal about the Papists, but I'll tell you what he thought; that if your Bible liberated England and Germany from the Roman Catholic Church and from the power of the pope it will liberate the Mormons from Joe Smith and Brigham Young. That's what he was afraid of. Oh," said he, "Perrie is sharp." And he laughed as he added, "But you and your Bible got away with him."

I was soon ushered into a large room, where we met some half dozen Mormon women who seemed pleased at my coming, and I was introduced to them in their given names (as is customary)—to Sisters Jane, Catharine, Mary, etc., etc. These proved to be the Bishop's wives.

Dinner over we were seated in the large parlor, when the bishop, addressing me, said: "Now, Doctor, I have a question to ask, and I wish you to answer it, will you?"

I replied that it might be a question that it would not be proper for me to answer.

"Well," said he, "I want you to answer it. I want no dodging. It is about the way I am living."

I replied that I did not know how he was living, and besides, it would be very impolite, after partaking of his hospitality, to in any wise criticise his way of living in his own house.

"Oh," said he, in great glee, "you can't get off that way, though you are a Yankee. I am one of those who are practicing polygamy."

"Well," said I, "I won't answer you in the presence of these your wives, but if I should answer I would say, 'I think you are living in a rascally way!'"

He clapped his hands and said, "You are a Yankee, sure enough. That will do," while the women chimed in and said: "We think you are right, Doctor. It is a rascally way, and none but Mormons and rascals live this way; we are ashamed and tired of it."

The old bishop laughed and rejoined, "But it is the order of the church and I must obey."

Soon the sleigh was announced and away we went, from ward to ward. As soon as we arrived all exercises in the Sunday schools ceased, and I was immediately introduced and addressed the schools, composed of old, middle aged and young.

Thus we visited and I addressed seven different

schools and societies. In the evening I also addressed a great company of young men and women in a large ward meeting house—a union meeting of the Young Peoples' Improvement Society. It was a day full of labor and interest. The old bishop rendered valuable service, by which I was enabled to make eight Bible discourses to as many different congregations. And on Monday night, by invitation, I delivered another address to a large audience.

My next visit was to Brigham City. Here Lorenzo Snow, an apostle, brother of Erastus Snow, another apostle, was president of the Stake, and his son was first counselor. I stopped with Bishop E., who had five wives living in town—three in the house in which I stopped. The old wife he had brought from England. She was very rebellious and "ruler of the ranch." To the wife living in the north end of the house the old wife would not speak. To the young wife up stairs she was kind and showed some favor; to the two in the other part of the town, who brought butter, eggs and produce she was also kind. They all took sacrament together at the hands of the Bishop, but the old wife would not eat at the table with him nor sit in the same room with him. She told me that she had procured a revolver and put it under her pillow and would kill him if he came into her room. I stopped with them several days but never knew of the bishop speaking to his old "first wife."

At my next visit I stopped with Bishop Z's family. He had four wives in a large stone house, and about thirty children. I boarded at the home of the youngest wife. Though the youngest she had nine children. The old bishop was at home while I was there, though he had other wives scattered around, some in and others out of town. This youngest wife told me with heart-rending sobs and tears that Brigham Young and the apostles came up to Brigham City and collected all the girls from fourteen years upward who were not married and discoursed about the beauties and rewards of polygamy, and finally told them it was the order of the church that they should marry the bishops and elders and raise up a generation of saints, and that all who were married at the next Christmas should be "blood atoned." She said she was born in Utah, of Mormon parents and knew her fate, and only knew to obey; and, to save her soul, she had been compelled to go into this degrading kind of life.

"Now," said she, "what can I do? Here am I, the mother of nine children. Where could I find a home? What am I to do? I have often thought of suicide, and were it not that I fear I should be lost I would have taken my life long ago. I would rather see every child I have dead and buried than that one of them should be compelled to lead such a life as I have lead."

And then, while the hot tears dropped upon the face of her babe, she said, in accents of despair, "I suppose I will have to endure this hell upon earth until death comes to my rescue."

Poor creature! She was only one of thousands who are the victims of men's lusts, held in bondage in the the sacred name of religion.

I organized here a county Bible society, and George Bretherton, a colporteur, supplied that part of the field with Bibles.

On my return to Salt Lake City I visited John Taylor, president, Seer and Prophet of the church. He received me kindly, and as I gave him my commission he said.

"I know where you have been and what you have been doing, and I most heartily approve your plans and work and your way of doing the work committed to your care among my people. I know that the Bible is the only book given of God to guide us in our duties in this life.

And, picking up a well-worn copy of the Scriptures from his desk, he said, "This book has been my companion for years. I carried it all through Germany, France and England, and have found that the Germans regard Luther as their great political advocate and leader as well as reformer, by reason of his translation and distribution of the Bible among the common people in their own language."

He gave me a letter addressed to Agnus Cannon, brother of George Q. Cannon, who was president of the Salt Lake Stake, directing him to arrange that I should hold a county Bible meeting in the great tabernacle in Salt Lake City.

Accordingly, I soon held a meeting there, in which I met more than a thousand of the priesthood of the Mormon church, addressing them and completing an organization, the only organization effected in fifty years among the Mormon priesthood outside their own plan and control.

I was, and am still the only gentile ever admitted to a purely Mormon priesthood meeting.

At the close of this meeting President Cannon endorsed on Mr. Taylor's letter the following address:

"To all the presidents of Stakes, Bishops, High Priests of the Order of Melchisedeck and of Aaron, and all Bishops and Elders and Priests of the church of Jesus Christ of Latter Day Saints, greeting:

"Whereas, John Taylor, president, Seer and Revelator, has given authorization to Dr. H. D. Fisher, bearer of these presents, to hold Bible meetings in the churches in Utah,

"Therefore, It is ordered and directed that every facility be afforded Dr. Fisher in the execution of his work, for the supplying of the people of said church with Holy Bibles."

This address and proclamation was so like that of Darius, on account of the deliverance of Daniel, that I felt truly that God was in this work.

Soon after this I made a trip to Southern Utah. Mr. Fredrickson and my son Frank accompanied us, as colporteurs, with a Bible wagon carrying supplies. A portion of the party consisted of Rev. E. Smith and wife, Miss Ida Bardwell, Miss Couch, Prof. Hilton and Rev. Mr. Court. These were missionaries and teachers. We traveled by wagon, holding meetings as we went.

Arriving at St. George, the most Southern settlement in Utah, we stopped at the Presbyterian Mission home, where a brother of Rev. Court was in charge. Here is the first Mormon temple erected in Utah, "a thing of great beauty," but, being gentiles, we were not permitted to desecrate it with unholy feet. We were permitted, however, to hold meetings both morning and evening in a magnificent tabernacle.

St. George is a perfect oasis in the desert, a town of over four thousand inhabitants, with soil and climate producing tropical fruits in abundance. Many of the older people are New Englanders, sent by Brigham Young to this extreme Southern corner of Utah to build a town and temple, both of which they accomplished, many Mormons traveling hundreds of miles to pass through the endowment house in the temple.

Bishop McCallister, formerly a Methodist, brought up in Philadelphia, by a pious mother, who was a member of the old Ebenezer Church, was president of St. George Stake. He welcomed us royally and wept freely as we carried him and his people in recollection back to childhood associations, mother, home and the Bible. He evidently still retained high regard for his early training and many of those grand sentiments instilled into his mind in childhood by his faithful, pious mother. I preached in the morning and my party were invited into the choir.

In the evening we had a most remarkable meeting. Bishop McCallister presided. My party led the singing. Prof. Hilton and I made Bible addresses, followed by the bishop, who eulogized the Bible in the strongest language, as God's Word and Will, superior to all other books in all the world.

Then he proposed to the congregation that all who wished to express thanks to Dr. Fisher and his companions for their visit and services, and a request for their return when convenient, should hold up their right hands. A sea of hands went up. Then he called for their left hands. Up, up, they went, a forest of them; while the shimmering, glancing light of the great central chandelier shown down upon them, presenting a phantastic scene. Then he called again. "All who want to thank Dr. Fisher heartily, keep hands up and rise to your feet!" The whole assembly with uplifted hands arose to their feet, and stood as if thrilled with delight.

"Thank God," we cried, while hearty "Amens!" went up, all over the house. Our party was fairly carried away with pleasure and the whole audience joined us in singing, "Praise God from whom all blessings flow."

I organized a Bible Society on Monday with Rev.

Brother Court, corresponding secretary, and we left St. George for the scene of one of the most atrocious massacres on record—the Mountain meadows—where one hundred and seventeen innocent, inoffensive and defenceless emigrants, were slaughtered by the Mormons and their allies, the Mormon Indians, under the leadership of John D. Lee and by sanction of the High Council of the Mormon Church and Brigham Young. The journey was a hard day's drive, and about nine o'clock P. M. we reached Pinto, a small town about five miles from the meadows. Here we were to spend the night, and finding a boy guide made our way to the Bishop's ranch in the corner of the town. Seeing the Mormon church lighted, we inquired what was going on in the church, and were informed that they were having a dance in honor of the visit of a very old saint, who had come to see the church and his friends.

My plans were immediately formed, and, leaving Brother Smith and others to care for the teams and prepare for the night's rest Prof. Hilton, Miss Bardwell and myself repaired to the church to capture the dance and convert it into a Bible meeting. It was after ten o'clock when we arrived. The seats were piled up in the yard, the fiddler was playing his best tune, and the bishop and people were dancing with great zeal. Dancing is great sport with the Mormons and a favorite means of grace. I sent the boy to ask the bishop out. He came to the door when I made myself and party known, as well as the object of our visit. We were invited inside, and the Bishop said to me:

"When this set is done I will introduce you, and you can address the people concerning your plans for supplying them with Bibles."

We went in. I had never seen a dance before. They were hopping around and "swinging the circle," while the violin squeaked and squealed like mad. I had no knowledge of dance phrases, and had never before seen a "set"; but the dancers looked like a "set," and they acted like a "set." By and by the music ceased, and the "set," steaming hot, and covered with perspiration, came to a standstill and vacantly gazed at the intruders. The Bishop had the company seated around by the walls, and introduced me and my mission.

I made a Bible speech, to which the panting company listened with attention. Then I introduced Prof. Hilton, who made a finished address, the best he delivered on our trip. Afterwards I introduced Miss Bardwell as a fine singer and performer on the organ, saying if they desired it, she would favor us with a song and some music. I asked them to vote their request. Up went the right hand of every one and Miss Bardwell sang grandly, "The Musician and his Lyre."

At half-past-eleven P. M., after capturing a Mormon dance and turning it into a Bible meeting, we retired in good order and the dance went on until the "wee hours of the morn." It was a remarkable achievement and grandly opened the way for our colporteurs, Fredrickson and Frank Fisher.

The next morning over we pushed on to the Meadows, a beautiful, sequestered and romantic spot. Here is the famous spring where the emigrants were getting water when attacked and when they first discovered their perilous condition. Yonder are the ridges covered with low, scraggy cedar and burr-oak trees, furnishing ambush for the treacherous Mormons and the few Indians who joined the murderers for plunder. Here is the great "carne" or grave in which were deposited by Conner's soldiers the scattered remains of the massacred men, women and children of the doomed party. Near by is a clump of bushes, gnarled and bullet-marked, behind which John D. Lee, in fiendish manner, shot with his own hand the young women whose rejection to become his concubines had incensed him and nerved him for the bloody work, though his son-in-law begged for their lives. And now we stand on the identical spot where Lee met his just deserts, under sentence of Judge Bozeman, he having been here shot to death by United States soldiers as he sat on his coffin.

It is a solemn, lonely spot, just where as the men were filing out of camp as prisoners they were mercilessly killed by Lee's orders in the presence of their wives and children, who likewise were afterward brutally shot down. The stone column built by Gen. Conner's order to mark the burial place of the dead had been destroyed by the Mormons, the rock hauled away and scattered, and we gathered up as much as we could of the stones and replaced them upon the "carne."

Having fully explored the Meadows and visited the spring we turned our faces toward Cedar City. Here we visited the Mormon church in which the decision for the massacre was reached, after the deluded people had held a meeting for plan and consultation before going to the slaughter. We visited the "Tithing House," where the clothing of the victims, reeking with their blood, was passed into the custody of the church authorities and from which they were distributed to the participants of this bloody work, according to the part each played. We met here some one who had been active in this fearful and yet unrequited drama. Here we met John Taylor and the Mormon apostles, on their annual visit to the stakes, and heard their lamentation about Joseph Smith and Brigham Young and their fate as martyrs, on account of spiritual wifery or polygamy.

The journey was a surprise and revelation; the colporteurs were enabled to supply the whole populace with Bibles, so that we had the field fully supplied before the "Edmunds Bill" took effect in the territory. It was most providential, for there never was before nor has there been since an opportunity to put God's word, without note or comment, into the hands of that deluded mass of people.

"God is His own interpreter, and he shall make it plain, vindicating His own truth and word. It shall not return to Him void."

CHAPTER XXXII.

BIBLE WORK IN MONTANA.

Our work in Montana was entered upon immediately after returning from Southern Utah. My son Frank and Mr. Fredrickson were commissioned and outfitted for the trip and work with two good horses, a well-arranged Bible-wagon, provisions, cooking utensils and an ample supply of Bibles. Traveling North they supplied the field as they went, as far as they could reach the ranches and settlements. I had ordered a number of cases of Bibles sent to the terminal of the Utah Northern Railroad at Dillon. When they reached Camas Valley I passed them, going to Dillon to prepare the field and in person supervise the supply of this vast territory.

Arriving at Dillon I repaired to the depot to learn if the Bibles had reached that point. My life-long habit has been to reprove profanity, and I have met but with two instances of rudeness or rebuff. Here the teamsters from far and near, with the trainmen and depot hands, were swearing as only that class of men in the wild West can swear. In this case I thought that if I should reprove them they would probably but swear the more, so I retired to await the coming of my colporteurs. Next day they arrived, and I obtained the privilege from Mr. Beebe, the depot master, to open our cases in the depot in order to fill up our depleted boxes in the wagon and condense the residue for shipment to different points, so that we might stock up on reaching those needy places. The men were still very profane. When we opened our boxes they drew near to see what we had. One fellow asked if we had any song books. Another inquired if we carried Bob Ingersoll's lectures. I replied that we were not allowed to carry anything but Bibles and Testaments. Another said he did not believe we could sell Bibles and Testaments in Montana; that if we had flasks of whiskey we could easily sell them all out. I replied that we believed the people would buy and read the Bible.

In the meanwhile a young man had picked up a copy of a "Brevier" Bible, and was quietly turning the leaves, when I noticed his lip quiver and his eyes moisten, and with an effort to suppress his emotion, he said, in a trembling voice, "I declare, if that ain't the very kind of a book my mother taught me to read out of when I was a little boy."

His words had a thrilling effect. We stayed there a day and a half and did not hear another oath. The thought of mother, home and Bible touched the hearts of those hardy, rough mountaineers, and turned away their profanity. I gave out a number of copies to the men before leaving.

On returning some months later Mr. Beebe told me that he never knew such a change among men. Instead of profanity and vulgarity, now when the men have leisure they read and talk about the Bible. I went unexpectedly to the depot, and there were three of the men sitting quietly reading God's Holy Word. One of them afterward ordered a beautiful copy and sent it over two hundred miles as a Christmas present to his father, saying, "It's the best book I ever read."

Subsequently Dr. McMillen, district superintendent

of the Presbyterian missionary work, included in my field of Bible labor, and I were together at McCannon, on the Oregon Short Line railway, awaiting a train to take us to Paris, Utah, in the interest of the missions and the Bible Society. After dinner, while sitting in the public room of the hotel, we were annoyed by the profanity of a party of men who were in the room. I called their attention to their language when one of the party attempted to provoke a laugh, to turn the point of my reproof. But I interrupted him.

"Gentlemen," said I, "let me tell you my experience recently at Dillon."

Then I related the foregoing incident. As I did so every ear was attent to hear, and as I described the young man's quivering lip, his moistened eye and subdued and trembling tone of voice a hush came over the company, like the awakening of conscience, and again at the thought of mother, home and Bible, eyes were suffused with tears. After a pause of but a brief moment one spoke up and said:

"Well, it is wrong to swear, and I would not have my mother know I swore for anything in the world. It would break her heart. I won't swear any more." They all joined in admitting that it was wrong to swear. Dr. McMillen often referred to the incident with great commendation and pleasure.

Our journey to Paris, and visit to the bishop, our Sabbath services, with our journey over the mountain range, a night in the Mormon camp, where they were sawing timber for the great temple at Logan, and my sermon to the Mormons in the mountain fastnesses, were all of intensest interest but must not be detailed here. Pages would hardly suffice to describe them.

Subsequently we reached the city of Butte, spending a Sabbath in this great mining camp, supplying the families and holding public services in the churches. On Sabbath afternoon at four o'clock I preached at the corner of Main and Fifth streets, the principal business streets, to a large crowd of miners and citizens. Mr. Fredrickson, my son Frank, and a number of Christians sang and the men came out of the saloons, faro banks, and other gambling dens by the hundreds, and crowded up about the corner until fully seven hundred people gazed at the singers and the speaker. We sang "Come thou fount of every blessing," many in the audience joining in this old and everywhere familiar hymn. A short prayer was offered and then "Hold the fort, for I am coming, Jesus signals still!" was sung.

At its closing line I glided very readily into an explanation of the origin of the patriotic song, then the parody by Mr. Bliss, and his sad and tragic end, and the hymn which was now so popular and its very appropriate use on this occasion, and announced my text, "A good name is rather to be chosen than great riches."

While I was preaching a drunken fellow came up near me and wanted to sing, insisting upon having my son's book to sing out of. Several in the crowd called out, "Arrest that fellow. He is disturbing the preacher." A policeman was about to arrest him and lead him away when I turned and said to the crowd, "If nobody wants that man arrested worse than I he won't be arrested." The officer stopped and I laid my hand on the man and said to him, "Be quiet, they want you arrested, but I want you to listen to me." He straightened up and stood as still as a man could, quietly and orderly.

From that moment the crowd were my friends. They listened with marked attention. In my discourse I referred to the value of the Bible as a safe rule of life and the source of prosperity, and related, as I had done to the Mormons, how, when Queen Victoria was young, a foreign prince sent his minister to inquire, "What was the cause of England's prosperity?" and how the queen in the presence of her lords gave the minister a beautiful copy of the Bible, saying, "Take this and give it to your prince, and tell him this is the cause of England's prosperity."

Just here a true son of the Emerald Isle piped out, "Be jabers, she had bether been after sending pertaties to the starvin' Irish."

This spontaneous sally of Irish wit caused an audible smile to encircle the entire congregation. But instead of reproof or attempted reply I pressed right on to convince my auditors that a good name is rather to be chosen than great riches, the Bible bringing spiritual and temporal prosperity. The crowd remained until the strange and impressive service closed. Scores came forward, shook hands with us, and thanked us for the songs and sermon. Some said it was the first sermon they had heard for years. One man said to me, "It is seventeen years since I heard the gospel preached."

Many other interesting incidents occurred in our work. At Blackfoot, Idaho, one of the colporteurs called at a store in which were a number of men. Opening his grip he began to show his Bibles. The men said they had no money, but maybe the man for whom they were herding sheep would buy one, as he was the only one in the crowd that had money

Mr. Fredrickson accosted him, whereupon the man replied, "If you have a book that has anything in it about sheep, I'll buy it." Quick as a flash Fredrickson turned to the 10th chapter of John and began reading: "I am the good shepherd, and know my sheep." Then turning to the first of the chapter and reading on, came to the 15th verse, when the crowd chimed in, "Buy it, buy it. That's just the book we need!"

The man took out his pocket book, paid the price and took the book, saying, "That's the book for me. I am going to read it after this." Before he left the company bought several other copies, and all of them were pleased that they had met the Bible man.

In 1883 we arranged a visit for the supply of Eastern Montana. There were two routes of travel open for us from Salt Lake City, our base of operations; one via Beaver Canon, Dillon, Virginia City, Bozeman and across the Eastern Divide at Mullen's Pass into the Yellow Stone Valley, thence South up the Yellow Stone river to Yankee Jim's, the farthest end of the valley, toward the far-famed Yellow Stone, or National Park, very appropriately named "Wonderland." Here we would have to double our track and retrace the usual trail or valley via Bozeman to Helena, thence to Fort Benton and Fort Assinaboine, on the Northwest Missouri river, and back to Helena, thence by way of Deer Lodge, Butte, Dillon and Red Rock to Beaver Canon, thus reaching the line of travel eastward to the Park. The other route was via Beaver Canon, thence due east one hundred and ten miles through an unbroken wilderness to the Firehole basin, thence through the National Park and out at the North side of the Park to Yankee Jim's Dugway, joining the valley at the Westerly traversed road, crossing the divide at Mullen's pass into the Gallatin Valley. This latter route we chose as giving us a shorter line of travel, the opportunity to visit the most noted geysers in the world, and as saving us from doubting our track, or retraveling the same road.

This field, in long centuries gone by, has doubtless been the field of the most powerful and active volcanoes on the whole globe. Here rivers of fire and volcanic lava, like molten iron, have been vomited forth until for hundreds of miles down the Snake River Valley the lava, in some places forty miles wide and fifty to one hundred feet deep, rolled in angry fiery waves, covering the whole valley through which the great Snake river runs.

Our party consisted of Mrs. Fisher, Messrs. Fredrickson and Foreman and myself, well outfitted with five horses, two wagons and complete camp equipage, and an ample supply of Bibles and provisions. We were out sixteen weeks and traveled over twenty-six hundred miles. When at Mammoth Hot Springs Dr. Foote, of Boston, and General Armstrong, of Carlisle, Pennsylvania, were with us at family prayer.

We were preaching frequently and singing on the journey, and distributing Bibles everywhere, only sleeping three nights in a habitable house. At Bozeman I preached at eleven A. M. in the Presbyterian church and at seven P. M. in the M. E. church. At four P. M. I held a service on the street corner in the principal part of the town. Quite a number of persons had gathered, when a man in great haste, followed by three physicians, came running by and the crowd followed them. We soon learned that Charlie V., who had been gambling as keeper of a faro bank all night and until Sabbath morning, had lost all he owned, and in a fit of desperation had taken poison and was dying in a disreputable house, surrounded by fallen women and debauched and drunken men and gamblers. Presently the crowd, greatly augmented in numbers, returned. We sang a hymn, and I preached a plain and searching sermon. We were surrounded on all sides by saloons and gambling houses, but the people listened with all possible attention. But to divert attention and defeat the impression made the managers of one saloon rushed around and organized some music. I closed my services in time to checkmate that, and the crowd was so indignant that instead of drawing the men to the saloon it repelled them, and the saloonkeepers felt the rebuke.

At the close of the services a very pleasant looking young man from New York came to me and said, "When I left my home and mother I had a good name and recommendations from my Sunday school superintendent, pastor and business men. I came here an innocent and pure young man but drifted into the saloon, gambling hell and other disreputable places. I soon lost my position, my good name and conscious innocence and am ruined. What can I do to recover myself and former good standing? Oh, if I were only back with my mother again!"

I advised him to go to his former employer, confess, ask his forgiveness and seek reinstatement that he might recover himself and raise enough money to return to his home and mother, and never stray from the path of virtue again. He promised he would do so and next day followed my advice with success.

We completed our work here, and at an early day moved on to complete the work in other parts of our vast field and hasten South, as winter was approaching. We crossed the great mountain range between Montana and Idaho just three days before winter broke upon that vast, mountainous region, closing travel for six whole months, but not until we had furnished a vast territory with the blessed book of God.

This was truly foundation work. The people and missionaries gladly received us, and I felt that while it was the most laborious it was yet the most important work in my ministerial career.

CHAPTER XXXIII.

COMPLETION OF BIBLE WORK IN UTAH.

American Fork Canon is one of the celebrated canons of Central Utah. Here Rev. F. F. Day, a Presbyterian minister, was resident missionary. We arranged to hold Bible meetings in his mission church. The town contained about two thousand souls. All except about twenty were Mormons. I called upon Bishop Harrington, the ruling bishop, and several other leading Mormons and had but little trouble in interesting them in the work. After Bible addresses by myself, Rev. Day and some of the bishops, we proceeded to organize a county society.

Bishop McCary was elected president, Rev. Mr. Day corresponding secretary, and some one nominated Mrs. Bishop Harrington (the ruling bishop's wife) as vice-president. I put the motion and she was unanimously elected. The secretary innocently inquired the lady's first name. Then came the tug of war. The bishop had several wives. Some had voted for one; several others had voted for a different one, and others still for number two or three or another yet. Finally Bishop McCray suggested that they would give the old bishop away to the gentiles if they did not look out, and they had better agree that they had elected Sister Catharine Harrington, the fourth one. This cleared up the very laughable predicament of a too-much married bishop and of a promiscuous vote on a bishop's wife in Utah.

The "San Pete" Valley is one of the natural divisions of Utah, a very fertile and populous part of the territory, almost wholly settled by Scandinavians. Canute Peterson (commonly called King Canute) was president of the Stake, including the entire valley. Bishop Mabin, his first counselor, lived and presided at Manti, near the south end of the valley. Here they have cut the point of a mountain, built three terrace walls, containing over twenty-eight thousand cords of heavy mason work and graded up to the site of a beautiful temple, which looks from a distance as though it had grown right out of the end of that mountain.

When I visited Ephraim, the resident town of President Peterson, for the purpose of holding a Bible meeting it was late in the day of an autumn month. After an interview with the "king," he said: "You need give yourself no anxiety about a congregation; I will have all the people in the church by 7:30. I have my own method of calling them together. You be on time; we will meet you in the tabernacle if you are there."

I repaired to the tabernacle about fifteen minutes before the time, and to my surprise and delight found the place packed full. I was the only person in the house not a Mormon. I occupied the pulpit with this petty king and his bishops, made my Bible speech, read the constitution, and called for a vote on its adoption. In doing this by uplifted hands I called for the negative to show their hands. The king cried out, "Stop; we never take the negative side, for those who do not favor our measures are not worth minding." So we adopted the constitution unanimously and elected our officers in the same manner, Mr. Peterson making the nominations.

One other incident, small in itself, but far-reaching and vast in importance, occurred in the South part of the territory in Frisco, where the Horn silver mines are yearly putting out mililons of silver bullion. Here Rev. Brother Hedges had organized a small class and Sabbath school. I visted the place to hold a Bible meeting, and preached morning and evening to good congregations, also addressing the Sabbath school. I was requested to hold a temperance meeting on Monday evening, and to organize a society for the boys and girls.

When the hour of meeting came a large company of men and women, as well as young people, assembled in the school house to hear the temperance speech. At the close of my address I read a constitution which I had prepared for the Boys' society, together with the pledge, and invited those who wished to become members to come and enroll their names. Three boys about fifteen years old, one a saloonkeeper's son, walked up amid applause from the audience and boldly signed their names.

When they were seated the audience was startled by a tall, fine-looking man named Peter Franklin coming forward to enroll his name as a member. He had been a Mormon, but in going through the endowment house had become disgusted and apostatized. He was quite intelligent and very successful in money-making, but had become addicted to dram-drinking and would often spend hundreds of dollars on a single spree. His signing the pledge led many others to follow his example.

Next morning as he went to his work men said to him, "Pete, you can't keep that pledge." He replied, "You will see; I intend to stop right here and now." The men at the smelter wanted him to drink, but he declined. Then some of them said if he would not join them in a glass of beer they would not work with him. To this he replied, "I don't have to drink with you, and you don't have to work with me unless you choose to. I am not going to drink rum as long as I live." He joined Brother Hedge's class the next Sabbath. In less than six weeks he was happily converted, and became quite active as a temperance and Christain worker.

In the mining regions the rule generally prevails that all who work in the mines and smelters pay one dollar monthly to the hospital fund. This, in case of sickness, entitles them to admission, on certificate, to the hospital. It so happened that my friend Franklin became sick from the fumes of the smelter, and was compelled to enter the hospital at Salt Lake City, where he lived. After being under treatment for several weeks he became convalescent and so far recovered that he was permitted to visit friends whom he had known in the Fatherland, before they or he had become Mormons. He told them of his changed life and now happy experience as a Christian. Many of them wanted him to read the Bible and pray with them, which he did. Then they wanted him to meet them in some hall or public place and preach this better way to them. But he was only a probationer, with no authority to hold meetings; and besides, his membership was at Frisco. So he came to me for advice. Being superintendent of the American Bible Society's work I authorized him to take copies of the Bible and distribute them, at the same time explaining the Scriptures to his friends. He became an excellent Bible reader and soon returned for more Bibles, saying the people were urging him to preach to them. I told him I would get the privilege for him to speak to the people in the lecture room of the M. E. Church and secured the use of one of the parlors of the church.

His first audience consisted of about forty Scandinavians, mostly old acquaintances. I was present, and told the people that as a Bible agent I had authorized Brother Franklin to explain and expound the gospel to them. Thus he opened his mission. His health was restored, he left the mining camp, and under the direction of the church began to preach and was finally licensed and recommended for probation in the traveling connection in the M. E. Church.

Bishop Wiley took his recommendation from the mission to the Nebraska conference but forgot to present it. From there he went on to Beaver, Pennsylvania, to hold the Pittsburg conference (my home conference) and there presented the recommendation and Franklin was received and elected to Deacon's orders under the rule for missionaries. Bishop Warren, returning from California, stopped in Salt Lake City for the purpose of ordaining Brother Peter Franklin and Brother Gillihan.

The Bishop lectured on Saturday evening on "The Powers of a Sunbeam." This, with much service on the coast, and long travel, had worn on him, and, although I had just returned from a laborious trip in Montana he insisted that I should preach the eleven o'clock sermon, prior to Franklin's and Gillihan's ordination. What a strange coincident that he who was converted to a Christian life under my ministry, so strangely set to work under my authority, and so strangely received into my home conference, should be ordained after my unexpectedly preaching the sermon the bishop should have preached!

Being a good scholar in his native tongue and a man of fine address Franklin was a very effective speaker. He visited San Pete Valley and created quite a stir among his Swedish and Danish acquaintances and countrymen who were Mormons. The day of his arrival among them to hold a Methodist meeting two of their principal bishops were carried out of the streets of Ephraim in a state of beastly intoxication. Franklin did not fail to make the best use of this event and delivered a powerful discourse on "Righteousness, Temperance and Judgment to Come." King Canute forbade his people to attend the meeting of this apostate heretic, but the more he opposed and interdicted their attendance the more the people pressed to hear the joyful tidings of salvation. Scores were converted and joined the Methodist church and subsequently built a mission chapel.

My judgment from the first of my acquaintance in Utah was that mission work could be most effectively accomplished among the Scandinavians. So it was proven, and the conversion and call of Peter Franklin to the ministry proved to be the opening of this vast and promising department among the apostatizing Mormons. Franklin's efforts resulted in building the first Scandinavian church in Salt Lake City, the establishment of a school for their children, from which the work is growing rapidly. Other brethren entered into the doors opened by Brother Franklin, when he had been called to wider fields of activity and usefulness in Minnesota.

I received much efficient help in the Bible work from all the missionaries and teachers in the field. They looked upon the putting of the Bible in the homes and hands of the people, backed by Bible sermons as "foundation work" which must produce beneficial results, especially as the people had little else to read. I was very greatly aided in the complete supply of Utah by an active, devoted and self-sacrificing company of colporteurs, whose Christian spirit and example contrasted beautifully with the sordid, secular and sensual lives of the chief Mormons. So that the Bible and corresponding example made a sensible impression upon many who were in the thraldom of the Mormon faith and teaching. The leaven was put in the meal, and has been working gloriously.

If the introduction of my work was, as I believe, providential, and if we were divinely aided and directed in it, then the fact of our having so completely and thoroughly canvassed and supplied the entire territory before the Edmunds Bill passed is no less providential, significant and gratifying. For, be it remembered, that this work was completed by the time this bill became a law, and such was the attitude of the Mormons all over Utah toward the law and toward all churches and all Gentiles that every pulpit was closed against us, and every neighborhood barred against our colporteurs because they were Gentiles. But the work had been done and so thoroughly done that the board of managers of the American Bible Society have not thought it necessary to put workers in the field since we closed the canvass. To me it was among the most satisfactory fields of ministerial labor ever occupied.

CHAPTER XXXIV.

WONDERLAND.

It was in 1882 that I, as superintendent of the American Bible Society work in Utah, Idaho and Montana, planned the trip of supply to which I have already called attention, from Salt Lake through Idaho and into Eastern Montana. The route which we proposed to take followed the Utah and Northern railroad line to Beaver Canon, thence through an unbroken wilderness one hundred and ten miles to the Fire Hole Basin. This would give us an opportunity to thoroughly see Yellowstone Park, as we passed through it from west to east, and from south to north. Thence we expected to go to the great Yellowstone River Valley, cross the ridge or great Divide at Livingstone, come into the Gallatin Valley, and travel north to the British line, near Forts Benton and Assinaboine.

Having thoroughly outfitted with an exceptionally complete supply of camp necessities, my wife and I set out in company with two colporteurs on a journey of twenty-six hundred miles. We took with us two wagons and five head of horses, and carried a large supply of Bibles. From the day we left until the journey was ended we slept but three nights in a habitable house.

After we were once under way we staid not nor stopped until we reached Beaver Canon, from which point, after a brief respite, we plunged into the wilderness. The trail we followed was an unfrequented one, and boasted in the way of roadside habitations but a single hut on the river bank, constituting a sort of rendezvous for lost travelers and explorers.

At Little Snake River we partook of cheer with one Mr. Ray, who for fourteen years had maintained in that lonely spot a fishing and hunting camp. A little later we were in camp at Goose Lake, then, passing Henry's Lake, we camped again near Riverside, and at last we pitched our tents on the very rim of the Fire Hole Basin. We did not reach this last point of vantage without diligent labor, having had to double-team and climb a mountain of obsidian glass and volcanic output, almost four miles long from bottom to top.

When we had crossed the River of the Basin we came into full view of the Fire Hole itself. Almost we seemed precipitated into the heart of some vast manufacturing center with belching smoke-stacks, so numerous were the columns of steam rising in front of us. Ugly-mouthed craters yawned at us, tall, geyser-throats reared before us, wraith-like pillars of white steam towered above us. It was a burning, hissing magnificence.

We hastened down the ashy rim until we reached a point on the Fire Hole River—of water almost scalding hot, fresh from the geysers—within forty rods of the head waters of the Madison, one of the three tributaries combining to give impetus to that greatest of all rivers—the Mississippi. A little further, and we have entered the Park, "Wonderland," where are massed the most beautiful natural effects encompassed in any one spot upon the face of the earth.

In 1882 the Park was almost geographically square, containing one hundred square miles—sections taken off Idaho, Wyoming and Montana, and by congressional enactment, introduced by a Kansan, Senator Samuel C. Pomeroy, forever set apart as our National Park.

About midway from where we had entered the basin and the upper end of the Fire Hole we again crossed the river and climbed a very precipitous elevation, composed almost wholly of the output of the "Sheridan Geyser," and so reached a small plateau, euphoniously called the Devil's Half-Acre.

Up here we made our first visit at close range to a hot spring or boiling lake. The surface area of the one we examined first was about one-eighth of an acre. Above water as clear as crystal floated and gleamed in the dancing sunlight a beautiful cloud of pink vapor. The walls of the lake were curiously inwrought and of variegated color. Dense volumes of steam were continually rising from the surface, yet when these would break and clear away momentarily we could see into immense depths through the crystalline waters beneath. One strikingly beautiful feature of the scene were the finely finished formations on walls and shores, worn smooth as glass by the play of the waters, some as small as the pearls of a lady's necklace, others as large as oranges, and even as large as large melons, and all rich in colored light. Some were yellow, some were emerald green, some were as pink as the inner sides of shells, some as blue as a summer sky. And as they caught the sun's rays and held back those colors they saw fit to, and sent out others with many a refractory glint, the prismatic play was marvelously enchanting.

Taking up positions at various angles and looking down into the unfathomable depths, we could see into fair and graceful formations below the water, and felt that we were in eerie proximity to the water-nymphs and sub-marine fairies. A fairy sun was there, and by his side, in modest companionship, the moon sat in benign splendor. Stars specked the water and shone through the intensely clear liquid as from the other side of the world.

We had up to this moment been so wholly absorbed with the hot spring that we were oblivious to the nearness to us of the Sheridan geyser. When our attention had centered upon it we found it to be a gaping crater, thirty or forty feet, with irregular and broken sides, holding a disturbed body of water some fifteen feet below the surface of the plateau upon which we stood.

The water was in great agitation and our awe and wonderment changed to terror when the angry, hissing, seething volume rose suddenly as if it would overwhelm us. We fled, like Lot's wife, to a place of surer safety, while the whole column of water was lifted with a deafening roar high into the air. Detonations as of terrific cannonading accompanied the agitation, while the hiss and rush and roar of the geyser continued and the column of angry water rose ever higher, until it had reached the altidude of full an hundred and sixty feet. From it, poised in mid-air, floated off bubbles as large as barrels, shot through with the sunlight and showing every color of the rainbow, bursting as they floated further and sending back a shower of hot water. My wife's heroism paled before the sublime manifestation, the colporteurs were terrified, and I was overwhelmed with a sense of the divine omnipotence. I wept and shouted and laughed, thrilled with wonder and amazement.

Part of the great towering column of water fell back into the crater, and part rushed like another Niagara over the sides of the plateau into Fire Hole River.

The agitation kept up for fully fifteen minutes. When it had subsided we cautiously wended our way out of the field by way of the wagon tracks we discovered. The whole crest of the plateau was blistered with little geysers and openings out of which steam was issuing. It was in a state of some trepidation from this latest experience that we continued our way up the valley to the upper end of the field of wonders.

As we sat in our wagons awaiting directions from our guide, to our great delight we were greeted with a display of the powers and beauty of "Old Faithful." This magnificent geyser has well earned her name, for every sixty-five minutes, day in and night out, from year to year, so far as known, "Old Faithful" makes her report "All's Well" and emphasizes it with her incomparable display. She stands like a sentinel on an elevation on the west side of the river. She never asks for a vacation, and her waters gush forth as beautifully today as they have in all these years. Her crater is built up of a product siliceous and limey in character, corrugated and wondrously carved and inwrought by flowing of the water. Her throat is oval in shape and is four by six feet in diameter. Her position is on an irregular plateau thirty feet above the river drainage. The volume of dense hot water rises by the exploding force of the pent-up gas and steam to an altitude of one hundred and sixty feet, and sways back and forth like a sapling pine. The sparkling column showers back myriads of drops and bubbles, bright and glistening in the sunshine, like a multi-colored sky rocket. Rising by impulsion the column pushes away, jet after jet, higher and higher, and carries heavenward with it the astonished game.

We made our way to a little plateau near by and parking our wagons pitched tent in the midst of one of the most active groups of geysers in the field. Scarcely had we adjusted ourselves to our new surroundings when we heard the thrilling shout of the guide:

"The Bee Hive! The Bee Hive! The Bee Hive is going to show up!"

The Bee Hive is a universal favorite and comes in for a great meed of praise for its beauty where all is beautiful. The crater stands five feet or more above the plateau, is eight or nine feet at the base and six feet at the top, with a throat large enough to admit of the passage of an ordinary barrel. The opening is oblong in shape, beautifully finished and as smooth as porcelain. There is connected with this geyser an undergroud vent leading to a very small indicator, or geyser, some twenty feet away, out of which a volume of steam issues for fifteen minutes before the Bee Hive begins to play, this signal serving as a steam whistle to notify visitors that the entertainment is about to begin. The valley is immediately alive with excitement. Citizens from all the vicinity, soldiers from the military posts who were en route to meet General Phil. Sheridan, and tourists from all countries, came rushing to the scene. A great company stood in breathless expectancy.

The indicator ceased. The steam and gas from the crater began to rise. Then the volume of water rushed up and up, as straight as a telegraph pole and as compact as the stream from the nozzle of a fire engine. As dense as the body of a great pine tree the column rose to the height of one hundred feet and then spread out in a beautiful waving spray. So dense is the column of water, gas and steam that, standing close to the crater, I put out my hand until I almost touched the ascending column. Then seized by a wayward impulse I took off my hat and tossed it in. As quick as a flash, to the amusement of the company, up went the hat more than a hundred feet, whirling and swirling with the steam and gas, cutting fantastic freaks.

During the demonstration on the part of the Bee Hive we were also treated to an amusing incident as one of the exigencies of the treacherous ground on which we stood and sat. A soldier was sitting on the ground narrating war stories to a crowd of interested companions when he suddenly shot up in the air, slapped himself vigorously on the place he had been sitting upon and cried vociferously, "A geyser! A geyser!" So it was, too. He had been sitting on a small crater, which had surprised him by a hot attack from the rear.

The beauty and grandeur of this most chaste of all geysers was kept up for fully twenty minutes; and scarcely had the excitement died away attendant upon the Bee Hive's demonstration before another shout was raised—"The Splendid!"

We rushed over logs and stumps and rough places for about an eighth of a mile to witness the display of a triple stream thrown out of a geyser with a large throat but with a larynx so formed as to divide the water into three streams. Strangest of all is the intermittent impulse upon which this geyser plays. After an exhibition of five minutes it takes a five minutes' rest, then plays again for five minutes, then rests again, and then comes the final effort of activity. One stream, two feet in diameter, rises one hundred and sixty feet in a perpendicular line, one spurts out in a northerly direction and the third and last cutting away to the southwest. The effect is best suggested in the name given the geyser. I went down into this seething crater and secured a remarkably fine specimen.

Most phenomenal of all geysers, and, as her name indicates, most powerful, is the "Giantess." At the summit of the plateau lies what to the seeming is a lake placid as a summer morning, smooth as a mirror. Out toward shore line is a formation much like extending ice. The depths are bottomless. Only once in a long while does the "Giantess" arouse to a determination to show the other geysers what a geyser can really do. Her domain is undisputed, her prestige unchallenged. The crater, of a diameter of twenty feet, is so near the level of the top of the field that she is not suspected of being a "spouter" at all; but when in action this great body of water is lifted solidly into the air for an hundred feet, when by internal propulsion it divides into five distinct columns, each of which rises nearly another hundred feet like fluted columns. These columns then begin to spread out like elm trees, until having reached the altitude of nearly two hundred and sixty feet the descent begins. Then it is as if the windows of heaven were opened. The torrent rushes madly down the sides of the plateau into Fire Hole River.

It is useless to attempt a detailed description of all the multiform attractions formed by the physical agencies at work in the heart of the earth in "Wonderland." They are too numerous and too marvelous for anything more than the typification of all by the illustrations given above, and the mere mention of a few of the other most prominent ones to which attention has not yet been given.

Among these "The Castle" is well named. It is a chimney shaped crater, some eight by ten feet, irregular, terrace-formed, while all around are curiously-carved basins full of crystalline water. Some of these little pools contain a pint of water, some a gallon, some of the water is orange, some of it is green, some sulphurous. The intervening partitions are wonderfully molded. The base of the crater is covered with a convoluted formation resembling cauliflower. One particular specimen in my cabinet might easily be taken by an anatomist for the cerebellum of a child of ten. When the Castle is on the verge of an exhibition the earth trembles for acres around, internal intonations and thunderings are heard, as if a battle had been drawn and thundering parks of artillery were engaged. There is a heaving, a hissing, a trembling, as when the engineer throws the throttle wide. The water is greatly troubled and rises and splashes and dashes like a caged lioness seeking escape.

The "Giant" further down the field is a guard on duty. It's crater resembles a large sycamore tree broken off ten or fifteen feet from the root. In the northwest side of this geyser there is a large rent and a heavy piece has been thrown off by some mighty shock or struggle within.

Not far from the Giant stands the Grotto and below in the same field is the Riverside and Falls.

Crossing the Divide we came to a lake of fire and brimstone. In close proximity is the Devil's Outlook, and not far away is the most inexplicable demonstration in the entire field—an opening in the side of a mountain, where a mud-geyser is in perpetual action, a veritable bit out of Dante's Inferno. Dark and smoky, there issue from it horrid, rumbling noises as of fire, and a cry as of some soul tormented. The smell of brimstone mingles with the stench of the debris—the base of all the extracts of cologne—into one foul malodorous odor. The murky mud gooled up toward us as if to overwhelm us, then receded in black sullenness, while we stood terrified before it.

Further on we found Yellowstone Lake, the source of Yellowstone River. Down the river are the Upper Falls with a descent of more than eighty feet. A mile or more below are the Great Falls, having a plunge of three hundred and sixty feet. It is here that the Yellowstone Canon begins, the most wonderful of all on the east side of the Rocky range. From Point Lookout we stand and gaze over the falls and as we gaze on yonder rocky summit is an eagle teaching her young to fly. Opposite us rise castellated precipices thousands of feet high. Cathedral upon cathedral, tower upon tower, rise in one grand amalgamating mass. We are charmed and chained by the awfulness of the wonders of nature. Out of the north flames before us a mountain of sulphur on fire. The very wagon road we travel is of glass, "obsidian." The forests we pass through are full of petrified trees, and the fields are haunted by hobos and goblins, hideous stone-forms, caused by the action of the water, frost and erosion of the wind, and so terribly fantastic that no Indian will go that way.

We pass, further on, "Young America," the "Minute Man," who, though a little geyser, spouts every minute. At almost the north limit of the park we come upon one of its chiefest grandeurs, the Mammoth Hot Springs, the wonder of all the tourists, vast and varied in formation and indescribably beautiful. Then comes Liberty Gap at the finish, and all reluctantly we bid Wonderland adieu.

CHAPTER XXXV.

RETURN TO KANSAS.

After two years of very arduous though successful work in the mountains I decided to return to the Kansas Conference and again engage in work on Kansas soil. It had so long been my field of labor and my life and history had been so intimately interwoven with her woof and warp that I longed for re-establishment in my home conference.

Again, the Bible work in the mountains entailed a great deal of physical hardship and I found it was beginning to tell upon me in most trying manner. The "jerkies," or mountain stages, were far from comfortable vehicles in which to ride over mountain roads, and not infrequently after a long and rough ride I would suffer excruciatingly with headache and spinal irritation, until life would be almost unbearable. This condition was aggravated by a misfortune which befel me which came near being serious. While suffering violent pain at one time by mistake I took a dose of tincture of Aconite, and but for the timely discovery of the error would have been sacrificed to the poison, the dose having been amply sufficient to have destroyed life. This poisoning increased the sensitiveness of my brain and spine, absolutely necessitating discontinuance of the mountain "jerky" method of jerky travel. My health was so rudely shocked by this laborious work that I was compelled to visit my doctor-son in Texas for treatment, and upon his advice determined at the earliest moment to retire from the mountain field and take up lighter labor. With this determination I purchased an interest in the Kansas Methodist and became its editor, at Topeka. In connection with my editorial labor I embarked in the church book and publishing business, in which combined enterprises I continued for some time. This work did not prove satisfying to my energies and ambitions, and after fairly starting both enterprises toward success I disposed of them to Rev. J. N. See, who for a long time continued the issuance of the Methodist.

During my editorship I was not idle ministerially. I was repeatedly called upon to dedicate new churches and lift church debts, in every instance in which my services were sought succeeding in accomplishing the work in hand. In several instances I succeeded in raising far beyond the amount needed, winning the gratitude of the people and assisting in furthering the cause of the church and her substantial and spiritual interests in this manner. This particular function has been one in which the most gratifying success has attended my efforts all through my church life. A list of my dedications and debt raisings would prove an interesting record, could I but get it together at this time. Perhaps in the future I may do so.

Among the churches dedicated by me, one in particular had a most peculiar history covering its origin, completion and dedication. It is located on an Indian Reserve strip, seven miles South of Eureka. Two or three families came all the way from Northwestern Iowa with wagons drawn by very poor spans of horses and correspondingly poor harness. With the men, the women and children walked most of the way.

The teams had all they could do in their skeletonness to draw the wagons containing the household goods, bedding and clothing of the movers. These families took up homesteads on the "Diminished Reservation," which had just been opened for settlement, and built a small temporary house from stones which cropped from the surface of the prairie ridge running through their homestead, the stones being laid in mud instead of mortar. In these houses they concluded to live until they could build a church and school.

Before long the time came for this much desired work to begin. Sister B. agreed to board the workmen, as her subscription. She had two small rooms in which were quartered the masons and their helpers while they were engaged in quarrying the rock and laying the foundation. Then came the carpenters, and these were taken in until the walls and roof of the church were ready for the plasterers. Meanwhile her husband solicited help and collected money, material and labor, and superintended in a general way the erection of the building. Then came the men to do the plastering, painting and glazing, and they, too, were boarded.

At last after a long and hard struggle the desire of these self-sacrificing Christian men and women was realized. On a prominent site in that primitive country stood completed a well proportioned nud neatly finished church, which will accommodate two hundred and fifty people, erected at a cost of nearly one thousand nine hundred dollars.

The day of dedication was at hand. I was called upon to preach and raise the amount needed to pay all the indebtednesses on the church. When I reached the neighborhood I was quartered with this Christian family, as they only of all the neighbors were prepared to entertain the preacher and visitors. Sister B. had baked a barrel full of loaves of bread, roasted two or three good-sized turkeys, boiled and baked half a hog, and had cooked nearly a quarter of a medium-sized beef. She was amply provided with table comforts for all. We had a meeting of the trustees and interested friends on Saturday night, after which we repaired to this hospitable home. In the room in which I slept, which was twelve by fourteen feet square, there were four beds. Three persons slept in each bed, except the one which the preacher was to occupy with the head of the family. In the other room, which was smaller and had the cookstove in it, there were five beds, and the intermediate space was occupied by the rising generation until next morning.

The day dawned auspiciously, and the people came in groups from far and near until the whole prairie around the church was alive with teams and the church was filled with people to its utmost capacity. As we walked to the house of worship my big-hearted hostess said to me: "That church has got to be paid for today if we have to part with our homestead. We can go West and take up more land and pre-empt it if necessary." All this time I was wondering, Where lay the secret of this zeal?

Before me gathered nearly one hundred young men and women of ages ranging from fifteen to twenty-five young people as intelligent as are found anywhere, who had come with their parents from older states where they had enjoyed the advantages of church and Sabbath school, but who without a house of worship would soon have passed into such indifference as would have foreboded moral ruin. The children!—this was the secret which led to so much joyful toil and self-sacrifice in the erection of this church.

The company of people was so great that many could not find room, notwithstanding the aisles were seated with chairs and wagon-seats from the numerous farm wagons in which the families came to the dedication. Quite a company of men were around the door and near the windows, which were opened so they could hear the sermon, for I was to "preach for all that was out"—as well as for all who were in.

We had had a feast of spiritual singing and I was preaching from a favorite dedicatory text, Galatians iv., 4, 5: "When the fullness of the time was come God sent forth His son, made of a woman, made under the law, that we might receive the adoption of sons." The audience had become deeply interested in the discourse, and I was about through its delivery, when out from the North came an old Indian chief with some of his tribe, his four squaws, and more than a dozen of his children. Some of them were pappooses on their mothers' backs, with all the wickups, poles and paraphernalia of a real Indian camp on their ponies. When they came in full view of the church, teams and crowds of men, they halted, then diverged to the left of the road until they came within about an eighth of a mile and stopped again. Some of the men went out to them and talked to the old chief, who, with his people, were on their way to visit tribal relatives in the Indian Territory, intending to remain "two moons."

Imagine his astonishment to witness such a change on the very grounds over which he had roamed from boyhood to manhood, and which his people had occupied in undisputed possession for centuries. The contrast of the situation, the difference between the Indian clan before us and the assembly of white people in their Christian homes and church, was so vivid as to afford me the opportunity of showing the advantages of revealed religion over the "light of nature" and unassisted reason. The Indian had nature for a teacher and nothing to do but study the book. He neither toiled nor did he spin. The procession of states and planets went silently in their incessant march before him. The mountains with their pinnacled tops pointed constantly toward heaven. But he knew not God, nor Christ who had redeemed him. But the Bible, the Church, the Christian Altar and Sabbath all told of immortality and eternal life.

It was a glad day for the neighborhood and people. The debt was amply provided for and the church duly dedicated, to become a center of attraction and a joy to the whole community.

CHAPTER XXXVI.

LAST YEARS OF PASTORATE LIFE.

The closing years of my life as a pastor have been pleasantly and efficiently spent in the Kansas Conference. Up to April, 1887, after having retired from the ownership of the Kansas Methodist, I served as organizer of the temperance forces of the state. At that date I concluded to re-enter pastoral relations and accepted the charge of the church at Marysville, Marshall County. This was a pleasant little city and the membership of the church, though not large, was composed of pious Christian people among whom it was a pleasure to live. I associated myself with Halcyon Lodge of Independent Order of Odd Fellows, by transfer from my home lodge, and otherwise became identified with the interests of my charge and its people. But little of unusual importance occurred during my two years' residence at Marysville, though many incidents serving to strengthen us in the service of the Master are recorded in our hearts.

At the close of my second years' pastorate at Marysville we were assigned the station of Wamego, on the Union Pacific railroad, and here spent two very delightful and profitable years of service. During our residence at Wamego we held a number of successful protracted meetings, at which there were many conversions to Christ. Among those converted was a bright young girl named Bessie Lilly. Her mother had been a Baptist, her father a Baptist preacher.

When the time came for the administration of the sacrament of baptism Bessie elected to be baptised by the method most commonly in vogue in the Methodist church and was sprinkled. Her grandmother, hearing of this, visited her and taking the little girl upon her knee expressed her regret that she had chosen to be baptised in this way, presenting most earnestly her objections to this method of administering this sacrament. The grandchild listened respectfully, but was only confused by the earnestness with which her grandmother urged immersion as a saving grace, and finally sighingly said to her, "Grandma, if you don't stop talking to me that way you will make me an out and out invalid." The child got the word mixed, but her grandmother saw the force of her reasoning and yielded the point at issue. Beyond doubt many men and women are made infidels by the confusion in doctrines and sacraments in the various church denominations. To them these differences seem to undo a great deal of the teaching of the church, and stand out in bold antagonism to the preached doctrines of a brotherhood religion.

From the time we used to hold union Sabbath school services in my boyhood days, and the time of the union meeting earlier recited as having occurred in which the Quakers and Methodists came together to serve one God, I have been a firm believer in the usefulness of union church services and have wished that the time may come when all Christian denominations whose doctrines are not widely at variance may worship the Master under one membership. I cannot but feel that through the union of all Christian forces greater good than now would be accomplished and more precious souls would be brought to believe in Christ and Him crucified. The confusion of almost innumerable denominations cannot but be confusing and unsatisying to the unbeliever.

May God in His own good time bring us together.

While at Wamego for my second year I had the satisfaction and pleasure, and a pleasure it was, too, of visiting the four conferences now in Kansas, which were formed out of the original Kansas Conference of which I became a member in territorial days.

The South Kansas Conference met at Chanute. I attended a lovefeast during the session, at which many gave testimony of the goodness of God. After a great many had spoken I arose near the altar and briefly related a part of my Christian experience, this prompting the recital of the conversion and entrance upon the Methodist ministry of the brother whose conversion was due to Mrs. Shugro's recital to him of my escape at the time of Quantrell's raid, as already recorded.

I next attended the Northwestern Kansas Conference in session at Norton, the county seat of Norton County. On the way to this conference I met with an accident which all but cost me my life. Upon reaching Mankato, on the Rock Island railroad, we were snow-bound for nearly ninety hours. There were a number of preachers and the presiding bishop, Bishop Merrill, on the train. A deep cut was packed full of snow and the plows were at work trying to clear the tracks, three locomotives being employed in the work. The passengers were irresistably drawn to where the excavating was going on. One of the party, Rev. Dr. Stoltz, had been ill and I remained behind with him for a time, but when he became better we started up the track to where the snow-plows were at work, not knowing that there was a locomotive behind us. We were walking deliberately up the track, unconscious of danger, when an engine under good head of steam approached from behind. We were not seen by either the engineer or fireman, they being otherwise occupied and not expecting that any one would be on the track with the snow banked high on either side. A cry of warning was raised from an adjoining elevator and heard by Dr. Stoltz, who sprung from the track in time to reach a place of safety. He cried to me to look out for the locomotive. We had not thought of danger from the rear, so I looked sharply ahead, thinking he meant that an engine might approach from that direction. He called loudly the second time, and turning I saw the locomotive with a snow-plow, looking like the end of a barn, directly upon me. I could neither turn nor run nor jump sidewise in time to be saved. I felt a sense of resentment to think I was thus placed in an unconscious danger simply because the engineer and firemen were not on the lookout ahead, and seeing no other chance for escape sprang with all my strength right on the pilot. The engine was approaching at such speed, however, that I was thrown from the pilot to one side. I was thus saved from being crushed to death beneath the ponderous machine, but as it passed me the stop-cock of an escape pipe caught me and held me alongside the driving wheels a prisoner, lying flat on the snow-covered ties, close to the rail, as the great engine with its snow-plow attachment passed almost over me. I was so close to the drivers that one of them wrenched my over-shoe from my foot. Brother Stoltz turned blind and faint as I struck the pilot and was hurled to one side, and marveled to see me escape alive. Though my danger was of a different nature, yet it was but little less pronounced than when the guerrillas entered my cellar at Lawrence in search of my life. I praised

God that I had again escaped a violent death, attended conference as planned, and returned home to recite to my wife who had saved me from the murderous hands of the Quantrell raiders how again I had had a narrow escape from imminent danger from which the Lord in His goodness had delivered me.

While at Wamego I lectured to the congregation and citizens on the Quantrell Raid, at the special request of numbers of the people who knew something of my marvelous escape, and who were, therefore, more deeply interested in my recital of the awful massacre than they would otherwise have been. The last time I delivered this lecture Mr. M. D. Embly, one of our citizens, said to a friend, "I have heard Dr. Fisher's lecture four different times; I don't believe I care to hear it again." When the hour came, however, he was persuaded by his wife to accompany her, and I noticed that he listened with marked attention. As he returned to his home he said to his wife, "I have now heard that lecture five times. I thought I should never care to hear it again, but I will give a five dollar bill to hear it once more." Though indirectly a compliment to the lecturer, perhaps, yet the thrilling incidents of the story had so grown upon him that it had failed to become an old story, and its recital for the fifth time had so aroused his interest in the part his state had played in the War of the Rebellion that he had come to be a ready listener to the review of the most deplorable of all its unfortunate occurrences.

At the close of my pastoral term at Wamego I was stationed at Westmoreland, the county seat of Pottawatomie County. I confess when my appointment to this charge was announced I was disappointed. It caused me to recall a story of Rev. George S. Holmes, under whose pastorate I served as a lad, and of whom I have repeatedly spoken in the earlier pages of this volume. Brother Holmes expected to be stationed at a certain charge at one of the conference sittings, but when the appointments were read out he was surprised to hear that he was assigned to one of the most uninviting of all the charges, a place to which he had not had the slightest thought of being sent. As soon as the Bishop had finished his appointments Brother Holmes rose in his place on the conference floor, addressed the Bishop and conference, and voiced the following words. "Bishop, and Brethren, I was taught to believe that the assignment of preachers at the sittings of our conferences is the work of the Lord and the Bishop. But since hearing where I am to go for the next twelve months I have reached the conclusion that this particular lot of appointments is more likely to have been made by the Devil and the Presiding Elder."

This was about the way I felt when assigned to Westmoreland. But in this, as in many other things in which my voice has been raised in doubt of the wisdom on God's movements as they have related to me, I was doomed to a pleasurable disappointment. Our station was a quiet town, off of any railroad. It first seemed to me like a burial of myself and wife to go there. It was so quiet that one of my little grandsons, in writing to his Papa about it, wrote, "Every day is like Sunday up here and Sunday is like a funeral." This quiet was almost unbearable at first, but I soon learned that it was just what I needed. Furthermore, the people were among the most hospitable and considerate I have ever presided over. Our church work was satisfactory to us in large degree, while our social life in Westmoreland was restful and in many respects delightful.

Among appointments I took in was one called Moodyville Springs, a popular summer resort. On one occasion at this station there were present under my preaching one hundred and eleven persons, young and old, immediately connected with a family named Siddens. A large number of them were professed Christians. This remarkable incident was made especially impressive by the fact that within a twelvemonth I was called upon to bury seven adult members of this family connection.

While pastor at Westmoreland I was stricken, almost without a moment's warning, with the most violent illness of my life, neuralgia of the heart. For a time my life was despaired of by physician, wife and friends. In the extremest moment of my illness I looked back upon my eventful past and could but feel that while there was many an hour and many a day and many a month and many a year in which I could do better, perhaps, had I my life to live over again, yet, after all, I had tried as best I could in an humble way to serve my Master, and I could but feel that all would be well with me were I called to leave my loved ones. Looking over my church life to see if there was anything upon which to depend for safety I was made comfortable and happy in the beautiful words that came to my mind:

>   "My hope is built on nothing less
>   Than Jesus' blood and righteousness.
>   I dare not trust the sweetest frame,
>   But wholly lean on Jesus' name."

I was ready to go if it were God's will. But under

His providence I was spared for other years, though shattered in health for a time.

It was during this severe illness, more than at any other time, that I was made to feel and understand God's providence in sending me to the good people of Westmoreland, whom I shall ever bear in grateful remembrance for their uniform kindness and support in this dark hour.

My own illness at Westmoreland and a serious illness which overtook Mrs. Fisher at conference, determined me to take a superannuated relation rather than again undertake the arduous duties of pastorate life. This step was not taken without much consideration and prayer. We possessed a comfortable home in Topeka. We were growing old. Our boys could not make it convenient to visit us at out-of-the-way points as they wished they might, and as we would have been glad to have had them do. During my alarming illness neither of my doctor-sons could get to us. So taking everything into consideration I decided I had better seek retirement from active pastoral duties and serve God as best I might be able in other lines of work.

A special reason which operated to cause me to reach this decision arose from the fact that I had decided to become a candidate for the chaplaincy of the United States Congress at its Fifty-fourth session, having received assurances from Honorable Case Broderick, representing the First Kansas District, and Honorable Charles Curtis, representing the Fourth District, at Washington, that I would most likely be chosen to this honorable position. I could but feel that this would be an acceptable closing of a life of usefulness in the service of the church and our country, and felt, also, that it would give me more of the leisure and rest than pastoral work, and would afford me opportunities for useful labor in a line of work which I desired to take up between sessions of Congress, were I elected. Therefore, I asked for and was granted superannuated relation at the session of the Kansas Conference held in Atchison in March, 1895, after more than forty years of active pastoral duties, above thirty of which had been spent in the service of the Master in the Kansas Conference.

CHAPTER XXXVII.

CONGRESSIONAL CANDIDACY.

In entering upon a formal candidacy for the chaplaincy of Congress I was gratified beyond measure at the warmth of support I received from almost every one with whom I came in contact in this relation. It was a case of where a prophet is not without honor in his own country. Every state elective official, almost the entire membership of the Kansas State Senate and House of Representatives, members of the Supreme Court of Kansas, and several of the District Judges of the State, the officers of the Grand Army of the Republic of Kansas and many of its prominent members, together with leading members of the church and citizens all over Kansas serving in private capacity, joined in signing my papers of recommendation and wishing me every possible success in this candidacy. Better than riches is a good name among the brethren and one's fellow men. I could but feel most highly complimented by the freedom and unanimity with which the support of the state officers and legislators was tenderd my congressional supporters and managers.

Armed with these recommendations and with promises of votes from members of congress from a dozen or more different states, I repaired to Washington in the fall of 1895 in the interests of my candidacy. Messrs. Broderick and Curtis had managed my campaign with admirable skill, and to my extreme gratification I found that it was generally accepted that I would be named for the chaplaincy on the ticket headed by Mr. McDowell, of Pennsylvania, as a candidate for the clerkship of the House of Representatives. This ticket was generally conceded to win in the caucus, therefore my name was most freely mentioned as that of the coming chaplain. The office had been long looked upon as belonging to the clergy of the District of Columbia, five of whom were in the race against me. Rev. E. H. Couden, of Michigan, a blind preacher of the Unitarian church, was also in the field.

When the caucus convened Mr. McDowell was easily elected as the candidate of the republicans for the clerkship of the House. The remaining candidates on the ticket headed by him were also successful, but the balloting was prolonged well in the night and the members were growing tired before the balloting for a candidate for chaplain began. Seven names were placed in nomination, my name being placed before the caucus by Mr. Broderick in an earnest plea that the Kansas Chaplain might be chosen.

The balloting began and I led the race, receiving just as many as all the balance of the candidates together received. One more vote would have nominated me. The second ballot was taken and again I received exactly as many votes as all the rest together. It was then after midnight, and the members were weary and beginning to scatter. Opposing friends conceded that I would be elected on the next ballot, and some of my supporters, hearing that the other candidates were to be withdrawn one by one in my favor, thought it not necessary to remain and left for their hotels. This was a fatal mistake. The third ballot was called and votes were being cast when a member from Massachusetts violated the rule of the caucus and in explaining his vote made an earnest plea that the blind preacher might be chosen, and thus the McDowell slate be broken on one office, at least. Sympathy was aroused for the blind brother and those of the candidates who had intended withdrawing in my favor were not able to prevent their supporters from going to Rev. Mr. Couden, who on the third ballot received the nomination which on two ballots was mine had I received but one more vote.

The most stinging part of my defeat was because it was accomplished by a representative from Kansas, through his not casting the necessary ballot for the candidate of his own state. Representative Miller, of Kansas City, Kansas, supported the candidacy of Mr. Henderson, of Illinois, against that of Mr. McDowell, for the clerkship, and refused to support me because I was the candidate of the McDowell ticket. Every representative from Kansas but Mr. Miller considered that it would be an honor for his state to have the office, but he preferred that Kansas should not be thus recognized than that a single candidate on the McDowell ticket should receive his vote. Had it been given when I lacked the one necessary to give me a majority of the entire number cast I would have been the nominee and the West would have had the office for the first time. But he preferred to gratify his selfish opposition to the McDowell ticket all the way through and thus defeated his townsman. The responsibility is his. I recite the facts without comment.

My vote on the second tie was one hundred and nine ballots against one hundred and nine for the other seven clergymen in the field.

It has been held that had Mr. Miller cast his ballot for the Kansas candidate it would have resulted in securing for the state the appointment of a number to clerkships, thus realizing to our citizens honors and many thousands of dollars now lost to them, and that among the results would probably have been the securement of the reading clerkship. Of this I have knowledge from congressmen, my information coming from sources of eminent reliability, in all probability fully correct.

To say that my defeat did not bring disappointment would be untrue. But whatever of disappointment I experienced and whatever of bitterness toward the defaulting Kansas Representative I have felt is materially lessened by the fact that the successful candidate in every way deserved recognition by his country because of his affliction, a result of the war. I cannot but feel that had I been a member of that caucus and had I not been pledged to some other candidate for personal or local reasons I should have cast my ballot for the blind man. Sympathy for his affliction elected him, but it was a commendable sympathy. May God bless him in the performance of the duties I aspired to perform, is my prayer.

I have said that my candidacy developed the fact that in this instance a prophet was not altogether without honor in his own country. During the canvass I received most hearty assurances of sympathy and support from many sources, some of whom which had not been hoped for nor thought of. After the question had been settled by Rev. Mr. Couden's election I was made to feel even more gratifyingly than before that both in church and state I am held in high esteem, and that my failure of election brought as great a degree of disappointment to many warm friends as it did unto me. I violate no confidence in appending some of the endorsements received while the canvass was on and expressions of sympathy and regrets after it was over. I cannot but feel that I would fail in the performance of a pleasant duty should I not take pains to express my gratification for these kindly expressions of confidence and publicly voice the thankfulness that in me is for that large warmheartedness of my Bishop, my state and my friends, in thus coming to me with support and sympathizing voice and heart in the closing years of an earnest life.

Petition of Kansas State Senate:

Topeka, Kansas.

Hon. Case Broderick,

Member of Congress, Washington, D. C.

We, members of the senate, learn with much pleasure that you propose the choice of Rev. H. D. Fisher, D. D., as Chaplain of the House of Representatives of the Fifty-fourth Congress.

His long and efficient services, his unswerving loyalty and devotion to the republican party, as well as his eminent ministerial labors, peculiarly qualify him for the position.

His loyal and faithful service in the army as chaplain of the Fifth Kansas Cavalry, entitle him to such a position and recognition. We heartily commend you for this generous effort and hope you will succeed.

Lucien Baker..................Senator 3rd District.
(Now United States Senator.)
James D. Williamson..........Senator 3rd District.
W. A. Morgan................Senator 23rd District.
E. T. Metcalf.................Senator 7th District.
Milton Brown.................Senator 38th District.
K. E. Willcockson............Senator 39th District.
J. W. Parker.................Senator 6th District.
John A. Carpenter............Senator 13th District.

CONGRESSIONAL CANDIDACY.

H. F. Robbins................Senator 18th District.
L. P. King...................Senator 27th District.
T. V. Thorpe.................Senator 5th District.
D. McTaggart.................Senator 12th District.
W. E. Sterne.................Senator 17th District.
S. T. Danner.................Senator 30th District.
Jas. Troutman................Lieutenant Governor.
Jas. Shearn..................Senator 19th District.
H. G. Jampar.................Senator 16th District.
Jno. Armstrong...............Senator 35th District.
Anson S. Cooke...............Senator 33rd District.
J. W. Leeds..................Senator 36th District.
G. E. Smith..................Senator 40th District.
W. P. Dillord................Senator 8th District.
H. M. Reid...................Senator 9th District.
J. H. Reilley................Senator 11th District.
Edwin Taylor.................Senator 4th District.
Geo. D. Bowling..............Senator 32nd District.
Alden E. True................Senator 21st District.
A. G. Farney.................Senator 28th District.
Jason Helmick................Senator 26th District.
R. E. Baldwin................Senator 31st District.
E. O. Bryan..................Senator 29th District.
Chas. F. Scott...............Senator 14th District.
H. S. Landis.................Senator 37th District.
Levi Dumbauld................Senator 24th District.
John M. Price................Senator 2nd District.
M. A. Housholder.............Senator 10th District.
A. W. Dennison...............Senator 25th District.
W. B. Helm...................Senator 34th District.
J. W. Leevy..................Senator 15th District.
Wm. Rogers...................Senator 20th District.
W. Senn......................Senator 22nd District.

Endorsement of Old Soldiers in Convention:

Lawrence, Kansas, October 15, 1895.

To Whom it May Concern:

At the annual meeting of the Douglas County Old Soldiers and Sailors Association, held at Lawrence, Kansas, October 15, 1895, it was learned that Chaplain H. D. Fisher had been named by the Hon. Case Broderick for the Chaplaincy of the House of Representatives, for the Fifty-fourth Congress.

Chaplain Fisher was a resident of Lawrence seven years, entered the service at the outbreak of the Rebellion, remaining until its close, serving as Chaplain (and known as the "Fighting Chaplain") of the Fifth Kansas Volunteer Cavalry, therefore,

Resolved, That in his selection for such place Representatives can make no mistake, but will secure a worthy, capable and deserving Christian gentleman, who will reflect credit upon the state he has so long and faithfully served, as well as upon those who may vote for his selection as Chaplain of the incoming Congress.   Albert R. Greene,

Stephen H. Andrews,   President.
Secretary.

Endorsement of the Fifth Kansas Cavalry in Reunion Assembled:

Ottawa, Kansas, September 4, 1895.

Head-quarters Fifth Kansas Cavalry Volunteers,
Ottawa, Kansas.

Hon. Case Broderick,

Dear Sir: It affords us pleasure to know that you propose the election of Rev. H. D. Fisher, late Chaplain of the Fifth Kansas Cavalry, as Chaplain of the House of Representatives, Fifty-fourth Congress. We assure you that we appreciate this honor as to our regiment, and that in his election our delegates in Congress will make no mistake. We request them to unite with you to secure his election.

Most respectfully yours,
The Fifth Kansas Volunteers in Reunion Assembled.

O. E. Morse,   Powell Clayton,
   Secretary.   President.

Expressions of Sympathy and Regret from Bishop Vincent:

Topeka, Kansas, December 1, 1895.
My Dear Dr. Fisher:

I learn from "The Capital" this morning that you failed, through a Kansas vote, to secure the prize you coveted and deserved. I am sorry; I am very sorry. And Representative Miller, whoever he is, ought to be required to give his reason—whether it be religious, denominational, political or personal. You have the confidence of the whole state, the love of your church, the testimony of a good conscience, and you crown everything by your magnanimity in defeat.

Your faithful brother,
John H. Vincent.

Explanation of Mr. Miller, from Hon. Case Broderick:

House of Representatives, U. S.,
Washington, D. C., December 6, 1895.
Rev. H. D. Fisher, D. D.,
Topeka, Kansas.
My Dear Sir:

I found among my papers the petition signed by all the state senators asking your appointment as chaplain. I was of the opinion when you were here that I had left all these papers at home.

I trust you have reached home safely.

The vote on the chaplaincy is still being discussed here. Mr. Miller's explanation that he was determined to defeat the combine, when they were complaining on the other hand that Kansas wasn't to get enough from the McDowell people, seems quite inconsistent. The Michigan members had all been in the combine on everything except chaplain, which shows that Mr. Miller's effort was to prevent Kansas from securing anything in the organization. He knew that every state senator in Kansas and nearly all the members of the lower house of the legislature, the prominent people in Pottawatomie County, and many Grand Army people had all declared in favor of your election, but it seemed to have no effect.

My daughters join in sending kind regards.

Yours very truly,
Case Broderick.

Expressions of Sympathy and Regret from Judge Guthrie:

Topeka, Kansas, December 1, 1895.

Rev. H. D. Fisher, D. D.,
Washington, D. C.

Dear Sir:

I have watched the progress of your canvass for chaplain ever since you left for Washington, and Saturday night remained at the Capital office until a dispatch came stating that you were elected chaplain with the McDowell ticket. But the Capital this morning reports a man from Michigan elected. I assure you I am greatly disappointed in the result. Kansas would have appreciated your success. But there is nothing to be gained by a post mortem discussion of the causes of misfortune. I suppose you will be home soon, when

I hope you will call at my office and tell me about your experiences.

Truly and sincerely,

John Guthrie.

Judge Shawnee District Court.

CHAPTER XXXVIII.

THE GRAND ARMY OF THE REPUBLIC.

Universal history has established the fact that war is barbarous and demoralizing in its effects upon those engaging in it, even though the outcome may advance civilization by affording opportunities for better conditions—as, for example, the great revolutionary war, which resulted in the establishment of a nation free from kingship and a national independence, and the late civil war. The latter was a terrible test of integrity, honor and morality, and, viewed from the standpoint of other great wars, many wise and philanthropic citizens contemplated with dismay the moral effect upon society and the nation of the disbanding of such an army of men, after such prolonged absence from home and civilizing influences as our citizen soldiers had endured. The world looked on with solicitude and awaited results. Never did the sun shine upon such a scene; never did pen of historian record such results. A mighty army of men, vanquished and conquered, returned to their homes to pursue a better life under the magic words of their conqueror, "Let us have peace;" while the conquerors returned to theirs, flushed with victory, won on the bloodiest battle-fields the world ever saw, the proud saviors of the best and grandest nation on earth and the brightest and most expressive and significant flag that the sunlight of Heaven ever gilded or the breezes of God ever kissed, for the most part wiser and better men and citizens than when they enlisted in their country's cause.

The fears of the nation were dissipated in an incredibly short time; for these conquerors had learned to obey orders, respect authority, magnify law, love home and admire and adore pure womanhood; and with very few exceptions they readily returned to the peaceful avocations of private business and professional life, to be at once recognized as sober and honorable citizens of a prosperous and re-united nation.

On the Fourteenth of April, 1861, the flag had been lowered on Fort Sumter; and just four years afterwards "Old Glory" was raised by Major General Anderson, who had so nobly defended our national honor when the first gun of the rebellion was fired at the heart of the nation by Beauregard. The ceremonies were appropriate and national in character and importance. In April, 1865, more than a million men were in military service, a still larger number had been previously discharged, and already over three hundred and fifty thousand noble patriots had been numbered as the grand army of the dead.

The total enrollment in the military service of the nation had reached above 2,860,000, which, reduced to an average of three years service, numbered more than 2,320,000. There had been killed in battle 67,058; died of wounds and other injuries, 43,032; died of disease, 224,586, and from unclassified causes 24,852, making a total death roll of 259,528. This was the number of heroes who gave their lives for the life of the nation.

The engagements numbered more than two thousand; many of them were mighty battles, displaying the splendid powers of the Americans on the field of conflict.

The navy numbered 122,000 men, variously employed, and made a record unequaled in the history of naval warfare, covering a line of coast patrol and defense from the British line on the north to the Rio Grande on the south, rendering incalculable service to the army on land, blocking posts and capturing forts.

When Gen. Lee surrendered to the "Silent Man of Destiny" Secretary Stanton proposed that the armies of Meade and Sherman should be reviewed in Washington before being disbanded. The armies of the Potomac, Tennessee, and of Georgia, therefore, rendezvoused in the neighborhood of the Capitol City to be reviewed on May 23 and 24, 1865, the necessary orders being issued by Lieutenant General U. S. Grant.

Washington never presented such a gorgeous scene of decoration as welcomed the war-begrimed veterans who marched those proud days through Pennsylvania Avenue with martial music and national songs, under the re-baptized folds of the dear old flag, now rendered doubly dear to loyal Americans because it had gained a higher place in the galaxy of nations. Such a pageant never trod the streets of any earthly city. The rarest welcome was accorded the victorious hosts, such a welcome as human pen cannot describe nor tongue of golden eloquence depict, nor painter's pencil imitate. It was the tribute to Liberty's choicest nation. Upon the front of the Capitol building hung in splendor an emblazoned canvas on which was the grateful acknowledgment:

"THE ONLY NATIONAL DEBT WE CAN NEVER PAY IS THE DEBT WE OWE THE VICTORIOUS UNION SOLDIERS."

Many states were represented by their loyal sons and daughters, who welcomed the returning heroes, especially those from their own commonwealths. President Andrew Johnson and cabinet, diplomats and envoys of other nations, with governors of many of the states, occupied reviewing stands near the White House. The war governors, notably John A. Andrews of Massachusetts and Andrew J. Curtin of Pennsylvania, were honored and welcomed for the promptness and steadfastness of their loyalty and sympathy for the soldiers. As they passed the reviewing stand, recognizing familiar leaders and feeling that thrill of comradeship by the touch of elbows, covered as they were with honor and glory, the occasion had yet a peculiar saddening and sanctifying effect which possessed all hearts, because of the absence of that sad yet intelligent face which would have been lighted with a halo of benignity at this hour, all aflame with love and gratitude from that mighty heart which had borne such great concern for long years of patient toil and waiting. That face was in every man's mind and heart all along the march up Pennsylvania Avenue, like a spiritual presence and benediction. It was the face of the martyred Lincoln. What memories rushed like phantoms through those soldiers' minds, even as they heard the shouts and plaudits of the welcoming multitudes! It was the triumphal march of the Grand Army of the Republic.

And now the absorbing question became, How shall its integrity be preserved and its comradeship be perpetuated; how shall its lessons of patriotism, loyalty and sacrifice be transmitted to the generations following, that what they achieve may be protected through the ages to come?

I have intimated that two great agencies were at work to aid in the preservation of this vast army of disbanded victors. One of these has not been properly recognized or valued by the nation—the loyal, loving women, the wives of soldiers, and sweethearts of the boys in blue. These noble women met the battle-stained soldiers lovingly and with tenderness. While the boys in blue had fought and won the women at home had prayed and worked and waited; they had kept their love burning like lamps towards the final home-coming, and now that that home-coming was realized they joined hand and fortune with the begrimed and battered men unshrinkingly, and went out in the world with them to build, and bake, and win. Tens of thousands of our comrades have been prosperous in business, happy in their homes, respected by their neighbors and useful to the state and nation, for the reason that our pure and loyal women were willing to ally their destinies for life with a soldier; willing to aid those ragmuffin boys-in-blue, unkempt, roughened by camp-life, penniless, to develop the good traits of character they had preserved during the war. All honor to the loyal women who loved the nation loyally and her soldier boys yet more, and who helped them and are still helping them to work out a higher individual and national destiny.

The other chief agent in making the soldiers of that cruel war the useful and successful men they have been was the early organization and successful maintenance of the "Grand Army of the Republic." No such organization ever existed in any clime or nation, and no companionships ever existed similar to the comradeships of our Grand Army. We marched and tented, we fought and bivouacked on the same field; we ate in the same mess, slept under the same blanket, drank out of the same canteen; we suffered in the same hospitals, buried our comrades in the common grave of heroes; we sang the same army songs, and helped to swell the same shout of victory. Over us ever waved the flag for whose honor we would have willingly died. Why, then, should not comradeship live forever?

"So it is, so may it ever be."

The solicitude felt for the welfare of the soldiers was not confined to those in the most commanding positions, but largely shared by the comrades in the ranks and the faithful Christian Chaplains. The first recorded suggestion which led to the formation of "fellowship of comrades" was made by Chaplain H. I. Rutledge, of the Fourteenth Illinois Infantry, while with his regiment with Sherman's expedition to Meridian, February, 1864. He and Rev. Dr. Stephenson, who were messmates, agreed that the soldiers at the close of the war would naturally desire to preserve the friendships and memories of their common trials, dangers and victories, and after the close of army service this subject was kept alive by correspondence until in March, 1866, they met by appointment in Springfield, Illinois, and formulated a ritual for the proposed organization.

Dr. Stephenson is doubtless entitled to the credit, tho' accrediting a large degree of the same to Chaplain Rutledge, of formulating this ritual. Both were aided in perfecting the plans and purposes of the Grand Army of the Republic by advising comrades. One of these comrades, J. S. Phelps, has in his possession a copy of the ritual of the "Soldiers' and Sailors' League of St. Louis." The name adopted, "Grand Army of the Republic," was perhaps suggested by the meaning of other organizations. The ritual agreed upon was printed with great care and secrecy, and on the sixth of April, 1866, Major Stephenson and Captain Phelps organized at Decatur, Illinois, the first Post created under charter.

Like all human organizations, the ritual needed revision and simplification. This it has received from time to time as exigencies have suggested. Among the declaration of principles is:

First—"The preservation of those kind and fraternal feelings which have been bound together with the strong cords of love the comrades in arms of many battles, sieges and marches.

Second—"To make these ties available in works and results of kindness, of favor, and material aid to those in need of assistance.

Third—"To care for the orphans and widows of comrades and for the disabled."

Dr. Stephenson, the founder of the Grand Army, was born October 30, 1822, and died August 30, 1871. He lived usefully, died peacefully, and sleeps in Rose Hill Cemetery, on the banks of the Sangamon, in hope of the First Resurrection. The commanders-in-chief of the Grand Army of the Republic form a galaxy of bright and useful comrades whose services shed luster upon the names and deeds of the citizen soldiers of the grandest army ever marshalled in the interest of Freedom's holy cause. Among these Fairchild and Logan shine most conspicuously.

Great national interests were subserved by the Grand Army under the wise and prompt action of General Logan when the arbitrary spirit of President Johnson had proposed the removal of the great war secretary, Edwin M. Stanton, by military force. General Logan bivouacked in the office of the secretary with Mr. Stanton, and the Grand Army patrolled the streets of the city, guarded the war department, and were ready at a moment's warning to protect the government from a military coup d'etat at the risk of their lives.

The world never before beheld the peaceful, quiet, orderly disbanding of an army of a million victorious soldiers returning to the peaceful pursuits of civil life without rioting or vagrancy. Triumphal war songs were exchanged for Christian melodies, and the hands which had learned the art of war took up the hammer, the plow, the spade and the spindle, and the land was soon filled with peace and plenty.

Other agencies wrought well and effectively to bring about this splendid state of affairs, but none so mightily and successfully as this Grand Army comradeship. The conception of such an organization was almost a divine inspiration—the results of prophecy fulfilled. The soldier-citizen is the highest type of sovereignty, and he has set the standard of morality and patriotism higher than ever before. The Post-room, the Camp Fire, the Reunion, and the Encampment are schools which cannot but continue to draw the lines of comradeships more and more closely, and further strengthen the ties of affection as the ranks of the Grand Army of the Republic are thinned by the recurring roll-call, ever attesting the promotions from the militant army to the grand rendezvous in The Land Beyond the River.

WOMAN'S RELIEF CORPS.

This chapter would be incomplete did it not record more fully that meed of praise belonging to the women of the nation for their deeds of heroic valor. These were not only shown in many helpful ways during the war and in esteem and affection for the returned soldiers, but especially is it noteworthy that the national heroines have organized the Woman's Relief Corps, composed of loyal women—whether soldiers' wives, widows and daughters or not—of all women willing to aid in perpetuating the memories of the loyal soldiers, in helping to make their work complete and in furnishing such help to the needy families of soldiers as devoted women can render.

This associate society has since its organization in

1879 raised and paid out for various charitable purposes, mostly for the benefit of the old soldiers and their families, nearly a million and a half dollars in money and supplies.

At the encampment of the Grand Army of the Republic held in St. Paul in September, 1896 the president of the Woman's Relief Corps reported that they had come into possession of a tract of land including Andersonville Stockade and Southern Prison Pen, which they proposed to restore and preserve as a colossal monument to the heroism and martyrdom of the nation's defenders who lost their lives therein. In this prison-pen thousands of the loyal patriots starved to death. The Woman's Relief Corps of the Grand Army of the Republic purpose furnishing convenient stopping-places for those who wish to visit this scene of martyrdom, that they may look upon the graves of those who here perished. These memories can no more perish while the nation stands than can Calvary and the Cross while the church and christianity live to bless the world. All honor to those who conceived the perpetuation of such a national object-lesson and such a charity!

A large class of intelligent and loyal women, believing that the Grand Army of the Republic Posts should have a corresponding organization into whose ranks none but those whose husbands, fathers, brothers, or sons had actual service in the army or navy of the Union should be admitted, united under the title, "Circle of the Grand Army of the Republic," for the purpose of giving greater emphasis to loyal service in the country's cause. This movement was perfected in 1883, having taken form in a representative meeting in Trenton, New Jersey, on December 15, 1891. The principles adopted indicated clearly the object of the organization—"To unite with loyalty love for each other; to practice the precepts of true fraternity of feeling towards all sisters of one Order, thus emulating the spirit which unites our fathers, husbands and brothers; to honor the memory of those fallen; to perpetuate and keep sacred forever Memorial Day; to assist the Grand Army of the Republic, aid and sympathize with them in their noble charity; to comfort the sick, help the needy, and to do all in our power to alleviate suffering." This is an organization of the direct blood-relations of those who shed their blood to save the Union for you.

The whole ultimate design and object of these organizations of the Grand Army of the Republic and auxiliaries is to preserve the trophies of war and its histories, to conserve peace and perpetuate and spread the gospel.

CHAPTER XXXIX.

CONCLUSION.

The Psalmist allotted unto man three score years and ten in which to serve God. I have reached this age, and am two and a half years beyond it. My wife, to whom I have been married more than forty-seven years, has also passed the Psalmist's limit, and is by my side as I close this volume, the sharer of my joys in old age, of such disappointments as have come unto me, and of my hope in Heaven. We are quietly enjoying our home in Topeka, resting as best we may after a long life of activity and toil. It would seem that we have been in the harness long enough to wish to lay it aside altogether. Yet it is difficult, after so many years of public labor, to accept a life of enforced idleness, and I rejoice in the fact that I am still able to serve the Master as opportunity affords. We also rejoice that in looking over an earnest past our lives have not been wholly spent in vain. Though falling short, no doubt, of the possibilities with which God endowed us we have yet tried to be of service in His cause, have tried to reach the mark of a high calling, have tried to do good unto our fellow-men, and are resting secure in the confident hope of a reward which shall come from On High.

The part assigned me in the glorious work of saving the Nation and freeing the slave, and my labors in bringing out of the house of bondage the thousands of contrabands who flocked to the Union armies in the

Southwest during the war between the North and South, is especially gratifying as I reflect upon it and as I contemplate the far-reaching effect upon the civilization of the nineteenth century of the War of the Rebellion. Yet not more gratifying are the successes of that bloody conflict than are those peaceful victories accomplished in the cause of the Master, in a contest of nearly half a century of ministerial labor with the agencies of the evil one.

It will have been observed that by far the major part of my career as a laborer in the Master's vineyard has been spent as a pioneer in His service; first, in Ohio and Pennsylvania as an itinerant circuit rider, then as a vidette on the outposts of Zion during the territorial and early state days of Kansas, and yet later on the plains of Nebraska and in the mountain fastnesses of Utah, Idaho and Montana, among Mormons and miners, in all of which fields, during my most active service, the religion of Jesus Christ was as a sealed book to the masses unto whom I was called upon to preach. Necessarily this class of service entailed great hardships, mental, physical and financial; but we have tried to endure them as true soldiers of the Cross. Our trust has ever been in God, and we have always been sustained by His grace. Whenever we have faltered or swerved in the least from the path of righteousness and duty we have been promptly brought to see the error of our way, and have straightway made haste to reconsecrate ourselves to His cause with the utmost satisfaction and soul-inspiring enjoyment. Verily, without God and His Son our lives would have been but failures, our efforts in behalf of our fellow-men unproductive of real results. With Him in our lives and with His grace to sustain us always, our sorrows have been softened, our crooked paths made straight, our earthly credits have been rendered compensating.

The Spirit has guided us for lo, these many years. Shall we falter now? Never! In the fullness of His time we shall reap our reward. For has he not said that there is a place prepared for them that love God and serve Him?

"In my Father's house are many mansions. If it were not so I would have told you. I go to prepare a place for you, and if I go and prepare a place for you I will come again, and receive you unto myself, that where I am there ye may be also."

www.ingramcontent.com/pod-product-compliance
Lightning Source LLC
Chambersburg PA
CBHW020225240426
43672CB00006B/416